LIVING IN THE SHADOW OF MUSIC ROW

Stories from the Heart of Music City

LETA LANGFORD

LIVING IN THE SHADOW OF MUSIC ROW
Stories from the Heart of Music City
Copyright © 2022 by Leta Langford

Library of Congress Control Number: 2021909669
ISBN-13: Paperback: 978-1-64749-461-2
        ePub: 978-1-64749-462-9

Printed in the United States of America

GoToPublish LLC
1-888-337-1724
www.gotopublish.com
info@gotopublish.com

CONTENTS

Psalms 65:12-13
"The little hills rejoice on every side, the valleys shout for joy.
They also sing."

ACKNOWLEDGEMENTS AND HEARTFELT THANKS

MY LOVE, MY THANKS AND GRATITUDE GO TO MY SONS, ROBERT, AND RICHARD.

OVER THE YEARS THEY HAVE LISTENED TO MY SERMONS AND MY EXPERIENCES

AS GOD WOULD SHARE WITH ME. I SHARED WITH THEM THE SCRIPTURES THAT

CAME ALIVE DURING MY DAILY BIBLE DEVOTIONAL TIMES.

TIME NOR SPACE PERMITS ME TO NAME EVERY PERSON WHO GAVE ME

ENCOURAGING AND INSPIRING WORDS TO WRITE ALL OF THE STORIES I SHARE

IN THIS BOOK. TO ALL THOSE WHO TAKE TIME TO READ THIS, YOUR LIFE WILL

BE CHANGED. GIVE GOD THE GLORY AND HE CAN AND WILL SPEAK IF WE LISTEN.

FOREWORD

It was in the summer of 1965 that I first met Leta Langford. My first impression of this lovely, tiny, vivacious lady was that she was someone I could trust. Her countenance glowed with the love of Jesus in all our conversations, whether we were talking about babies or personal difficulties. Even though I been saved in an Assemblies of God church, my upbringing had been very legalistic; therefore, meeting the Langford's, who were so joyful and real yet never judgmental, was a breath of fresh air.

Our friendship has lasted 50 years, and Leta is still trusting Jesus with the same fervor and enthusiasm with only slightly less energy. Though challenged with raising two sons, heartbroken after losing a tiny one, losing her beloved mother and father and losing the love of her life, the Reverend W.C. Langford, much too soon she has persevered in all her faith in Jesus and continues to encourage anyone who will listen.

Leta will always be my spiritual mother as she has been to hundreds of other women. Sometimes I lived close enough to see or speak with her frequently; other rimes I lived far away. Once while living in California and going through an extremely difficult time, my telephone rang, and it was Leta. She asked, "Betty, is everything alright.... I have been praying for you" She always had my back. God has richly blessed my life with Leta Langford, and I pray her story of struggles, pain, love and victory will encourage you to overcome whatever you face. She is the example of the woman I want to be.

Betty was the wife to John Hartford when he wrote the million
selling song:
"Gentle On My Mind"

INTRODUCTION

In our forty years of ministry here, the commitment and the dedication have placed our family in positions and situations causing us to share in many lives. Our home has been used as a bridge necessary for many to cross over difficult and seemingly impossible circumstances. We have become a part of the lives that transformed Nashville into Music City, USA. This transformation brought about the stories I have written. These stories and experiences are true. They show the power of God in the lives of our family as well as in the lives of those to whom we have ministered.

I have newspaper articles, photographs and handwritten notes that may be used with many of the stories. We have experienced the height of joy and the depth of despair always trusting God to be our great stabilizer. Some names have been changed to protect the privacy of those of whom I have written.

The theme of my book is, God does all things well. This proves the promise in Mark 7:37

(NASV):

> "and they were utterly astonished saying, He has done all things well". God has been faithful in every area of my life, as the wife, the mother and the daughter of a minister.

God does all things well, (Mark 7:37) is the theme of my book and my life as the wife, the mother and the daughter of a minister.

In our forty years of ministry here, the commitment and the dedication have placed our family in a position to share in many lives.

We have become a part of the lives that transformed Nashville into Music City, USA. This transformation brought about the stories I have written. These stories and experiences are true. They show the power of God in the lives of our family as well as in the lives of those to whom we have ministered.

I have newspaper articles, photographs and handwritten notes that may be used with many of the stories. We have experienced the height of joy and the depth of despair always trusting God to be our great stabilizer.

Some names have been changed to protect the privacy of those of whom I have written

CHAPTER ONE

GOD DOES GOOD ALL THINGS WELL

Billy and I had been engaged for over a year. However, in the back of my mind were the ever-present nagging questions, "Why are you doing this?" "What in the world are you doing?" "When are you going to tell him how you really feel?" "Do you want to be a minister's wife?" And always following with a quick reply, "No way"

It was on a Sunday afternoon when I decided that the time had come to answer these questions once and for all including the all-important question Billy had asked, "Leta, will you marry me?" This was in spite of the fact I had sent my engagement ring to him just this past Wednesday. Billy was aware of my feelings about marrying a minister when we first met but he thought I was getting over it. And I convinced him that I could handle this fear and frustration and because I hadn't said anything about it at all.

I could not accept the responsibility of becoming of all things a minister's wife, no matter how hard I tried. That was when I decided the only thing to do was to take my beautiful engagement ring off, put it back into the blue velvet box and send it back to Billy and end this relationship; the sooner the better for both of us.

Billy was holding a revival in Jackson, Tennessee when I reached my decision. I knew that the postman had delivered my ring to him because I had sent it special delivery. He had not called or driven up yet although it was only one hundred and forty miles from Nashville. It was getting into the late afternoon on Saturday. I felt sure that I wouldn't hear from him.

Finally, our engagement was over, and the pressure was easing and the questions were answered at last. Each time I thought about it I would breathe a big sigh of relief but also there was a deep empty, heartache filled with unhappiness. My heart was light and heavy at the same time.

Late Saturday night the phone rang. When I answered, Billy said, "Honey, what's wrong? Why did you send your ring back?" I felt weak all over; I couldn't respond to him. I knew that I loved him, and said to myself, "God, I'm not ready for this."

I thought about my dad and home life in the parsonage. And I remembered that I had learned from my childhood days the sacrifices that mom and dad had made for the ministry and realized that my time would definitely never be my own; knowing only too well the rigid lifestyle of a minister, his wife and his family.

The requirements, the duties and the responsibilities were not what I desired or needed. My mind was spinning with all kinds of thoughts on 'why not to marry a minister,' when Billy broke into my concentration by asking, "Leta, Leta, are you still there?"

"Yes, I'm still here." After a long pause Billy said, "How about my coming up and talking with you tomorrow afternoon after church?"

Perhaps it would be easier to tell him in person. Maybe tomorrow I'd know more about how to say what I wanted to say. I just couldn't think of anything right now. Nothing I said came out sounding like I meant for it to sound. "Okay. I'll look forward to seeing you tomorrow."

I hung up the phone with a sigh of relief; I'll take care of this tomorrow. However, after talking with Billy I could not get my mind to slow down and quit thinking of him and how out of the ordinary his attitude toward life was compared to mine. I kept busy getting my clothes ready to wear to church and trying to decide on what to wear when I talked with him; and also did some extra cleaning to the house and especially to my room.

When he comes tomorrow I want him to remember the parsonage as being very clean even though it is a very humble home in East Nashville on Burris Avenue. This would probably be his last visit. I fell into bed totally exhausted. I tossed and turned, thought and argued with myself all night. I am so tired. Why can't I sleep? What is the matter with me? I was wide-awake when the rays from the rising sun beamed through the window. I walked over, pulled the curtain back and stood looking at the stars in the sky as I had all through the long night knowing I had reached the only decision that could possibly be made; it did not include marrying a minister.

However, God dealt with me all through the night. The question kept ringing so loudly in my head, even when I put my hands over my ears to keep from hearing it, "Is the real problem conforming to the ministry or could it be submitting your life to God?" I didn't want to admit what the real problem was. I didn't realize I really wanted God to take second place in my life.

Sunday School and church were over and we had just gotten home when Billy arrived to have dinner with us. After dinner we borrowed daddy's car and drove to Shelby Park in East Nashville to talk about our future. Billy was so certain about his call to full time ministry.

Until last night I didn't know what I wanted for my future. We walked around the lake, resting every once in a while on a park bench. After all these months, over a year and after all the questions, suddenly what Billy was saying sounded familiar yet strangely different. From deep within my heart and without a doubt I knew what he was saying was logical and for the very first time in my life I was admitting it.

All afternoon my mind was spinning with the thoughts and the scenes and even the voices from last night. Every detail was still vivid and even the smell and stench from the dark pit seem to remain in contrast to the sweet and fresh aroma of the field.

The gentle yet firm way God had dealt with me, filling my heart with joy and the love of Jesus and realizing that God was calling me, personally into the ministry. In my heart I was asking, "Lord, why didn't you tell me this before?"

Every few minutes Billy would ask, "Why are you so quiet?" "What are you thinking about?" "You seem to be in another world." His beautiful blue eyes were sparkling and I felt they were looking straight through me. He smiled and shook his head from side to side slowly. He gently squeezed my hand and added, "Leta, have you heard anything I have said?"

With a deep sigh I replied, "Well, about being in another world, I guess I am." Silently in my heart I prayed, "God, help me!" I reached over and put my other hand on top of Billy's hand and sighed as I said,

"Billy, last night something phenomenal happened that I would never have thought of in a million years!" I began to unfold my experience from last night. After a long pause I continued my statement. "God gave me a vision. You and I appeared to be in the living room sitting on the couch talking about the things you have to give up to become a missionary or a minister. The many comforts of life we take for granted such as a home, your friends, and everything you have been accustomed to your whole life.

Then we seemed to be separated from everyone, looking across fields in the country at something in the distance. We were standing there in silence and suddenly there were people standing all around us. As far as we could see there were people pushing and shoving. The people were pushing against us so hard they were almost knocking us down. They were desperately trying to get away and move back from something.

Then a huge black hole appeared getting bigger and deeper as it came between us and the people. I was trying to look over into it to see the bottom but there was no bottom to it. While still looking down at it people were coming by me and falling into the pit. I could see their arms reaching out and they were kicking their legs and I heard their screams as they were tumbling into this pit. They didn't know it was there and didn't know what was happening to them.

The pit moved back into the distance and between me and the pit there was something moving in almost a straight line. It was coming directly to me and then I realized the line was people. In the front, leading the long line was a person with their arm raised and stretched out pointing their finger at me. They stopped and stood directly in front of me and still pointing their finger at me, spoke very distinctly saying, "You are the cause of me missing that" as they moved their arm and hand and pointed to the huge dark pit. Then they stepped over and stood beside me. The others following behind them in line said and did the same thing. They were still coming toward me as this scene faded from my view.

Then we seem to be in another part of the country and we are each riding on a horse. You were talking to people on one side of the road and I was talking to the people on the other side. A handsome yet sort of rugged-looking middle-aged man with a tiny bit of gray in his hair and beard, wearing a small torn-like cap that matched his robe-like shirt, dressed with bright colored beads on his gray robe-like garment was sitting on my side of the road playing some sort of an instrument. When I got closer to him I saw it was a tambourine he was playing.

He spoke first and asked, "What kind of book is that?" I felt relieved and replied, "A song book. Would you like for me to sing for you? It probably isn't the kind of singing you are used to hearing, but I hope you like it." Thumbing through my song book, I then turned to "What A Friend We have In Jesus" and started singing it. When I came to the word 'Jesus' he touched my arm and said, "Who is that?" I said, "You mean, you don't know, who Jesus is?" He scooted over and made a place and motioned for me to sit down on the ground next to him. I explained to him the wonderful story of Jesus from His birth, to His death and then our blessed hope through His resurrection and the hope we have in this life because of Him.

We talked back and forth for a while then I asked "Would you like to know this man personally and if you do you will have life forever." He nodded his head "yes" and said "Oh yes!" We prayed a prayer together. With a big smile that showed his beautiful white teeth and his eyes filled with joy and excitement he said, "I'm so glad that you told me about Him."

Such inner joy I had never experienced! Slowly he begins to fade in the background until he is completely out of sight.

The big black pit is appearing again with people falling head over heels into it. In an instant my joy turned to sadness and utter despair. But it also suddenly fades into the distance. From somewhere in the distance the most beautiful voices were singing very softly, "Who Will Go?" and at the exact same moment a beautiful illuminated cross appeared. Jesus was nailed to it. The cross was moving closer and closer to me. When it stopped I could have touched it. It seemed as though the voices were coming from the cross. I was trying to speak but the words would not come out. I barely whispered and choked out the words, "I'm no preacher, my dad is but I'm not; besides, I have my own plans." I turned my head and looked away so I couldn't see the cross.

Everything was silent for a few minutes then a voice called me. I lifted my head and turned back around. The voice was coming from the cross. "Leta, what if you were in my place?" "What if you didn't know there was such a place as Heaven or that there was a Hell?" and "What if someone else knew this but didn't tell you; how would you feel?"

While still looking at the cross and still unable to say anything the cross begins to look entirely different. After gazing at the cross and looking at Jesus and trying to figure what made it change so dramatically I realized I had never really seen Jesus before. I saw Him in a way I had never seen him before. I realized the fact that what we call living on earth is just getting ready to live eternally.

The pit appears again still off in the distance and there is an old lady modestly and simply dressed. She is marked by many years of hardships showing on her face yet with a beautiful smile she walked between the pit and me. She was carrying a bucket and gently swinging it back and forth as she was singing, "Oh, Tell me His Name Again."

I had to decide if the most important goal in the world is Jesus. Not ourselves, not our ideas, not our plans. We must be completely yielding in every part of our mind and body to serve Him freely without reservation knowing His Will will be the perfect will for our happiness and our future.

While all these thoughts and questions were going over in my mind, from the cross came the question, "Don't you understand?" following these life changing words, "The decision is up to you."

"Yes, Lord, I understand now. You are my highest goal in life. I surrender my plans and desires to you completely." That decision was made not only for that Saturday night but for an entire life time.

All the while when I was telling Billy of my experience he never interrupted me one time. After looking away, off in the distance, for a few minutes he said, "Now I understand why you have been so preoccupied." With his big, beautiful smile and his blue eyes sparkling he pulled me over to him and held me close to him and said, "I'm glad the Lord helped me with you!

Billy said, "If you love me, don't you want to spend your life with me?"

I said, "I really do love you and would love to spend my life with you."

He reached into his shirt pocket and then took my left hand and put the ring on my finger and said, "Okay. Let's go ahead with the marriage in May as we planned." Continuing, he said, "I may not be able to keep you in silk hoses, but I will give you the best of everything that I possibly can. How about May 29, the night after you graduate from Litton?"

Billy began to make plans and started talking about what we would do after the wedding. I said, "Hey, wait a minute. You haven't asked me to marry you yet. You just slipped the engagement ring back on my finger." He pulled me close to him and said, "Leta, I am asking you for the second time, will you marry me?"

Sometimes now when we are talking with friends, he will say to them, "Go ahead, ask Leta if she didn't ask me to ask her to marry her." There is no way to deny it and I have discovered there is no need to try. So, I smile submissively and nod my head 'yes.'

My life and Christian testimony did not seem to have the depth and seemed empty compared to the fullness of God's grace and power that was so evident in Billy's life. He was totally committed to God. So for over a year and every day since our wedding my prayer was, "Oh God, help me to be filled with your love, your grace and your understanding. Help me to have the compassion for others and be totally committed to you like Billy. Let Christ be made real to others through my life."

Billy was elected as associate pastor and I as the music director for the First Assembly of God in Kingsport, Tennessee. After several months finally the good news came! We were expecting a new arrival at our house and we were so excited and could hardly wait! We were hoping for a boy. It was four weeks until my due date but the labor pains had started. They did not let up and after twelve hours our beautiful little boy arrived, twenty-one inches long and weighing six pounds. Oh, we were so thrilled and off all things he had red hair. My dad proudly reminded my mom, "I told you that one day we would have a little red headed offspring. My side of the family has always been proud of its red hair."

On the tray when they brought my lunch there was a small card the size of a business card on it. It was slipped under the napkin with only the corner of the card showing. It was from the Women's Auxiliary of the First Presbyterian Church in Kingsport. (I still have the card.) These words were typed on the card, "And we know that all things work together for good to them that love God, to them who are called according to his purpose." Romans 8:28

This gave me the assurance that everything was going to be all right even though we were going to have to leave little Larry at the hospital when we went home. I held the card in my hand and thought, "Well, this is the reason the Lord gave me this card."

When we arrived home Billy and I went into the bedroom. One side of our bedroom had been made into a nursery, a very modest nursery. The bassinet was trimmed with blue ribbon and the shelves above it were filled with the gifts from the baby showers. Everything was going to be just perfect for him when we brought him home. My mind went back to the little card on my lunch tray and I was so thankful for the assurance that "we know that all things work together for good to them that love the Lord."

I was not ready nor did I accept what was getting ready to occur. I entered into one of the darkest times of my life and into an experience of fear, doubting God and everything that I had ever been taught and bitterness beyond description which would almost destroy me. When Larry, our precious gift of joy and delight was ten days old and had been home for only seven days he began running a fever. We held him and walked the floor holding him all night and when daylight finally came we called the doctor. He came to our house and said we must take him to the hospital immediately and he would meet us there. He had developed a respiratory infection. He explained that one of his lungs had not full developed and he should be placed in an incubator. The condition he had was Hyaline membrane disease. Today when a baby is born early and the lungs are not fully developed they are immediately placed in the incubator and it is not removed until the lungs have fully developed. However forty years ago they did not do this.

Having been up nearly all night I was exhausted. It was taking me so long to get dressed to go to the hospital. Billy and Mom took Larry and went with the doctor. Dad stayed to drive me. I was shaking on the inside as well as on the outside. Dad said, "Leta, why don't you lie down just a minute or two, Billy and your mother are with Larry. You look so tired."

I walked down the hall and went into the bedroom. The sweet aroma from the baby powder filled the room. Before I reached the bed, the phone rang and dad said, "Let me get that. It's probably about Larry." He lowered his voice but I could still hear enough to realize the tone of his voice was changing. I just knew something was wrong. Out loud I kept saying "Oh God, don't let it be Larry. Not our little Larry. Not now. Don't take him. Oh God, No." The crushing of my heart, the disappointment, the fear, and the helplessness that instantly covered me is indescribable.

I ran back into the hall looking at dad. He just stood by the phone holding the receiver in his hand, with his head bowed. I looked at the expression on his face as he stood motionless for a long time. I knew that death had reached into our home and had taken our most prized possession; our little red headed son. Dad turned, facing me and reached his arms out to me. I almost fell into his arms. He spoke firmly yet softly and said, "Leta, the doctor said, because Larry has been born early, his lungs aren't fully developed. He developed pneumonia and died shortly after reaching the hospital."

While dad was walking back into the bedroom and talking to me I began to hear something else in the back of my mind. It was coming through clearly and almost overriding his voice. It was my prayer that I had prayed many times, "Let me feel what people feel so that I might have a real understanding and a genuine love for them; so they can see Christ in my life." I began to cry out loud and almost shout. "Not this way, oh God, not by taking Larry. Please God, does it have to be this way? Oh, God, not like this."

Dad was holding me in his arms as we stopped and stood in the doorway to my bedroom. Then he said, in his stern yet gently voice, "Leta, do you remember what I preached about this past Sunday?" Knowing I was unable to speak for crying, he continued, "What I preached about was a grain of wheat. It is only when we completely give our life, our will, our hopes, our dreams, our successes, and our failures to God that we become like Christ and become pliable in the hands of God. God can then use us to bring others to a relationship with Him."

Continuing in the same tone of voice he said, "Sometimes the requisite for finding God's will is in the surrendering of our own will."

He was leading me over to the bed to sit down. Finally, I managed to ask him, "What does the verse say, exactly?"

In his clear and very distinct voice he began, "Verily, verily, I say unto you, except a corn of wheat fall into the ground and die, it abideth alone: but if it die, it bringeth forth much fruit." Then he smiled and added, "That is in the Gospel of Saint John, the twelfth chapter." Dad did not know it but each word went straight to my heart like an arrow. He was not aware of the longing in my heart and the prayer I had prayed since Billy and I married.

Never have I experienced a night so dark. Each night grew darker and every day I became even more bitter. I resented everyone and everything. This is just the opposite of what I thought I needed to become - an ideal minister's wife. I felt hate instead of love. I felt revenge in my heart instead of understanding. Now I was even having a feeling of rebellion that was unbelievable. This attitude and frame of mind continued for months; if there were any changes at all, it was for the worse.

I knew I needed prayer but I couldn't pray. I would sometimes, just in a casual way, ask friends, "please pray for me when you have your prayer time." I knew this was my only hope, yet I was so helpless. During this time I would tell God over and over in the night time and in the day time, "God, this is not what I prayed for. Please help me."

Many months passed and it was over a year from the time of Larry's death before I could pass children on the sidewalk or in the stores without going out of my way to avoid being close to them. And if a mother with a small baby or child happened to pass close by me I would quiver deep inside.

Until this day if I hear a baby or child crying while we are shopping or eating out, I feel a certain pain deep in my heart. I look around and it is all that I can do to keep from going over to them and asking, "Why are you letting your baby cry?" or, "Please don't drag your little one by the hand while they are crying, they are so tired." Then at other times I seem to become paralyzed and can't move. I don't mean to stare at them.

Gradually the bitterness and rebellion began to slowly fade; in its place, there was a feeling of compassionate understanding, wrapped in an unusual kind of warmth and over flowing love. What a relief was coming into my mind. It had been so long since I had wanted to play the piano. One morning I sat down on the piano bench and after a while before I was hardly aware of what I was doing I began to play and realized I was playing 'Amazing Grace' saying the words to the verses to myself. When the words of the third verse came so did the warmth of the Holy Spirit.' Through many dangers, toils and snares, I have already come. 'Tis grace hath brought me safe thus far, and grace will lead me home.' The sweetest peace came into my heart and the terrible heaviness and ache finally lifted and the bitterness and turmoil were gone.

During this time of heartache, bitterness and hurt each flower, card and phone call was such an encouragement. A very close friend, Margaret Meek, who was several years my senior and had several years of experience as a pastor's wife, must have understood what I was experiencing when she sent this prayer to me. At the bottom of the prayer were the words, "Source unknown" but I felt it came directly from God at a time in my life when I could not pray. I would hold the prayer and place it to my heart unable to say anything but inside my soul was crying out for relief.

"I asked for strength, that I might achieve;
I was made weak that I might learn humbly to obey.
I asked for health, that I might do greater things;
I was given infirmity, that I might do better things.
I asked for riches, that I might be happy;
I was given poverty, that I might be wise.
I asked for power, that I might have the praise of me;
I was given weakness, that I might feel the need of God.
I asked for all things that I might enjoy life.
I was given life, that I might enjoy life.
I got nothing I asked for - but everything I had hoped for.
Almost despite myself, my unspoken prayers were answered
I am among all men, most richly blessed."
Source Unknown

On a cold January day thirty-two years later, we were sitting in the Family Section of the Phillips Robinson Funeral Home. Once again we encountered the unwanted experience of death invading our home. The memorial service was being held for my dad.

While sitting there my thoughts went back to the telling of some of his experiences that he had shared through the years. He accepted the Lord as his Savior and began preaching in 1912. He was ordained by the Assemblies of God into the ministry in 1914 in Russellville, Arkansas He moved to Missouri shortly thereafter. He pastored in Malden, Puxico, and Chaffee. In 1923 he moved to Cape Girardeau to pioneer a church (which sponsors a great Teen Challenge Center).

In 1930 he moved to Poplar Bluff and constructed a wooden tabernacle. A year later he moved to Kennett to pastor. He saw the Sunday school grow from under 100 to over 300 in average attendance and become the largest church in Kennett. He later moved to become the Pastor of South Side Assembly in St. Louis.

In 1940 he moved to Tennessee and was elected Superintendent of the Tennessee District of the Assemblies of God. He lost his eye sight due to cataracts. After an operation his sight was restored and he was re-elected Superintendent and continued in that position until his retirement.

Dad had such a marvelous memory. I envied his knowledge of the scriptures of the Bible. He read the Bible through over twenty times and studied it every day. When he died, I felt the great loss of not only his life but the knowledge of the Bible which he possessed. Many many times I have told him, "Daddy, my heart's desire is to have the same knowledge of the scriptures as you. I wish I could understand, correlate and explain the Bible like you do." His usual reply was with this question, "Leta, how much time do you spend studying the Bible?" When he lost his eyesight, the agency for the blind sent 'The Talking Bible' to him. The books of the Bible are recorded on individual records. We were so grateful for them. I don't know what he would have done without them. He looked forward to their arriving each time when he returned his last one. He listened to it every day.

He had the neighborhood children in his home for a Bible Study every Saturday morning. After the Bible Story, my mother would serve them milk and her homemade cookies.

One story I remember was his telling of his early days, when he, my mother and my older sister started on a train to hold a revival. The train had an unexpected overnight layover on the way, which used up the money he had saved from working on the farm to pay their fare. After staying in a rooming house close to the station, they set out for the railroad station early the next morning without any money.

He took mom and my sister, Sylvas, and found them a seat. He turned back and was walking around and was walking toward the ticket window. He said, "A nice looking stranger with a very pleasant expression on his face walked through the door and walked right up to me. He was taller than anyone else in the train station. His hair was medium brown and his brown eyes were sparkling. He was dressed in neat cleanly pressed dark pants and a light colored shirt and appeared to be about thirty years old. He did not speak, but when he got close to me, he reached out his hand toward mine. I reached up for his hand. He put something in my hand. He did not say a word. I looked down and there were several dollars in my hand. After he handed me the money he turned around and walked back through the station and out the door. It was the exact amount needed to purchase the train tickets. The ticket man asked me, "Why did you wait so near the time for the train to leave to buy your ticket?" I explained to him that I had no money until that man came in and gave me some. He replied, "Sir, I've been standing right here all the time and there has not been anyone that has come through those doors." Then daddy would always add, "To this day, I wonder about this stranger and wish I knew his name."

And I remember the times that dad told me about their coming back home from preaching revivals. The train stopped at Clinton or Shirley, Arkansas. They would have to wait for the mail hackney to make its run before they could get back home and up the mountain. Dad would have to run alongside of the horse-drawn mail-hackney going up the steep, rough road that had big boulders in it, to the top of the mountain called Round Top, because he didn't have enough money for both he and my mother to ride. I can hear him saying, "It wasn't too hard. The rough roads kept the horses from going too fast and the driver would let me ride when we had to cross the river and the streams. I could always rest then."

I must admit, I heard very little of the funeral message, words of encouragement or songs. Again the feeling of loss, the terrible heartache, and the emptiness that only death brings had come to our house. It is hard to accept the fact that in this life we may never know why some things happen. When questioning different situations that would arise during our ministry on Music Row, I would always seek advice from Dad. He would say, somewhere in our conversation, "Leta, God knows a few things that He is not going to let you know. You just have to trust Him."

Suddenly filling the Family Section was the voice of the Lord speaking clearly. "If heaven is like your dad preached all those years and if heaven is a real place and if you believe that it is like the Bible says it is, then why the sorrow? Is it or not?"

I sat up straighter and looked back over my shoulder and then looked all around the room at each individual. The voice was so loud I was sure that the rest of the family sitting there had heard it. Then realized as loud as it was, they evidently had not heard the voice. I settled back in my chair, wiped my eyes and whispered very softly, "Thank you, Lord."

Relaxed in the love of Jesus, deep peace came to me and from that moment, I have not shed another tear neither have I felt the overwhelming feeling of sadness and grief for my dad. For the first time in a long time dad is able to see again.

Dad had problems with his eyes for many years. I remember one Saturday night while he was preparing his message he suddenly began to have sharp pains in his right eye and due to the pressure from glaucoma, before anything could be done, his eyesight was gone. Ten years earlier he had lost the sight in his left eye due to a detached retina. I remember all the times that I heard the different doctors say the words, "Nothing can be done to help you have any eye sight at all."

He had gone completely blind due to glaucoma fifteen years before his death but now his eyes can behold all the splendor of heaven. He is able to participate in the life beyond the grave, the life which he looked forward to, and was to him, and is to me, as real as this present life.

If dad were to speak to me today I'm sure he would say, "Leta, take courage, I'm not dead. I'm alive. I've just gone home." And he would probably quote the scripture, "For as in Adam all die, so in Christ all will be made alive." I Corinthians 15:22.

Since 1986 I too have experienced many problems with my eyes. As I write this, I again feel the terrible fear, frustration and even despair when the doctor speaks these words, "Mrs. Langford, it's not your glasses that need changing. You have developed a rapid growing cataract on your right eye" continuing, he further stated, "You also have a cataract forming on the left eye however you can wait about having this one removed as it does not seem to be growing so rapidly." "I will make an appointment for you."

With the marvelous progress made in the medical field especially concerning the eyes I had less pain and difficulty. Dad had to lie two weeks in the hospital with nurse care around the clock. He was not even allowed to turn his head for days. This consequently led to his having a complete nervous breakdown. Also he had to wait so long for the operation. For me, Dr. Arrowsmith met me at his office at seven in the morning. The cataract was removed, and an implant was inserted. I was home and had eaten lunch by noon.

A year later it was time for my annual eye exam. Before leaving town for Lafayette, Indiana, to stay two weeks with Kori, my granddaughter, I decided to get the check-up over with as we passed Dr. Arrowsmith's office on the way out of town. Little Bobby me was driving me there and Billy was coming next week. Billy went by the office and met us there just to be sure everything was okay. He knew the apprehension I always had about going to have my eyes checked.

Sitting in the little office waiting for Dr. Arrowsmith to return with the results brought back memories of my being with dad so many times before. Dr. Arrowsmith returned hurriedly into the room, closed the door behind him and reached for my hand. He placed his other hand on mine. He leaned over and said, "Leta, you have a hole in each retina and also a tear in the left retina. Surgery should be done immediately. My office is scheduling it now. You must be very careful. Do not read; do not hit your head in anyway."

I was paralyzed with fear and could not move. My heart was pounding. The room was filled with a deafening silence. Finally, I slowly turned my head and looked over in the corner of the room where Billy was sitting. Big tears were running down his cheeks. He knew only too well how the words 'tear in the retina' went to my heart with numbing fear stabbing me like a dagger when he said each word. I felt like the world was falling out from under me. Absolutely overwhelmed!

The next words I heard him say was, "Leta, the operation is scheduled for the day after tomorrow, October 11th at seven o'clock in the morning." He explained to Billy that cryo surgery is what the doctor would do to freeze the hole in the retina. With much fear and trembling I was concerned about Dr. Arrowsmith performing the cryo surgery in his operating room across from his office. However before I could have the cataract removed I had to go to Baptist Hospital and have the tear repaired. This was repaired with an Argon laser. In December 1989 the cataract was removed and a lens was implanted in my left eye.

Then I began experiencing problems with my left eye sight. Since it was about time for my annual examination the anxiety and anticipation was building. June 14, 1993 Dr. Arrowsmith brought the bad news again. A secondary cataract had formed. Surgery was scheduled and performed on June 18 using a Yag laser. This past August my eyesight was checked. With my glasses I now have 20/20 vision. I only need them when I read, write or do close-up work.

Through the years we have found that of all the responsibilities involving the ministry, conducting a funeral is the hardest and most difficult. Dealing with the sadness, heartache, and often unbelievable situations causes much apprehension and uncertainty during this time. Billy and I have become physically ill following a funeral. I learned early not to ask for Billy's advice about my appearance when getting dressed to attend a funeral.

Billy asked me to read a poem the daughter had written for her mother at the beginning of a funeral service. This would not be too difficult except she forgot to bring the poem the night before and I would not be given the poem and would not even see the poem until just before the service and I had to begin playing the organ thirty minutes before the scheduled service. We arrived early but they were running late. While pacing back and forth looking out the window I frowned at Billy and asked, "Why did you volunteer me to read a poem that I have never seen before." He calmly replied, "One of the family members wrote it and it will mean a lot to them." Still frowning and trying not to raise my voice I whispered "I don't mind reading it. I would just like to at least look over it before I stand up to read it in front of everyone." He smiled patted me on the arm and said, "Oh,

Honey, don't worry. You'll do fine." I gave a big sigh and said, "I knew that was what he was going to say!"

We had already had a conversation pertaining to this before we left home. Richard and Robert were on their way to school and finally I was dressed. I decided to wear my new black hat that Billy had bought for me to wear on Easter. It was a beautiful wide brim black straw hat with a tiny black ribbon around the crown yet not too overpowering. I had placed it over another hat in the shelf in the closet so it would not get folded or bent out of shape.

Billy was already in the car. I was getting ready as fast as I could. I grabbed my hat out of the closet put it on while rushing down the stairs and jumped into the car. Billy had already opened the car door for me. I didn't remember the hat feeling so uncomfortable when I tried it on. As I was closing the car door I asked Billy, "Does my hat look alright?" Giving me a quick glance he said, "Yeah, it looks fine." I decided that I just wasn't accustomed to wearing a hat this large.

After the funeral at which I played the organ, I opened the funeral by going to the front and reading the poem, then singing with the trio. After the service, I talked with the family at the grave-side. As was our custom, Billy always stayed with the family around the grave after everyone else left and I always walked back to the car and waited for him.

My hat was so uncomfortable I decided to take it off in the car instead of waiting to get home. When I took it off I still felt as if I had it on. Holding my hat in one hand I reached on top of my head with the other hand. I felt another hat! Then I remembered that I had placed this new hat on another hat to keep it in shape.

I was so embarrassed! I felt terrible. By the time Billy got to the car I was crying. I blurted out through my tears, "I can't believe you. Why didn't you tell me I was wearing two hats? You let me get up there in front of all those people like that."

Billy reached over and took my hand that was holding the new black straw hat and said, "Honey, I'm sure no one noticed. I couldn't see that you had on two hats. I'm almost certain there was not a person there who was aware of it. So don't feel so badly.

Stop crying. People don't pay that close attention to what you are wearing at a time like this."

"Okay, then why did you pay $15.00 for a hat, if it doesn't matter?" I had told him several times that he had paid too much money for a hat when we needed other things. Even though it was the prettiest hat I had ever had.

He squeezed my arm, smiled his beautiful smile and looked straight through me with his beautiful sparkling deep blue eyes and said, "How 'bout me taking you to a real nice place for dinner? Would that make you feel better?" "It will make me feel better but it sure won't help the way I was dressed standing in front of all those people at the funeral." I held up my hat and managed a small smile.

Still holding my arm and reaching for my hat with his other hand he said, "The family gave me an envelope with a check enclosed. We will use that to pay for our dinner and give you the rest." He took my hat and tossed it in the back seat. I handed him the other one and said, "Here, put this one with it but not on top of it." We chuckled and as we were driving out of the cemetery Billy continued, "Let's make a deal! From now on, any money given for weddings or funeral services will be yours."

Cutting my eyes to the back seat then back at him I said, "Deal." Through the years this has created a special and a loving bond between us as we refer to as 'our deal' following a wedding or funeral. It was necessary sometimes to remind him, "A deal is a deal!"

Following the question to Billy, "How do I look?" or "How does this outfit look?" You can be sure, I always double check his answer.

Through the years I have learned that I cannot govern situations that come to me in life. Many times I wouldn't have chosen them to be the way they have been. Experiencing the death of little Larry taught Billy and me one of the greatest if not the greatest lesson needed in our ministry, the importance of words needed to be spoken and words that should be unsaid in the time of great sorrow as well as other times of stress and anxiety.

People who meant well said to us, "You'll have other children." "Be glad it happened while he was still a baby." "You'll get over it." "You and Billy are still young." "You just need to get your mind off of it."

I have often wondered if their well-meaning words of comfort and comments may have influenced my very difficult time following his death. You can be assured this made Billy and me aware of every single word spoken in any situation at times of difficulty. We learned that at a time of heartache people need your presence, not your advice or comments.

Like the story of the little girl who was gone too long when she went to the store for her mother. Her mother asked her why she was gone so long, she replied, "My friend, Mary, broke her doll, and I had to stay and help her cry."

God prepared us for the most difficult task there is in the ministry and He prepared us by personal experience. We have been there. As I reflect over the years of ministry on Music Row; death is one of the saddest and most final of all life's experiences. Death brings our darkest night and most hopeless and terrifying experiences of life. Although we have conducted hundreds of funerals we have never become accustomed to facing death. It has never become routine to sing or play the organ for funerals. Words fail at this time. There are no answers for the persons grieving.

It is difficult to know exactly how to deal with death and the heartache it brings. The feeling of loneliness and despair is difficult to handle. Life can deal cruelly and harshly with us. We then often become weary, tired, resentful and bitter. We can come to know God amid the tragedies and disappointments of life. These are the experiences that can make us better persons through them we can have a better understanding of God's Word and develop a close relationship with God and the reality of heaven brings us hope and becomes a sweet and blessed relief from suffering.

Through sorrow, disappointment and despair, I must remember that the fact remains, this is for today and it won't last forever; this too will pass. If I can live for today, quit struggling and not step over the boundary into tomorrow with its uncertainty, I can be assured that tomorrow is another day. The sun will shine again. With the bright sunlight of the morning we will once again have hope.

We have been there!

CHAPTER TWO

MOVING TO MUSIC CITY

The brisk, cold mountain wind was blowing and a light freezing rain was falling on this blustery November day. It was six-thirty in the morning and the darkness of the night had not lifted. The previous night we had packed everything we owned in our 1948 black Mercury.

The boxes were stacked and crammed in the car with our rocking chair wedged in between the front and back seat. Billy could barely see out the rearview mirror; there was hardly room to move. My husband Billy, Robert, our tiny son, only nine weeks old and I started for our new home - Nashville, Tennessee, which was later to be known as Music City, U.S.A.

We were leaving the beautiful little city of Kingsport, located in the mountains of East Tennessee, and the security of our home, our parents and our friends, Billy had resigned his position as Associate Pastor of a nice church with a lovely congregation.

The Tennessee District Superintendent of the Assemblies of God asked Billy to come to Nashville to build a church. Billy felt that he should answer this call. The minister who planned to build the church had to take his little boy to Arizona due to health reasons.

The question kept going over and over in my mind all through the day. Why did Billy feel such a strong urge to go to Nashville without a congregation rather than to accept either of the positions he had been offered in two large established churches, the one in Memphis or the other located in Milan?

Never at any time had we thought that we would go to Nashville to build a church; even though we helped in a tent revival on the corner of Sixteenth and Division across the street from the Tony Sudekem

Park, now called West Park. It is located across from the Country Music Hall of Fame on Music Square. The Speer Family provided special music, Billy preached and I played the piano.

Three very tired people arrived in Nashville on November 16, 1951, after completing a very long and tiring trip. The temperature was dropping, causing our windshield wipers to freeze. The freezing rain finally stopped falling and the wind had stopped blowing so fiercely while we were driving in the mountains near Cookeville, about 100 miles east of Nashville. Without the interstate highways, the never ending, winding narrow roads made it seem a lot farther. It was cloudy, overcast and dark all the way. Now night was approaching and we were still driving.

Billy said, "Honey, since it has gotten dark when we get close enough, you will be able to see the beautiful and picturesque skyline of Nashville. The State Capitol is located on a hill. It is the tallest building in the skyline and has lights shining on it. You can see it for, miles." After a short pause he continued, "At night from the Capitol grounds you can look in every direction and see the lights shining all over Nashville; and you know Nashville is completely surrounded with a range of hills. It's so pretty!" I thought to myself, "I know all of that. Why is he telling me this?" He looked at me with such confidence and gave me a big beautiful smile.

We drove into the city where a dense fog mixed with heavy coal smoke had settled over the entire downtown area. One could barely see the street lights in the next block; much less see the skyline or the lights of the city.

Robert had slept most of the way, waking up only when he was hungry or needed his diaper to be changed. What a challenge to change his diaper in the cramped space. I'm sure he could sense my anxiety. I was having a hard time with the large diaper pins when he was squirming. Disposable diapers with their Velcro tabs were far in the future. He was getting very restless. It was time for another bottle but his milk was cold.

Billy said, "We're almost there!"

After another few blocks, we arrived at the big, dark and drab two-story house, with the address 1028 Eighteenth Avenue South. The heavy smell of smoke was filtering into the car. The terrible smell followed us inside the dimly lit foyer. Billy pointed toward the dark stairs. We finally made it to the seconded floor. Over in the corner looked like a big refrigerator. We passed three doors before coming to the apartment which was to become our home.

Billy was loaded down with boxes and the diaper bag was hanging on his shoulder; he nodded his head toward the door across the foyer from where we were standing and said, "That's our kitchen over there." Then I knew, that was a refrigerator in the corner.

Going into the bedroom I laid Robert on a clean quilt that was on an old iron bed. The linens and utensils were also furnished. On the wall next to the door was a scratched up chest-of-drawers and a fireplace that was covered with boards and nailed shut. Billy put the boxes and the diaper bag in the straight chair on the wall opposite the bed. He said, "I'll get the rocking chair in a few minutes. Let's go see the kitchen and we can warm Robert's bottle there."

We went across the foyer and passing by the refrigerator he said, "We share the refrigerator with the other apartments." Clinching the bottle more tightly I quickly asked, "How many?"

He said, "Three."

The tiny kitchen was dismal and felt so empty. There was a round table, two chairs and a stove. Billy turned on the hot water faucet and let it run until the water was warm enough to heat the bottle. By this time we could hear Robert crying. Some of the doors cracked open from the other apartments but quickly closed when the occupants saw us. It had been dark for hours and seemed awfully late at night but when I looked at my watch it was only 8:45 p.m.

I was restless inside also and felt like crying just as loudly as Robert, but trying not to let Billy know the terrible frustration I was feeling. I was so quiet Billy knew something was wrong. There didn't seem to be anything to say. Billy said, "Honey, in the morning everything will look better. Nashville is really a beautiful city. I know you'll like living here." It has always been so easy for Billy to be optimistic about everything at the time of writing this initially, I remember thinking.. We just celebrated our forty-eighth wedding anniversary. I have come to greatly admire his attitude.

Wanting to make the best of things I was trying to act happy and calm but inside I was so apprehensive and scared but still in my mind was the vivid memory of three years ago when Larry, our first little son had died of pneumonia at ten days old. The memories and the feelings again of desperation, helplessness, and fear were almost overwhelming.

Also I developed phlebitis in my left leg when Robert was seven days old. The painful ache was almost unbearable especially when standing in one position for any length of time. Even the elastic ace bandage did not keep the intense pain from hurting or stop the terrible throbbing ache. From my heart went a prayer, "God, you must help me. How can I bathe and take care of Robert? Please, help me."

We were to share the bath, which was across the hall next to the kitchen with these other people. It was very difficult to get used to this. Sunday mornings trying to get ready for church was the worst time. After we had been there a couple of weeks the other families slept later on Sunday morning or they stayed in their rooms until we were gone because the bathroom was always empty on Sunday mornings.

The apartment was as dark and gloomy inside as it was on the outside. The first morning we were there, while giving Robert a bath the landlady came up and knocked on our kitchen door and said, "You are keeping the lights on too much and you are using too much electricity." She came up to our kitchen and knocked on our door every day when I was bathing Robert and said the same thing. There was a one hundred-watt electric light bulb hanging from the ceiling in each room.

I guess I did keep the lights on nearly all the time, especially when it was so dark and dreary outside. We lived in this apartment for eight weeks; then another move and other adjustments were necessary as our lifestyle changed dramatically. Surely it would be for the better!

For the next four years we lived in three rooms in the back of the church. The church was located only one block down the same street from the apartment house. There were three Sunday-School rooms and a restroom behind the platform. Our back door opened up into the alley behind the church.

A couple of men attended the church and helped Billy build a cabinet and sink in the room we used for a kitchen. They also built a closet in the middle room. We used the church restroom, but went across the alley to our members Joe and Bess Citti's home to take showers. Bess and her dad, Mr. Rousseau, had come over to help us change and build the rooms. They were so excited for us to be there. They said, "You kids are welcome to make our home your home. Don't only come to take showers but come anytime during the day or night and stay as long as you can. Remember, our home is your home."

In the first Sunday service, only nine people were present and three of them included Billy, Robert and me. When we decided to move to the church our furniture consisted of all pieces given to us from attics, basements and garages. Not having a large congregation there was not a lot to choose from. However, we enjoyed those days. Even thinking about the squeaking rocking chair and the mirror on the dresser that so badly needed to be re-silvered brings back a smile and memories, some pleasant, some not so pleasant.

Since we did not have a television, Bess would call us to come watch programs in the evenings and also eat supper with them. She and Joe made our living in the back of the church much more enjoyable and their love for us helped us get through some really tough times. We shared many wonderful hours there with them. Robert took his first step in their living room.

Living in the back of the church was quite different and was a learning experience for sure. My dad was a minister and the one thing I said while growing up was, "I will never live in the back of a church." But I had also said, "I will never marry a minister."

On the corner of 17th and Division where the ASCAP (American Society of Composers, Authors and Publishers) building is now located, stood a large brick two-story house. The first floor had been converted into a gospel-recording studio. The couple had come down from Nebraska and opened one of the very first recording studios on 16th Avenue which was to become known as Music Row. The Sunday following our church service they approached me in a hesitating manner. He squinted his eyes and gave a small sigh and asked, "Would you consider my calling you when someone comes into the studio and needs a pianist? The pay won't be that great but it would really help us to have you on standby, if you could possibly do it." He didn't know how glad I would be to bring in some extra money. Our congregation was growing but still very small. That was our first involvement with the recording industry and meeting the hopeful entertainers.

DOLLY and JOE

◇◇◇◇◇◇◇

Billy would spend his days going out to invite people to church. If they had children, he would offer to pick them up for Sunday School. He would drive up to church on Sunday mornings with our 1949 black Mercury filled with kids of all ages.

One Sunday morning he came bringing a little eight year old boy and a little girl of five into the back of the church to our living room. Billy said, "Honey, I want you to meet Dolly and Joe." As I came through the door I stared in amazement. Such dirty children! Their little hands were filthy; their faces were dirty with marked streaks around their mouth and nose. Their hair was not clean nor combed. Their clothes were not only dirty but were ragged.

Billy was getting a washcloth and towel from under the sink and was running water into the basin. "It won't take long and they will be fine." The big smiles on the children's faces and the twinkle in their eyes as they watched Billy, made them look beautiful. They said in unison, "We're comin' to Sunday School today." Billy visited them on Bush's Lake (now Metro Center). He mentioned to me earlier in the week about visiting some children that lived on the lake, but I was pretty sure that the parents wouldn't let them come.

Billy was so excited when he went after them and saw them sitting on the steps in front of the house waiting for him to pick them up. We washed them every Sunday morning and they came for two years without missing a Sunday. We bought them a set of clothes including shoes. We kept them in our bedroom at the church. I washed the clothes every Monday morning and had them ready for the next Sunday.

Then one Sunday when Billy went by to pick them up they were not there. He knocked on the door, went all the way around the house but there was no one to be seen. He opened the door and there was nothing inside other than old newspapers, cold drink bottles and grocery wrappers. He tried every possible avenue he could. Billy continued to round up children from all over Nashville. Sometimes he had to make two trips to get them all to Sunday School.

FIRST COUNSELING SESSION

◇◇◇◇◇◇◇

Three blocks down the street toward town was the Florence Crittenton Home for unwed mothers. Each afternoon the girls were permitted to walk around for a couple of hours for exercise. Our church was located between the home and the grocery store where the girls usually went to buy candy, potato chips and knick-knacks. In the afternoon Robert would be out in the churchyard playing. The girls would often stop to talk and play with him. Our house became a regular stopping place for them. Sometimes they would spend their entire 'free time' talking with me.

Billy was usually out making hospital calls. After winning the girls' confidence that I would not repeat their story the girls were more at ease and felt free to share with me what events in their lives led to their unfortunate situation. Their situations were different. The girls were different. The locations were different, but as each began to reveal her sad, tragic story, it would coincide with the stories of the other girls. The girls were attractive, some very pretty, some heavy set some thin, nearly all with exceptionally sweet and gentle dispositions. Almost all were in their mid-teens although occasionally there were those who were younger or older.

The stories unfold. The father of the unborn child was married, not yet divorced, but planning to get a divorce as soon as he could get things worked out between he and his wife. He really wanted to go ahead and get married but couldn't right now. If he was unmarried the story was that he did not want the responsibility of a child and marriage now but would when he got a better job, better apartment and better car. It would be better for her if they waited. The same story over and over. I knew what the girls were going to say before they finished their sentence. Each girl was convinced that the father really loved her, after the baby was given away, things would be worked out and everything would be okay between them.

Some of the girls' parents didn't know that they were at the home for unwed mothers. They told them they were living with friends and were only trying to get a job in Nashville. Sometimes the baby's father would make all the arrangements and pay all the expenses.

Listening to them and hearing the heart breaking stories over and over was very difficult to handle. They were not asking for advice. They wanted someone to talk to and listen without being judgmental or critical. I just happened to be there for them. As I think back now, I believe that God placed me exactly where the girls had to pass by each afternoon.

When you were in the vicinity of Music Row in the afternoon, any day of the week, you could see the girls walking. They were laughing and talking with one another, suppressing their fear and anxiety. If you were not aware of the cry of their heart for sincere love, you would surmise them as handling their situation very well. Another heavy-hearted girl, another dramatic story, another life overshadowed by disappointment, engulfed in Music City.

Since the Crittenton Home had relocated out of town, I no longer had the opportunity to visit with the girls in this relaxed manner. I will never forget seeing these beautiful girls wearing the big oversized shirt, sitting in the church yard and hearing the sound of their weeping as they unfolded their tragic experiences. There is a deep sharp twinge in my heart when I think of them and I silently pray the prayer that I was privileged to pray with so many, "God, please be with them through this difficult time."

There is always a lot of traffic, cars, buses and tourists. In almost all the houses in this area there are small apartments or recording studios. Our church parking lot was used often for "out of towners" when they were unable to find a motel room. They slept in their car, camper or their bus. They seemed to always find our church parking lot. We did not mind this except when there was no place for church members to park when they attended church services.

One Sunday a church deacon told Billy, "You should do something about the people parking in the church parking lot. Do you know I had to park on the street almost a block away?" Billy said that he would take care of the matter. The people would usually be gone by the time church was over and he wouldn't have to say anything. We did place a sign asking them to please leave by church time if they parked there overnight.

GUNMAN

◇◇◇◇◇◇◇

During Billy's sermon one Sunday morning, a man wearing a nice navy blue sport coat, sport shirt and beige slacks came walking into the service. He was holding his arm in a ridged position down at his side. Taking a closer look, he was holding a small gun in his hand. He walked up the aisle directly to where Billy was standing at the pulpit. He walked up the aisle and he was biting his lower lip. He squinted his dark eyes just slightly and looked all around the church on both sides of the church very slowly and carefully. He did not change the serious expression on his face. He turned his head as his eyes scanned every person in the building. When he reached the platform my heart was pounding. I could not move, neither did anyone in the congregation. Billy walked over and leaned over towards him. He talked with him for a minute or two. He slowly turned around facing the congregation and walked over to the front bench and sat down. He put his hand holding the gun into the right side pocket of his sport coat. The morning worship service continued without further incident. I don't know how much of Billy's sermon was remembered; I would imagine very little, if any. Everyone was relieved when the benediction was given. Immediately after the benediction the man followed Billy directly into the office. Even though they didn't stay in the office very long I was still very apprehensive about this.

While we were eating dinner, I ask Billy, "What did you say to that man during service and what did he say to you?" Billy said, "He thought his wife might have attended our church today. He was looking for her and was going to take her back home if he found her. I told him, this is the House of God and you are out of order. You need to sit down until the service is over and then we will talk. I will help you if I can." Billy handled this situation very well. He was just twenty-four years old and this was our first of many exciting experiences to come on Music Row.

As I think back, I guess this was our first of many exciting situations we were to experience while ministering on Music Row. Had I known about this as well as the many other unexpected events, on that cold, rainy, foggy November night (I assure you); I would have had reason to be even more apprehensive and frightened.

PLEASE, DON'T LET IT RAIN

◇◇◇◇◇◇◇

Our faithful yet small congregation always prayed especially hard and very sincerely, "Please, God don't let it rain on Saturday or Sunday." Our roof had started to leak and we had to place pans on the benches to catch the water from the leaks.

Sometimes right in the middle of a service a new leak would develop. Whoever was sitting under it would have to move very quickly to another bench. We had plenty of water without having to prepare for a baptismal service and could have easily had a baptismal service anytime during any service whether or not it had been planned. It took several homemade ice-cream suppers, yard sales and car washes but we finally raised $300.00 to repair the leaking flat roof. What a relief! Now we could pray for something besides our leaking roof, or so we thought.

We were waiting for the next rain and to our dismay after a few hours the roof was leaking more than it had been before. There was more water than ever before. It leaked constantly now. We put all the pans back on the benches but still mopped up the water before every service. It was terrible!

The next day following the hard rain was Sunday. On Monday morning Billy called the roofing company. The telephone operator said, "I'm sorry, this number is no longer in service." We knew there must be a mistake. But after several tries Billy decided to drive down to their office. He wasn't gone very long and I met him as he was getting out of the car. By the look on his face, I knew something was wrong, He said, "Honey, there was not anyone in their office, in fact the building was empty. The door was unlocked and I went inside and there was no one around anywhere."

He was still sitting in the car with his elbow on the steering wheel leaning his head on his hand. After a few moments of silence Billy sighed as he said, "I inquired at the building next to the roofing company and the gentleman there said, "They moved out this past weekend. You're not the first person that has come over here to ask about them. We don't know anything about them, but you're welcome to check back again in case we should hear something from them."

Once again we started our projects for raising money. One of the ladies in the church had heard that pin cushions, doll clothes, pillow covers and other small items could be made from satin ribbons. Another lady mentioned that a church was doing this and they acquired the ribbon without any cost. The ladies were getting permission from cemeteries to gather ribbons from the discarded wreaths that had been placed in the trash at the back of the cemetery.

Joyce, one of the girls at our church said, "I will go, if you go with me." The next morning we met at the church and left about eleven o'clock. We started at Spring Hill cemetery on Gallatin Road then decided that we had time to go to another one. So, off we go across town to Lebanon Road to the historical Mount Olivet Cemetery. The marker outside the cemetery was established in eighteen fifty-six, the care-taker was in his office just inside the gate. We asked his permission to go to the back of the cemetery to check about the ribbons. Towards the back of the cemetery were huge antique monuments from the days of old. Joyce stopped the car several times as we read the engravings but we didn't get out of the car until we reached the huge pile of wreathes and flowers with ribbons.

It was later than we realized and the sun had already gone down. We heard a motor that sounded like it was about to stall and suddenly this old beat-up truck was coming up from a back road which neither of us had noticed. It turned and came directly toward us. There were three men sitting in the front seat. Joyce and I almost fell. We were trying to hold onto all the ribbons as we were rushing to get down from the large heap of wreathes. Our arms were filled and streaming down to the ground were all colors and sizes of beautiful satin ribbons.

The men must have been looking for something else because they threw the wreaths over to one side and kept looking on the ground under where the wreaths had been. We didn't stay around but headed directly for the gate. Finally it came into view! The gates were closed and when we got close enough to see, the window to the little house was closed and there was a sign hanging on the gates. "Cemetery Closed. Open each day from 8:30 to 5:30." Joyce and I looked at each other and we were both wondering about what could have happened. Joyce said, "Leta, What do we do now?"

We decided the care-taker had forgotten all about our being in the back. Joyce said, "The only way we can get out of here is that back road." I reminded her of those guys with their truck in the way if we tried that. She said, "We will have to get out that way but I'll go around their truck and we can make it." It was not easy to turn her big car around at the entrance with the gates being closed.

We followed all the little roads and finally got to the back and that truck was still sitting in the road and the guys were still looking around on the ground. Just beyond the cemetery were three houses. They had big backyards that came to the line of the cemetery. A driveway came across the middle yard and we hoped it led into a street. It was getting dark very quickly and our hearts were beating so fast. We made it fine until our back bumper got stuck on a small tombstone that we didn't see. Joyce finally worked it loose by going forward then backwards. It came loose and we checked the bumper on the car and the tombstone. Neither had been damaged. The men must have heard us because when we looked back they were standing on top of the heap looking at us. They were probably wondering what we were doing there as much as we were wondering what they were doing there.

The people sitting in their backyards surely gave us some hard looks. A man yelled, "Hey, where do you think you are going?" Joyce didn't stop to tell him. I wasn't going to tell Billy why we were later getting home than we had planned, until he wanted to know where all the sacks in the bedroom had come from then I showed him the ribbons.

After this fund-raising project and others, we called another roofing company. Billy checked on this one and the Better Business Bureau said it was a reputable company. The owner of the company said, "We know how to fix a flat roof." We were so glad that he knew about flat roofs. What a relief! We again waited for a rainy day. The rain came and so did the water. This time it almost poured inside. We were so perplexed. What else can we do?

The small congregation lost heart in trying to make money. The ladies had baked cakes, candy and cookies to sell every Sunday morning and tried to make craft items and now all the money was gone.

It was early fall and winter was coming. Billy asked the congregation, "If I try to fix this roof will anybody help me?" Everyone agreed to help: men, women and children. The next Monday morning he went to the hardware store down from the church and asked, "How much material would it take to roof our church?" The clerk helped him figure it out. Billy told him what had happened each time. Then Billy asked him, "Would you let me buy this material on credit?" The clerk said, "I will not only give you credit. I know someone that will let you borrow some roofing equipment, without charge."

Everyone in the church put on their work clothes and came every time they could. The part that bothered me most was getting off the roof and climbing back on the ladder. By the end of the week on Saturday late in the night, all the material, tools and people were at last off the roof. We were a tired congregation this Sunday. Following the next rain we were thrilled and greatly relieved. There was not a leak in the building then or ever again.

Billy didn't know being called into the ministry also meant becoming a roofer, carpenter, plumber, electrician and painter. He had learned to do all of these extremely well and surprisingly enough, he really enjoyed every one of them. In fact he worked closely and supervised the building of our new sanctuary on Franklin Road in Oak Hill.

THE VOO DOO DOLL

◇◇◇◇◇◇◇

One Sunday morning after the service, a tall heavy-set dark haired, and modestly dressed middle aged lady approached Billy and handed him a three by nine white envelope and asked him to come to her apartment later. She said, "the directions are in the envelope."

Everyone had left the church. Billy and I went into our back church apartment. He closed the door and handed Robert to me. He reached into his inside coat pocket, pulled out a white envelope and said, "The lady that came up front after the service this morning handed me this envelope. She asked me to come visit her next Friday afternoon. She said the directions to her house are inside. I haven't opened it yet. Let's eat lunch then we will open it while Robert is taking his nap." He put the envelope on the dresser.

Lunch was over, Robert was taking his nap. Finally, Billy and I could relax until service time tonight. Billy picked up the envelope as we passed the dresser. We sat down on the couch. He opened it and something was falling out of the envelope all over his shirt and suit pants. It looked like sand but as we examined it more closely it looked more like salt or sugar. Billy moistened his finger and put it on his shirt then put a grain of it on the tip of his tongue. He said, "This tastes like salt." Billy held the letter so that no more salt would fall out and we read the letter together. The letter stated, "My mother is tormenting me with witchcraft day and night. I will explain it to you more thoroughly when you visit me."

The directions to her house indicated that she lived three blocks from the church on Seventeenth Avenue South. Her apartment was upstairs leading up the back steps from the concrete driveway. We drove by and Billy located it on Monday before he was to go. From the outside of the house it looked like the other houses and apartments.

When Friday came following lunch Billy said, "Honey, pray for me while I'm gone. I will need divine wisdom to deal with this situation."

He drove to her house and following her directions went around to the back of the house and up the back stairs to the door that she described. There was a small cream color burlap cloth doll about eight inches long held by a big safety pin to the number on her door. Billy knocked and she very quickly answered the door. He said she was wearing the same pantsuit and her dark hair was pulled back like she had worn it to church. She invited him inside. He could see the kitchen as he walked through the door. Caught in the refrigerator door was a black linen cloth doll about twelve inches long. The refrigerator door was closed tight with pins sticking into the doll.

The lady pointed to the doll and said, "That is my mother and she is causing all my trouble. I am just getting back at her. I'm making her have pains in all the places in her body where I have stuck the pins." She started telling Billy the things that were happening which she attributed to her mother. She stopped talking a few minutes then looked at the refrigerator and said, "Now, I am going to tell you what I am going to do and let you see all the trouble that I can cause my mother."

Two hours passed before Billy came home. He said, "I can't believe that I heard her say the things she was saying and doing. She wanted me to pray for protection from her mother and for her to have power to do her witchcraft. She said, "I believe in voodoo and witchcraft but I am afraid to practice it."

Billy said, "Let me explain the plan of salvation to you. You undoubtedly believe in prayer or you would never have asked me to come neither would you have given me the letter last Sunday. The blood of Jesus Christ can set you free from the bondage of fear and witchcraft." Then he prayed for her but she would not say the sinner's prayer.

Walking down the back stairs as he was leaving Billy said to himself, "This can't be, not in America. Not down the street from our church. The pain in her eyes, the fear in her voice, there was such hopelessness and the feeling of reaching out for help. Oh, God, thank you for the power of the cross which is the only thing that can set people free."

We have received letters from her through the years. In each letter there is salt and also a voice of hopelessness because she is determined to get even with her mother and she thinks she will only get even with her through witchcraft. (By the way, I have no idea what the salt represented).

This visit made us aware of the fact that Music City, the city of bright lights, entertainment and high hopes, is also a city of darkness, evil and superstition. This was one of Billy's first pastoral calls and our very first but regretfully not our last encounter with voodoo, witchcraft, and the demonic powers of evil.

John Cherian, from India, was attending Vanderbilt over thirty years ago, getting his Doctor of Divinity Degree. He said to Billy and me many times, "America is opening its doors to voodoo and witchcraft. It has been spared many, many horrible things that we experience in India. God has protected the United States."

John told us many stories concerning the consequences of such practices. He presently lives in New York and is the editor of a monthly paper called 'Christian Anthropology'. It is received and placed in the libraries of Harvard Divinity School, Princeton Theological Seminary, Wheaton College among others.

Over the years the students from the colleges have enriched our lives and our ministry. Our church was located one block from Scarritt Methodist College, four blocks from Belmont Baptist College, six blocks from Peabody College and four blocks from Vanderbilt College. Many students attended our church. We still keep in touch with some of them. Especially those from other countries became a part of our ministry and our culture for such a short time. What a blessing they were. Some whom we loved so dearly have been killed for their Christian testimony. Our hearts are filled with deep sadness but are quickly replaced with joy when we remember the assurance we shared as we worshipped together. We are so thankful for the resurrection and delivering power that we have through Jesus Christ our Risen Lord!

MEANEST MAN IN NASHVILLE

◇◇◇◇◇◇◇

On a Friday night after our Youth service, everyone had gone and Billy was locking the front door. The man who lived across the street in an apartment house came across the parking lot headed toward the door. He staggered through some water that had been left by the rain that night. Still standing partly in the water he pointed to Billy and said, "Hey, preacher, step over here." The stench of alcohol was terrible. It was obvious that he was unsteady on his feet.

The young man continued, "Brother Langford, you know I don't have anything against you but I am the meanest man in Nashville and I'm gonna prove to you just how mean I am. I'm going to knock the h--- out of you." His fists were clinched and he was drawing back his arm to swing and hit him.

Billy spoke quickly and with a deeper than usual tone in his voice and very loud, "Dan, you're drunk and if you swing at me and miss. I'm going to flatten you right here in this wet parking lot."

In my mind I was wondering, where is all the traffic that is usually here? Where are all the people that are always walking up and down the street in front of the church? My heart was pounding. There was no one to be seen around anywhere. I laid my hand on Robert's shoulder. We stood as if we were frozen.

Billy said, "Why don't you give me your hand and let's shake hands?" Dan squinted his eyes and drew his mouth and lips tight together. He almost fell while standing there. Then he dropped his arms down to his side and stuck out his right hand and said, "Okay, preacher that sounds good to me." With a sigh of relief, Robert and I began to breathe normally again.

Then Dan continued, "Preacher, I like you."

Billy said, "Dan, I'm sure that you're a fine man and God wants to help you live a good life. He can help you if you will let Him. I was a sinner just like you before God saved me and changed my life."

Dan looked at him and held his hand. He then staggered down the walk. He almost fell as he turned around to throw up his hand and wave at Billy.

Several days later someone was knocking on the church door so hard that it frightened me. I said, "Who's there? Who is it?" The answer came, "It's me, Dan from across the street. Is the preacher here? I need to talk to him."

By the time Billy came from his office to the door I had opened it enough to see that Dan appeared to be sober. Billy said, "Come on in. We'll go into the office. Leta, hold my calls, Dan and I need to talk." Billy gave me his beautiful smile and winked at me as if to say it was okay. The office door closed behind them. I had mixed emotions watching them go in there. However I knew that Billy knew what he was doing and could handle the situation. Two hours later the office door opened. They were both smiling. Billy said, "We have had a good talk and Dan has accepted the Lord as his Savior."

This was the beginning of a good and pleasant relationship. We saw Dan many times after this incident; he was always sober and so respectful. We heard from him several years later. He moved from Nashville to a small town nearby and is taking an active part in a church. God is so good. He turned what could have been disastrous situation into a blessing.

CHURCH DOORS

◇◇◇◇◇◇◇

A lovely middle aged couple moved to Nashville from Ohio to continue their education at Vanderbilt University. They would be living here for two years while working to complete their degrees. They joined our church and attended regularly. The Sunday before Christmas following the morning church service they were the last to leave. When Jerry shook Billy's hand he placed a one hundred dollar bill that was folded into his hand and said, "This is your Christmas present from us." Billy handed it to me while we were eating dinner at the High Ho Restaurant (now McDonalds) on Hillsboro Road. It felt good to have that much money. I was so excited and began immediately thinking of things we could buy; things we really needed. Billy could get a much needed suit and shoes; Robert could get clothes and new toys, and for me a new winter coat.

The next morning at breakfast Billy said, "You know, Honey, one hundred dollars would probably buy two new front doors for the church and probably pay for the installation too."

My heart sank. "You're not going to buy doors. Are you? Oh, you just can't."

He didn't mention the doors again until after the Christmas and New Year's holidays were over; neither did I.

One afternoon he came in from making his hospital visits and said, "I went by and checked on the price of doors on the way home. We can buy them and get them installed for fifty dollars each." Then he added, "It would certainly make a big difference in the front of the church and it would make it look so much better."

There went all of our much needed new clothes and Robert's toys. I finally managed to say, "Billy, I can't believe you're going to take our Christmas money and buy doors. Jerry and Nita gave the money to us, not to the church."

He smiled as he walked over to me and put his arm around my waist. He pulled me close to him and said, "Well, okay, if you really don't want to."

I thought, "Why do you have to say, if I really don't want to."

Needless to say, after a few days I reluctantly consented to buy two church doors. They were purchased and installed and they really did make a big difference.

Billy was so proud of them but I really prayed sincerely, "God, please change my attitude. Every time I look at these doors this feeling swells up inside of me; I don't want doors. We need clothes and toys. Please help me. I don't want to be a selfish person." I felt so guilty that these feelings were there. Gradually and many days later, I was able to really and genuinely be thankful for Billy's love for the church. I must admit though, the doors really made the church look so much better. (And those clothes would have been worn out by now anyway and the toys would probably have been broken.)

As I write this I am again reminded of the scripture, "A man's life does not consist not in the abundance of the things which he possesseth". Luke 12:15 Over the years I have become aware and have seen the truth in this statement.

OUR UNNEIGHBORLY NEIGHBORS

◇◇◇◇◇◇

The elderly couple that lived next door to the church had used the front yard of the church as their yard. They planted a flower garden. They even built their fence to include the church yard. The gate opened into their garden which became the parking lot for the church. They weren't very neighborly toward us from the very beginning. They didn't like our moving into the Sunday school rooms and they especially disliked the church.

Mrs. Davis was about five feet and seven inches tall. Her flaming red hair was always frizzy and stuck out from the small brimmed straw hat that she always wore, even in the house. Her thick glasses made her eyes look extra-large. She always wore a long sleeve blouse over a cotton print dress. She was sorta on the heavy side as far as her weight was concerned.

Mr. Davis was about the same height. However, he was thin and did not look as large as Mrs. Davis. He was slightly bald. He also wore thick glasses but they were not as thick as Mrs. Davis'. He always wore an old tattered black dress hat when he was outside. He drove a T-Model car occasionally that they kept in the garage that was practically touching the back of the church (which was our living quarters). There was only three feet between us. His fence really was on our property. He was a plumber by trade and he stayed in the garage a lot. This put him right at our door.

Our rooms were in the back of the church. It was almost impossible to hear when anyone knocked at either outer door. Until writing this, just now, I had never thought about the fact that we were living on the alley! Usually when anyone came to visit us they would honk their horn, not loud, just a tap.

We suddenly became aware of a "No Horn Ordinance" in Nashville. Mrs., Davis would call the police department and report that someone was honking their horn, saying we had broken the law. By the time we could get to the door to answer it, the police would be driving up to also greet our visitors.

The policemen would drive up to the church and they came often to make calls to our house, sometimes several in the same day. We became well acquainted with both the night and day crew. They were always polite and considerate. We would invite them to come inside along with our visitors. If they had time they would have a cup of coffee with us. Then the police would drive off and be on their way only to be right back to answer another call about someone "disturbing the peace."

For weeks there was no let up at all. They did not like our living there. We kept thinking things would get better. The police department was working on a solution to help us with the problem. The next time the policemen came they said they had decided what needed to be done. The policeman said, "Place a sign on this big tree beside the church door that reads, 'PLEASE DO NOT HONK HORN'. When we or any of the other policemen drive up and see the sign, they will not have to stop and bother you again." The department has to answer all calls but when we see this sign that will take care of the problem."

One Sunday the Sunday school rooms were so hot that the younger classes met outside, under the big tree - the same one, with the sign concerning the horn ordinance. Our neighbor, Mrs. Davis brought out a radio and placed it on their outside screened-in back porch with the volume turned as loud as it would go. She and Mr. Davis stood looking at the children sitting under the tree. The other classes inside the church could even hear and their classes were disturbed.

A young man just home from serving the Navy was attending the church and heard the music from the radio. He left his class went outside and walked over to the fence facing them. He asked them to please turn the volume down. Our neighbors just ignored him and kept standing on the porch, looking at him. The Naval Officer said, "I fought for freedom to worship when I was overseas and I'll fight for it again today if I have to come over this fence to turn down the radio." Mr. Davis quickly reached over and turned off the radio and took it in the house with Mrs. Davis following closely behind. She closed their screen door very quietly. The classes continued with their lesson. All was well, or so we thought.

Until one Monday morning a familiar knock came on the door. When Billy opened the door there stood a well-dressed (wearing a brown uniform) middle-aged nice looking man from the Health Department Office. He was holding a small piece of white paper. He said, "Is this nine fourteen, Eighteenth Avenue South?" Billy answered, "Yes Sir, it is" The officer continued, "Well, we have a complaint that you have a flat roof that holds water, breeds mosquitoes, and is a nuisance to the community." By this time I was standing next to Billy. We couldn't believe this!

Then the officer asked, "Do you all live here?" We both nodded our head, "Yes." He was already stepping closer to the door when he asked, "May I come inside?"

We turned and he followed us as Billy directed him into each of our rooms and explained to him why we were living in the back of the church. He slowly walked back into to our poorly furnished living room. He had his hand under his chin as he just stood a minute or two. Billy looked over at me and sighed. He gave me a wink and managed to give me a small smile. He was standing with his hands in his pockets but walked over and put his arm around my waist when he realized I was so scared. My heart was beating so fast I could hardly breathe.

Finally the officer raised his head and looked at Billy then at me and then back to Billy. Without changing his expression he put his hand on Billy's shoulder and said, "Let me tell you what to do. Get a quart of oil and pour it on the water on the roof. That will take care of the problem."

After a short conversation, he left. As he was driving out of the parking lot Billy gave me a big hug and kissed me. We both breathed a big sigh of relief as we walked back into the church. When he told us about the complaint we didn't know what we were going to do, thank goodness, that's over.

Three weeks from that Monday we heard a knock on the door and when Billy opened the door. I could hear a man and Billy talking. As I listened more closely, I realized that it sure sounded like the Health Officer that had been here. He said, "I have a complaint that you are putting garbage in the alley, along the side and the back of the church." They came through the living room on the way to the back door. He was holding another white piece of paper the same size as before. He folded it and put it in his shirt pocket. I wondered where they were going.

Billy and I followed him outside and around the church to see what he was talking about. Sure enough there was garbage scattered along the side and back of the church and in the alley. We said at the same time, "We did not do this." He walked slowly around the alley and church and kicked the garbage with the toe of his shoe. Billy and I just stood there quietly and watched him walk back and forth along the side of the alley.

He pulled his jaw in as to be biting his jaw.

He walked over to Billy and me and motioned toward our back door of the church.

"Could we go back into the church?" and continued talking as we were walking. He said, "You see, whoever is making all these complaints is really unhappy. Think of all they are going through trying to make things up, just to irritate and bother you. Just remember, kids, this is bothering them a whole lot more than it is bothering you. I'm a member of a church across town and we have problems too. So don't take this personally. It will all work out."

Robert would play outside and sometimes his toys would roll inside their fence or Richard, who was only one year old, would walk over to the fence and throw his toys between the boards in the fence they would not get them for us. They would come out pick them up.

Put them on their back porch where Robert and Richard could see them but could not get them. We had no money to buy more. This still upsets me when I think about it.

One Thursday night, several years later, a nurse from General Hospital called our home. In fact it was three o'clock early Friday morning. The nurse asked, "Is this Reverend Langford who pastors a church on Eighteenth Avenue South?" Billy answered sleepily, "Yes." She continued, "A Mrs. Davis left word that if her husband died, we were to inform you and then you should go tell her. He died at two forty-five a.m. Please let me know what we should do about making arrangements." What a surprise to both Billy and I.

Billy got dressed as quickly as possible and drove to her house. He said she wouldn't open the door for the longest time. Finally, she recognized his voice and unlocked her door. He told her to sit down that he wanted to tell her something. She was still half-asleep. He told her about her husband and that the nurse had called him. Mrs. Davis took hold of his arm and asked, "Will you make all the funeral arrangements and call the hospital for me? And will you conduct the funeral service and would Mrs. Langford sing and play the organ?" When Billy returned home about six o'clock and told me what she had said, I could not believe it. I kept saying, "You've got to be kidding. She doesn't want us to do that, surely not."

For the next seventeen years Billy took care of her. He took her to the doctor. He took her to buy groceries; she even let him pick out what he felt she needed for her diabetic diet. She wouldn't let me change her grocery list but would let him. Each time, on their way home, she wanted to stop at Wendy's for a hamburger and a soft drink for them to take home to eat. She would always say to him, when they turned in their order at the drive-in window, "Get whatever kind of hamburger you want, but don't get those fixin's; they cost a dime extra."

One day returning from their monthly 'outing' as she called it, she said, "Reverend Langford, does your wife need a coat?" Billy said, "No, she's got one." (Thinking that she was not financially able to buy me a coat). And many other times she asked him, "Are you sure that your wife could not use a winter coat?" He would always answer, "No, she has one."

One thing I have learned for sure through the years is that things change, situations change, people change and our ideas change. Almost nothing stays the same. I am reminded of the scripture, Ecclesiastes the third chapter and the first eight verses and especially verse eleven, "He has made everything beautiful in its time," I must always remember that.

Billy helped her when she had fallen. She had injured her back and could not walk or even get out of bed without someone helping her. He was bringing her home from the hospital when she said, "Reverend Langford, the doctors don't think I'll ever be able to walk by myself anymore. What do you think?"

Billy said, "Let's not worry about that. If I come each day, will you help me and try to walk? We will ask God to give you strength just for that day to take a step or two. Let's leave the problem with Him,"

That was a commitment that took over a year to accomplish. She finally managed to walk with a walker and was able to get out of bed without assistance. Billy did not miss one day going over there even through the cold winter.

He said, "If other people can get to their work then I can get to mine." One cold, blustery day we had four inches of snow on the ground and freezing rain. The radio and television announcements were saying, "Do not travel or be on the roads unless it is an emergency - very dangerous driving conditions."

As I expected, Billy ignored my pleading advice which was, "one day will not make that much difference. You better not go."

His answer, as always, "Don't worry, honey, I'll be home before you know it. I'll be okay." Out the door he would go. Sometimes he had to try several times before the car would make it up the slippery hill in front of our house to the top of the street. I would stand at the living room window and watch him until finally he would make it. I knew he was on his way to make the eleven-mile jaunt across town.

He brought the wood in for her cook stove in the kitchen, checked to see if she had enough food to eat and if she had eaten, if not he would fix her something to eat. He checked on the little gas stove in her bedroom to be sure she would stay warm. Sometimes when he came back home he would say, "She's not getting her strength back. I think she has just given up and is not trying." However, Billy never gave up.

With Billy's persistence, after several months she was able to get out of bed by herself and walk with a walker. Then Billy bought her a walking cane and with the help of the cane she got more confidence and finally one day she took several steps without Billy's assistance. She began to improve rapidly. She would call every day after Billy left her house. She would say, "Hello, Mrs. Langford. I was just checking to see if Reverend Langford has made it home safely. He says, I'll be walking real good before long. Thank you all." Before I could respond she would hang up the receiver. After weeks of this one-sided short conversation she suddenly started talking to me. She would talk almost an hour sometimes. She said in one of our lengthy conversations, "I told Reverend Langford, I want you all to have my bedroom suite whether you want it or not; especially the chest of drawers and he agreed that he would take it." I told her we appreciated it.

She was walking much better now yet Billy checked on her almost every day. One day when he went by she was sitting on the front porch swing. She said, "Reverend Langford, I have been waiting for you." She shuffled across the porch to the door. Billy opened it for her and followed her inside into her dark, dreary, bedroom on back into the kitchen. She told him to sit down at the table. She handed him a piece of white paper about the size of a large envelope. Billy unfolded the paper and started reading,

"I authorize Reverend W. C, Langford to cash any check of mine" signed and dated January 31, 1981."

Billy said he thought about the things she had done many years before and wondered, "Can this be the same woman who had years previously seized our children's toys and caused us so many problems with the police and health departments?"

She brought him back to realization by saying, "Read it out loud," He read the note. She added, "and while you are here I want you to get my money for me." He had no idea what she was talking about. She continued, "Look behind the ornamental woodwork on the mantle, pull the board out just a little and you will see a can." There behind the panel was a flattened small eight ounce size tin can with the wrapper pulled off. It was stuffed with five and ten dollar bills.

"Now" she said, "Go get my vacuum cleaner out of the closet over there and look inside the bag." There was a small package wrapped in aluminum foil with ten dollar bills. "Now, look behind the refrigerator." Billy said that he had trouble getting this flattened can. It was down near the floor and the refrigerator was next to the wall. But she kept reassuring him, "Keep looking there is one back there." He finally touched a coat hanger. She said, "That's it. Keep pulling on the hanger." He said he pulled it very slowly until he could get hold of it. At the other end of the coat hanger was another flattened tin can with a hole in one end of the can. The wire ran through the top of it. There were more bills.

"Now," she said, "Look in the back of my wood stove toward the side and you will find another can." She laughed and said, "One time I forgot about this one and built a fire in the stove." Billy took his coat off and rolled up his shirt sleeve but he still got black ashes on his shirt. She insisted that he keep reaching farther back and sure enough he felt the end of the can. He pulled it out. The ashes were all over it. When he pulled it completely out, ashes fell on the floor. Inside the flattened can were more bills. The money was scorched but the foil around the can had protected it.

"Now, go look in the refrigerator under the bacon." As Billy opened the refrigerator door he said to her, "Now 1 know what having 'cold cash' means," He lifted the bacon and under it was another flattened can containing more bills. Before he shut the refrigerator door she turned and was shuffling back into her bedroom to a couch that was covered with newspapers and magazines. She said, "Come in here and bring all the cans with you." She motioned for Billy to sit down. Billy started to hand the cans and the foil to her. She said, "Don't do that. I want you to take this money to the bank for me. Put it in your name and keep it for me until I need it." Billy did that before he came home. He brought the cans and the foil for me to see. I could not believe it.

Twenty years later, at her death, we brought the chest of drawers to our house. Looking inside we found an old dusty, dingy cotton bag in the bottom. It was filled with something soft. I told Billy to take it outside and open it out there. He insisted on opening it in the den. After he got the string untied which had been tied several times he reached into the bag and said, "Honey, reach down in there and see what you feel." I quickly replied, "No way."

He turned the bag upside down and out fell a beautiful reddish brown coat. He reached on the floor and held it up. It was a beautiful full length fur coat. Standing there with my eyes and mouth wide open, Billy said, "Leta, she has been trying to give you this beautiful full length fur coat for years." He walked over to me and placed it around my shoulders. I slipped my arms into it. The coat was about four inches above my ankles. Believe it or not, the way the coat was made across the shoulders with the sleeves turned up it fit me fine. It felt wonderful. I was walking around in the den with a beautiful, soft, reddish brown full length fur coat. I was squealing, "I've got a full length fur coat! A real fur coat!"

All of a sudden my thoughts flashed back to those terrible four hard years we lived in the three tiny rooms in the back of the church. Our younger son Richard had been born while we were living there. Then we moved into a small new four room house on Sentinel Drive in West Nashville. We lived there six years. Then because we were always taking children having someone in our home we needed another bedroom. Billy asked Jim, a friend of ours, to help build another bedroom onto our house. He said we will talk about this later.

The next Sunday morning Jim and Frances, his wife, attended our morning worship service. Following service Frances said, "Would your kids like to live in East Nashville? We have a building site and are building some houses. If you want a house there we will build you the kind of house you want." Billy said, "That would be great if we could afford it."

Jim said, "It won't cost you much more than adding that bedroom you need on the house you have now. All of our equipment is already on the job." We decided upon a beautiful eight-room split-foyer Colonial house. We could never have afforded such a lovely home but God provided it for us through Jim and Frances, who are members of Glen Leven Presbyterian Church located just up the road from the location of our new church on Franklin Road.

The next fall we were moving into our new house on Tiffany Terrace. We spread what little furniture we had in as many rooms as we could. We didn't have a thing in the living room, dining room and one of the bedrooms. During the winter we brought the picnic table in from outside to us as our dining room table. Gradually we added a piece or two, until over the years, we finally have it completely furnished, not with the newest styles, but filled. In fact every once in a while Billy says, "We need to have a garage sale." And I always add, "Whenever you're ready."

From our kitchen window you can see the glow of the Opryland Hotel. All through the house can be heard the ever so faint sound of the beautiful, light-hearted music of the calliope. "Take Me Out To The Ball Game" from the General Jackson Showboat making their regular daily trips of the Cumberland River Riverfront Park to Opryland Hotel.

Just this side of the river is Cornelia Fort Airport for small planes. A plane was flying over the field gently gliding in for a landing and the roar of the motor could barely be heard; and looking still farther past the small plane in the distance was a large plane making its dissent to land at the International Airport.

Yesterday, Billy and I were sitting out on the patio listening to the birds singing and enjoying the fresh air. Beyond the back yard fence and across the river was a beautiful outline of green trees against the clear blue sky. Not a cloud could be seen. A soft cool breeze was gently blowing from the east. It was filling the air with the sweet fragrance from the white and vanilla flowers from the honeysuckle vines on the backyard fence.

With no feeling of apprehension or anxiety at all, I said, "Billy, you know what? I would rather have this house and live right here than anywhere else in the whole world." He looked straight into my eyes. After a few seconds he said with a teasing smile, "How do you know? You haven't lived in many other houses or in many other places, have you?"

My thoughts went back to that cold, dreary night in November many years ago and remembering also for the first time in years, how badly my leg was hurting that night when Billy said, with such optimistic certainty, "Honey, in the morning everything will look better. Nashville is really a beautiful town and I know you'll like living here."

I looked up into and away beyond the clear blue sky with a grateful heart and a prayer of thanksgiving to God for all of His many blessings to us and especially thanking Him for healing my leg of Phlebitis forty-three years ago, even before Robert had his first birthday.

Through the years we have shared the love for the four distinct seasons of the year which Nashville embraces. Many streets are lined with beautiful trees. We have seen freezing rain and snowfall in the winter making each tree stand out in its own beauty with every individual limb covered with ice. What a glorious delight to see the snow completely blanketing the lovely hills that surround the city. In the spring we have seen the budding Dogwood trees sprouting new leaves and bursting into beautiful blooming pink and white visions of splendor.

Soon to be followed by the magnificent Magnolia trees with their big beautiful, bold white flowers and the variety of colors from blooming plants and shrubbery. Then my favorite season of all, when summer gives way to autumn and the leaves turn to blazing red, gold and orange resplendent in their foliage with the fragrance and aroma of burning leaves filling the air with a warm nostalgic feeling.

Billy was right, everything did look better in the morning. Nashville is a beautiful city and at night the lighted and picturesque skyline is gorgeous. The tall and stately two tower South Central Bell Building is the tallest building in the state and looks pretty. I do like living in a city completely surrounded by gentle rolling hills and where the air is fill with the sound of music.

CHAPTER THREE

THE FLIP SIDE OF COUNTRY PEOPLE

Nashville is a city of melody where the clear and distinct notes of the guitar and the rhythm of a bass can be heard. Even as I write this, music is filling the air from the house next door. The music of a beautiful country, western or gospel song blends into the life of a busy city and they become one.

Music Row is about one mile long and the area is known as the streets where country music is alive. There is not just one street named "Music Row," but several streets make up this area. Two of the streets, 16th Avenue South and 17th Avenue South, are one-way streets; 18th Avenue South is a two-way street. Some of the connecting streets are Music Square North, Roy Acuff Drive and Music Circle. Music Row is located off Interstate 40, near downtown Nashville.

Music Row is made up of very ordinary-looking streets and looks like a residential area with some of the houses being made into recording studios, music publishing firms, management, promotional offices, and songwriting studios. Despite the varied operations of each they all work side-by-side. There is always constant construction of new buildings, such as the large modern ASCAP (American Society of Composers, Authors and Publishers) office.

The resulting array of old and new gives Music Row a charming and pleasing mixture. The tourist related shops, exhibits and museums create much interest from all over the world. The traffic is much heavier now than it was in October 1951 when we moved to Nashville.

We lived in the back of the church on 18th Avenue South. Our church began in a tent revival that was held on the corner of 17th and Division Street which is now the 'Music City Park,' The Speer Family provided the special music.

Driving around in the Music Row area you can see the tour busses parked up and down the street and hear the loud roar of the motors. The buses run regularly and seem to always be there anytime, day or night. Their excited passengers, climbing off or on the bus are often wearing cowboy boots and cowboy hats. Their arms are loaded down with souvenirs and always swinging from their shoulder is their camera.

While touring Music Row, you will likely see your favorite stars who will smile and wave at you and they won't mind stopping to talk to you. You can even take a tour in a 'trolley' that runs from the Riverfront Park through Music Row. In the last few years they have added horse-drawn buggies in some areas of town. We have had friends from out of town to visit us and when they arrive, the entire family would be wearing cowboy boots, cowboy hats, jeans, plaid shirts and red bandana scarves around their necks. Billy says that he and I should buy a complete 'country outfit,' we never did.

Billy does have his own tour of the country stars' homes. He has become acquainted with them over the years and when they see him drive up they will wave to him and invite him inside along with his visitors. They often serve them coffee or tea. Usually the Boones would pop them some pop-corn.

Working in the restaurants, department stores, service stations and every place of business you can count on there being a hopeful, optimistic artists, waiting to be discovered, thus making his or her golden dream come true.

MARTY ROBBINS

◇◇◇◇◇◇◇

Who is Marty Robbins? Martin David Robinson known as Marty Robbins and his lovely wife, Marizona moved to Nashville in 1951 the same year that Billy and I moved here. They started attending our church, Belmont Assembly in 1954. Marty was unable to attend regularly due to his being on the road. Marizona and Ronny, their small son was faithful to every service. Ronny would fall asleep during the church service when he was growing up and Marizona was unable to carry him to the car. She would lead him to the car and she said, "Ronny doesn't wake up even when we get home."

One Easter Sunday Marty was not on the road and attended the service. We gave everyone there a calendar. On the front of the calendar was a picture of Christ, standing in a boat behind a man who was steering the boat. The waves were high and some water was coming into the boat. The hand of Christ was on the man's shoulder. Marty said he kept thinking about that picture and could not get it out of his mind. He then wrote the song, "With His Hand On My Shoulder" which he recorded on the album

"WHAT GOD HAS DONE".
WITH HIS HAND ON MY SHOULDER

WITH HIS HAND ON MY SHOULDER I'LL SAIL THE SEA OF SIN.

WITH HIS HAND ON MY SHOULDER I CANNOT HELP BUT WIN. I'LL FOLLOW AS HE PILOTS ME THROUGH WATERS DARK AND COLD.

WITH HIS HAND ON MY SHOULDER I KNOW I'LL REACH MY GOAL.
MY EVERY HOPE IS ANCHORED TO THE FAITH I HAVE IN HIM.
I KNOW ILL REACH THE SORE LINE THOUGH AT TIMES THE LIGHTS ARE DIM,
HELL TAKE ME PAST THE ROCKY CLIFFS FROM LIFE'S STORM I'LL BE RELEASED.

WITH HIS HAND ON MY SHOULDER I'LL HAVE EVERLASTING PEACE.
SURROUNDED BY AN ANGRY SEA THAT'S MADE OF HATE AND SIN,

BUT I WON'T SINK AS LONG AS I WON'T LET
THE WATERS IN.
AND WITH THE HELP OF GOD I KNOW I'LL
NEVER LOSE MY WAY

WITH HIS HAND ON MY SHOULDER I CANNOT
GO ASTRAY.
I HAVE A HOME UP IN THE SKY HE MADE
IT JUST FOR ME.
BUT TO PROVE THAT I DESERVE THIS HOME
I HAVE TO SAIL THIS SEA. THE WAVES OF SIN
SOMETIMES ARE HIGH AND SPRAY MIGHT
TOUCH MY CLOTHES,

WITH HIS HAND ON MY SHOULDER IT WILL
NEVER TOUCH MY SOUL.

MARTY ROBBINS

◇◇◇◇◇◇

Marizona felt God leading her to start a church in an area of South Nashville near the State Fair Grounds. A church was not in that area. Billy and I were going to help her hold a tent revival. We decided that instead of having a bus ministry to our church that it would be much more beneficial to the neighborhood to have a church. Billy went to the houses in the neighborhood inviting the residents to the revival. This helped him to get acquainted with the neighbors. Also they would not be surprised when they saw a tent being put up on the vacant lot with the sign, "Revival with W. C. Langford preaching with special singing every night. WELCOME."

Marizona led the singing and I played the piano. The cool night air in the tent did not help the sore throat that I was battling. The third night my temperature would not go down and Robert was also running a temperature. There was no way that I could attend. That left Marizona and Billy to conduct the revival. However Marty was in town and he agreed to play his guitar and sing. The revival went on for several weeks and he continued to participate in the services.

One night after a service when everyone had gone Billy asked Marizona, "What does Marty think about the revival and does he think we are reaching the neighborhood and does he believe we would be able to start a church? I want to talk with him about this before he has to leave for his tour."

Marizona, in her very quiet and reserved manner smiled her beautiful smile and replied, "Marty said, the neighborhood was receiving us well and you have really done some great preaching." She bit her bottom lip looked off and then looked back at Billy and after hesitating just a moment she continued, "On the way home last night he also said in his sermon I think Brother Langford and I were the only ones there guilty of committing all the sins he was preaching about."

Then Marizona told Billy that he had said in his sermon, "I don't care if you have committed all the sins recorded in the Bible, God will forgive you. I don't care what you have done; I have committed all the sins in the Bible." Marty was characterized by his wonderful good nature and playfulness. Through the years we have shared a lot of good times and laughed about this many times.

During the revival, several people from the community attended regularly. Following the revival Marizona and Billy found a vacant building across from a tobacco barn on Martin Street. They rented it and we held services in it. Later, a house on White Avenue was secured for services.

My Dad, due to his eye problems, had recently retired after serving sixty years in full time ministry. He was still teaching the Wednesday Night Bible Lesson and teaching a Sunday School Class at our church. Billy asked him if he would fill in as pastor for the congregation on White Avenue until another minister was secured. Dad was delighted and pastored there for five years.

Calvary Assembly of God located on McGavock Pike is the outgrowth of the original church. They have built a beautiful new sanctuary and provide a wonderful day-care program. The pastor, Glen Burks and his lovely wife Shirley, are among our closest friends.

God is the reason Marizona and I have been so close through the years. One morning as Billy and I were finishing breakfast I told Billy very emphatically, "Billy, we need to see Marizona today." We had not been in close contact with them for a while. I continued, "Last night I tossed and turned all night long. Even after I prayed for her I could not get her off my mind; she needs us." This was about five years after we met. Billy said, "I was wondering why you were already dressed." I asked him to hurry and get ready. So by our usual breakfast time we were already across town in Brentwood standing on Marizona's front porch. While waiting for her to answer the door Billy reached over and took my hand. We asked the Lord for wisdom in telling her what had happened during the night because I didn't have a clue as what to say.

Marizona came to the door wearing her housecoat looking extremely tired and needless to say, shocked seeing us standing there, especially so early in the morning. She just stood there looking at us for a minute or two. She motioned for us to come in. She slowly followed us through the foyer and stopped at the beautiful step down living room entrance. We exchanged short greetings then I said, "Marizona, I know you are wondering why we are here so early."

She pointed to the couch as she sighed deeply and slid into the chair next to the window. She smiled her sweet, beautiful smile and answered softly, "Yes, I sense that you have come for a special reason." I said, "I don't know what to say except to tell you what the Lord revealed to me. And to tell you that I prayed for you most of the night. God assured me that when we pray, He will answer our prayer." Tears began running down her face and she nodded her head, 'yes' as if to say "I know what you are talking about." A little smile came even through her tears.

"Leta, I have told no one. But I have been going through a terrible time. I have been experiencing great fear. I have been unable to sleep. I am so tired that it has actually made me physically ill. I could not bring myself to talk to anyone. I know God sent you here this morning." With a great sigh of relief I replied, "Billy and I have come to anoint you with oil and pray the prayer of deliverance for you." She said, "Oh, I'm so glad you have come."

God gloriously met with us there in her living room, and we can say another prayer was answered. As I write this, I am reminded of the prayer she prayed many years ago. When she was eleven years old she began to pray for the Lord to send her a "singing cowboy and pretty clothes to wear."

Sometimes when we are together she will smile her beautiful smile, remind me of that morning and say, "Leta, I'm so glad you obeyed the Lord and came to my house early that morning." Marizona is a much stronger Christian than I, and with her quiet mild temperament, a much better example of Christ. I wish I were like her. Yet God sent me to pray for her. I do stand amazed at how God works. Through the years we have prayed together and seen God answer prayer many times.

Marizona and Marty's daughter Janet wanted to be married in Centennial Park. There is a huge gorgeous sunken flower garden just over to the right of the Parthenon. There is an array of beauty permeating the garden with the beautiful colors and the aroma of the flowers filling the air. Of course when the visitors to the Parthenon and the park heard the news that there was to be a wedding there, the crowd began to gather.

Cars could not get through. Some people, not knowing what was happening, began to blow their horns. However, this quickly stopped. I guess someone informed them that a wedding was taking place. Marty and Marizona finally made it through all the traffic and people. They finally arrived in his Rolls Royce. I said his because Marizona always says, "You never know about Marty and his collection of cars. I never know what he will be driving." He enjoyed driving his cars. In fact in later years he had a race car and raced professionally.

The sun was shining and it was a beautiful and perfect day for a June wedding. It was a very hot and humid day. Nashville is known for that during the summer months. And today was no exception. By three o'clock it was almost unbearable. Billy and I arrived at the park early. Billy did not put his robe on until just before the ceremony. Already perspiration was running down his face and running down the back of his collar. Because of the crowd, the wedding was late getting started.

The girls wearing their long pastel dresses and holding their pastel bouquets did not look a bit wilted. They were beautiful with the background of flowers behind them and looked just like a big picture. Janet and Marty were standing behind the cars. They were lined up on the little bridge leading from one garden to the other garden where Billy, the best man and the ushers were standing. Twenty white lawn chairs were set up for Marizona and the family members. They were placed close to where Billy was standing. The other guests were standing during the ceremony. Finally, the noise quieted down except for the birds chirping among the branches in the bushes and trees. In the distance you could hear the busy traffic on West End Avenue.

It was amazing how much the small electric organ that we brought from the church sounded like a large organ. The wedding songs sounded absolutely magnificent. The music was clear and each word of the songs could be understood. Neither the outside noise nor the organ was over powering. The flowers from the garden surrounding the wedding party were giving off their sweet aroma. The wedding vows were easily heard without straining. When the people realized there was a wedding ceremony taking place they were really very respectful and it became unbelievably quiet.

The reception followed at the West End Holiday Inn. Janet lives in Los Angeles. Several years later, on a cool brisk Sunday afternoon Billy and I arrived at the home of Marizona and Marty. Billy was there to perform the wedding ceremony of their son, Ronny to Cathy. Billy brought his robe to wear. It was a very formal wedding and their home was decorated absolutely exquisitely. When you walked into the foyer and looked down into the formal living room it took your breath away.

The only interruption was when a tour bus would stop in front of the house and then when the buses would start again their loud roar of their motor could be heard. Billy would just hesitate a few moments and then continue the ceremony. Cathy looked absolutely radiant with her beautiful dark long hair and dark eyes sparkling. Her long bridal gown and veil were so formal and oh, so beautiful! She was gorgeous.

Ronny and Cathy had met just a few weeks earlier at Fan Fair. This was definitely 'love at first sight' for both of them. They were standing facing Billy and exchanging their vows and listening to the beautiful ceremony. Everyone's wish and the unspoken words, "I wish Marty could have been here" was in everyone's heart.

A lovely reception followed and was held in their spacious dining room which was decorated as eloquently as the foyer and the lower living room. It was a picture perfect afternoon and evening from the moment we stepped out of our car until the moment we pulled out of their driveway. The time had flown and it was close to midnight.

Ronny and Cathy have a beautiful little girl, Courtney Leigh, and a very active little boy Michael Martin. The other day while talking to Ronny he said, "I think I'm too old for this."

Several years ago when Marty had heart surgery, Marizona called Billy to meet them at St. Thomas Hospital to have prayer with Marty before the surgery. Billy arrived at the Hospital. They had already taken Marty from his room and Billy was rushing down the corridor and calling to the doctor, "Wait doctor, wait just a minute," He got their attention just as they got to the elevator. Catching up with them Billy breathlessly said, "Marty, I came as quickly as I could."

Marty reached for Billy's hand and in his teasing way said, "Doctor, you're going to have to wait until my preacher prays for me. I need his prayers." Marty was among the first group of patients to have the procedure done at St. Thomas Hospital. His picture was on the cover of the annual report of Saint Thomas Hospital for the fiscal year 1981-1982. The words were Mending Broken Hearts. He was standing holding his guitar. In 1970 following his first heart attack he underwent a triple-bypass.

He was the first country music star to perform in Las Vegas and was the first to use horn at the Grand Ole Opry.

Marizona called on a cold morning December 8, 1982. The weather had been blustery and the snow and ice from last week's storm was still on the ground. It was in middle of the morning. She told us Marty had died and asked Billy to preach his funeral on Saturday at 11 o'clock at Woodlawn Funeral Home.

Marty made his final appearance and entered into the eternal throne room of God. His music career began anew, never coming to an end, with his beautiful voice giving praise to our Savior and King.

Billy's usual procedure was to read Bible verses from the Scripture when he conducts funerals rather than just preach a sermon. Becky Hughes sang "Take Up Thy Cross and Follow Me." Billy turned to the family and quoted the 23rd Psalm followed by John 14-3. "Let not your heart be troubled. Then he read assuring us of the Second Coming of Christ in I Thessalonians 4:13-18, I Corinthians 2:9,10, II Timothy 4:6-8, and Psalms 91:9-15.

Brenda Lee sang "One Day At A Time" before Billy preached the following message:

> Who is Marty Robbins? What is it about this man that when his name is mentioned, feelings of warmth, love and hope are evoked?

> As a note of ironic fate, a supplement to the *Nashville Tennessean* and *Nashville Banner* newspapers had on its cover recently, a picture of Marty with a headline that read, 'Mending Broken Hearts,'

As many of you know, twelve years ago Marty was among the first in our nation to undergo a heart by-pass operation. The operation was a success. Marty regained his strength to go back into areas of life with as much excitement as humanly possible.

At that point the true depth of the statement 'Mending Broken Hearts' comes into focus for Marty's life. While it is true that the doctors at St. Thomas Hospital did an outstanding job of mending Marty's heart physically twelve years ago, Marty has mended thousands of broken hearts each year through his songs which touch the very soul of America as well as countries overseas.

Marty Robbins was an example of the hope and achievement of a goal that brings thousands to Music City. We, as a city, take note of the vast contribution he has made to our lives. Marty's life symbolizes hope and inspires us to never settle for mediocrity. His life inspires us to never settle for complacency or compromise but to always strive for excellence. Today Marty has reached a new platitude in his career. Today, Marty Robbins has joined the choir in heaven singing of the glory of God and rejoicing in the eternal throne room of God.

Marty has set a high standard for each of us to follow. As in everyone's life there are a number of trials and challenges, but in his life, he turned them into achievements.

He received many awards, ranging from being the first Grammy Award winner for Country Music, as well as many other awards including one of the most coveted awards in the music business, that of being inducted into the Country Music Hall of Fame.

What is striking about awards is that they are in recognition of merit and accomplishment.

> 'The awards of this earth can be surpassed only by the God-given rewards of heaven. Just as we are all inspired by the awards that Marty has received, we should take his life as a pattern of simplicity and greatness woven together with God's love. Let us prepare our heart and live our life so that we may share with him the rewards of eternal life and also receive an award as we remember the words of Jesus Christ our Lord and Savior, (Revelation 22:12) "Behold, I am coming soon! My reward is with me, and I will give to everyone according to what he has done." Let us pray.

About two weeks after Marty's death, Marizona called me and invited our family to her house. She prepared a lovely Mexican dinner. She said that was Marty's favorite meal and she wanted us to share with her a memorial dinner. It was delicious and most eloquently served.

During dinner she mentioned preparing a proper yet meaningful grave marker. She asked Billy if he would write Marty's epitaph for the beautiful bronze plate that covers his grave. It is the same size of Elvis Presley's marker so there needed to be quite a bit written. After several weeks and many papers thrown in the waste-basket Billy called Marizona and asked her if it would be okay for him to ask Robert about writing it. She said that would be fine she just felt that either he, Robert or Richard should write it. Every few days Robert and Richard would call and say, "Mom, I just haven't got anything. Nothing is coming. When you talk to Marizona tell her I know it will come and tell her not to worry about it."

Late one evening Robert called from an airplane saying, "Mom, I got it. It just came to me as I was leaving the Washington airport. I started writing and I think it is exactly what Marizona wants." He wanted Marizona's phone number. He called her and in a few minutes he called me back and said, "Mom, she said, it is perfect and she also said, you know what Robert? Marty wrote most of his songs while flying."

MARTIN DAVID ROBINSON

September 26, 1925 December 8, 1982

To those who knew him, MARTY ROBBINS was a deeply religious and sensitive man, who loved his family very much.

It wasn't hard to get to know Marty, because if you knew his music, you knew the man.

His repeated references to his faith in God and his admiration for his wife shone through in his songs ranging from "With His Hand On My Shoulder" to "She Was Made of Faith."

His commitment to his country and his love for his fellow man was evident in "I Love You In Every Special Way" and "The Performer."

His endless zest for life was recognized by all who knew of his love for racing or witnessed his stirring performance of 'El Paso.'

His personal courage and strength was manifested through his pioneering heart surgery. He touched the soul of America by allowing his God given "golden voice" to be used in a public way. Yet the recognition he received on earth has been exceeded in a very private way. His faith allowed him to rank among the best in the choir above, leaving each of us the comfort of his songs, the presence of his memory and the anticipation of being with him in his "Little Spot of Heaven" for eternity.

We love you, Dad.
Janet, Your Daughter, Ronny, Your Son

Marizona, Your Woman, Your Wife

and Jesus said, "Let not your hearts be trouble, ye believe
in God, believe also in me. In my Father's house are
many mansions; if it were not so, I would have told you.
I go to prepare a place for you; and if I go and prepare
a place for you, I will come again and receive you unto
myself that where I am there ye may be also."
John 14:1-3

After his death he was inducted into the Cowboy Hall of Fame.
On Marty's birthday, September 26, 1983 Billy prayed at the ground
breaking ceremony of the Marty Robbins Memorial Showcase which
has been moved from Twitty City to the Grand Ole Opry Museum
located inside the park. The Memorial Showcase was developed to
cover his entire life span from his childhood through his career. It
combines music, photographs, exhibits, and memorabilia to offer an
in-depth look at his background and lifestyle. There are numerous
items of clothing which he wore on stage as well as a showcase of his
albums and awards. His museum has been combined with the Grand
Ole Opry Museum in the Opry Plaza complex and his NASCAR
automobile is also there.

Marty's last recordings included 'Tie Your Dreams To Mine'
and 'Some Memories Just Won't Die.' Truly memories of Marty,
his beautiful country and western songs, his distinct sound of music
and his unmistakable golden mellow voice will never die. We enjoy
a long and lasting relationship with Marizona and truly treasure her
friendship.

BARBARA - SONGWRITER

◇◇◇◇◇◇◇

A few weeks ago Bob called to let us know that he, his wife Wynnelle and his daughter Kori had returned safely from their weekend trip to Branson, Missouri, "Hey mom, guess what? While we were having dinner with Barbara and one of their friends, Brent, who is a songwriter, joined us. We began talking about Nashville and where we lived while growing up.

After a while the conversation turned toward dad and his being a minister and building a church on Music Row. Brent asked me, "Exactly where is the church located?" I explained to him it was on Eighteenth just down from Grand Avenue. It was the first building and we bought the house on the corner and used it for our Educational Building before we moved to Oak Hill on Franklin Road.

Bob said, "He squinted his eyes and said, you mean on the corner of Grand and Eighteenth - the house with the front room glassed in?" I told him, "That's the one. The glassed in room had been a front porch and dad suggested making it into a room. He enclosed it and placed glass around it and it became a beautiful office. It really turned out nice. People would take pictures of it all the time." "Then I told him, we hand dug the basement of that house."

Raising his voice, until the people at the other tables turned to look at us, he said, "You got to be kidding! I have written some of my best songs down in that basement!"

"Mom, I experienced a great feeling of satisfaction. I felt like I sort of had a part in his writing since we spent so many weeks digging and working in the basement. When we first started I thought it was an impossible task and didn't think that we would ever get it finished. But you remember how dad kept telling us, "It's going to look great when it's finished. Every shovel full makes a difference. And mom, remember the hand grenade he found down there? The pin was pulled halfway out and the Metro bomb squad came and got it and took it to Fort Campbell in Clarksville to detonate it?" I told him, "Bob, I not only remember it. I have the newspaper article telling about it."

When I placed the receiver back on the phone, I also had a great feeling of satisfaction remembering "for with God nothing shall be impossible" (Mark 10:27). God always helped us finish, what sometimes seemed to us, an impossible task.

The very day the money was due on our contract for the new property on Franklin Road this house was sold. As soon as this transaction was completed, Billy hurried to the bank downtown to make the deposit before closing time. Mr. Haley was surprised when Billy walked into his office and handed him a check to pay for the property in full.

Mr. Haley said, "Since we had not heard from you and it is so near to our closing time, we just assumed that it would not be possible for you to close the deal on the property today." He knew we did not have a large congregation and he also knew the contract had been signed by faith that God would provide the money.

God directed us in the planning and building of our new church. Many times we were not even aware that He had intervened until we looked back over our decisions and realized 'God had worked miraculously His wonders to perform.' An elegant colonial brick edifice with a tall lighted steeple is picturesque as it stands on eleven beautiful landscaped acres for everyone to see and it truly is a living tribute to God's faithfulness.

JOHN HARTFORD

◇◇◇◇◇◇◇

The one and only John Hartford. To know John Hartford is to know that he is uniquely different. One Sunday morning in 1965, John, his wife Betty and their one year old son, Jamie, attended church and since that time there has always been a very special spot in our heart for them.

Following the service we talked with them and found that John was from St. Louis and Betty was from Gideon, Missouri. Gideon is a small town near Kennett, in southeast Missouri, in what is called 'the boot heel.' My dad pastored in Kennett for seven years. My sister Sylvas, who had just celebrated her 83rd birthday was married and lived in Kennett. Since we were acquainted with that locality a kindred spirit was created from the very first time we met.

They drove to Nashville on weekends until they decided to move here. John was starting in the recording industry. John was both singing and writing. They attended church regularly on Sunday morning and evening. Betty and Jamie attended the Wednesday night prayer meeting and they would stay for choir practice which followed the service.

John sang and played his banjo in the church services. Betty would sing with him sometimes. Occasionally he brought his guitar but most of the time, especially after the first few months, he brought and played his banjo. When he was in a rare mood he would sing two songs and other times he would sing one song. Billy always insisted that he participate in the services and John had a deep respect for him. They had a wonderful relationship.

Betty had a beautiful clear soprano voice and she added greatly to our choir. She sang for our weddings, during special events and funerals. Betty was our featured soloist for our worship services, radio and T.V. Her wonderful serene spirit was always evident even as she sang. She also sang in our trio. For several years we met one day each week to practice. A very close relationship was formed and is treasured to this day.

When RCA Victor released his first record he brought us a 45 RPM demo the day they gave it to him. It was "The Tall Tall Grass" and the flip side was "Jack's in the Sack."

John and Betty were in my Sunday School Class. We always enjoyed discussing the scriptures and he made my class very interesting. Sometimes John and I agreed and sometimes we disagreed however we always disagreed agreeably and following our class he would come up to me with a smile and give me a hug.

John was best known as the songwriter of "Gentle On My Mind," a song that became a hit for Glen Campbell in 1967 and which went on to become the most recorded and performed songs of all time. He won three Grammy Awards for that song and in 1976 he earned a Grammy for the solo album Mark Twang.

The words to "Gentle On My Mind," gives one an insight to John and his wonderful unique personality. He wrote the words to this song on a napkin in just a few minutes one evening while sitting at a booth while they were eating supper. John, Betty and Jamie moved to California. John appeared on "The Good Time Hour" with Glen Campbell. John's song "Gentle on my Mind" became the theme song.

John has made a television special telling about his love for the river and riverboats. He wrote the theme song, "Down on the River" used by the paddle wheel boat General Jackson Showboat. It makes several daily runs from Riverfront Park downtown Nashville to Opryand Hotel. He and Jamie perform individually and also together on the General Jackson Showboat. Speaking about singing and riverboats, he says, "This puts both of my loves together."

Katie was born just before they moved. Betty brought her from California to be dedicated by Billy. They moved back to Nashville after a couple of years. Betty and Katie were very active in the church activities. When Katie was 13 years old she began to sing in the choir.

Jamie had followed his dad's profession and joined John occasionally when performing. Jamie and his wife Connie have a beautiful daughter. Katie is a beautiful girl with blond hair that came down just below her shoulders. Her eyes still sparkle and look like the clear purple blue sky as they always have. She has one of the most beautiful, sweet smiles that I have ever seen and it fits her beautiful reserved personality perfectly.

Katie married Eric in our church on December 19, 1993 at 2:00 p.m. They met while attending The University of Tennessee in Knoxville. It was a gorgeous wedding, yet simple in an elegant style.

The wedding reception was held at the home of her dad and step-mother Marie. Their house is in Madison which is in the suburbs of east Nashville. It is a lovely comfortable country house located on the high river bank and overlooks the smooth flowing Cumberland River. Across the river is a spectacular view of the area located between downtown and Opryland. It is the most picturesque scene you can imagine, absolutely beautiful. In the far distance coming into view is this big, colorful General Jackson Showboat filling the air with the sound of the calliope. The riverboats come very near their house. What a sight to behold! It would be nice to stay here forever away from the hustle and bustle of the city.

While sitting on the porch during the reception for Katie and Eric, John and I were talking and I mentioned to him that I was thinking about writing a book. I said, "John, can you believe after all these years

I am writing a book?" He replied, "Sure I can." He smiled his big pretty smile, winked at me and reached over to hug me as he continued. "Leta, it's your time to roll the barrel."

Betty, her mother Bertha Beck, her uncle Jimmy Payne and his family attended our church. Katie lived in Knoxville. Whenever and wherever we see Jamie or John they always make their way to us and give us a big hug. The warmth that was felt many years ago still lingers between us. How good it feels.

Update: John died June 4, 2001 at the age of 65 after a 21 year battle with non-Hodgkin's lymphoma. Johnny Cash wrote about him saying, "John is great, but doesn't know it."

BARBARA FAIRCHILD

The first time we met Barbara Fairchild was on a beautiful Sunday Morning following the morning worship service. She came with a couple who attended our church. They were also involved with country music and songwriters. From the moment we met Barbara we were very much aware of the great spiritual influence of God in her life.

Barbara asked Billy to come to her house the following Thursday Night. Bea, Barbara's housekeeper and nanny, had prepared a lovely supper. As we stepped into the foyer, Barbara took Billy by the arm and said, "I am so glad you all could come to eat with me but I really wanted you all to come so that I could talk to you all about the Bible."

While we were eating Barbara said, "Let me tell you what happened last Sunday. On the way home from church Bea said, 'Miss Barbara, on the way to church this morning you should have told me to be quiet." What happened was that during the morning worship service Barbara sang, "What a Friend We Have in Jesus." The song really touched Bea. Following the message Billy asked everyone to come down and stand at the altar and pray. A lady acquaintance of Bea's had come with them. She also came down to the altar for prayer. Previously Bea had been upset with this lady however Barbara and Bea went by and picked her up and she came to church with them.

Bea gave this lady an expensive dress that she had only worn one time but she thought the lady needed it. When Bea asked the lady why she didn't wear that dress she replied, "Oh, it didn't fit me just right so I gave it to my daughter and she cut it up and used the pieces for her school project."

By the time they arrived at church, Barbara said "Bea was steamin' and still upset during the service. But, she said, "You know, when I knelt at the altar the Lord started blessen' me and I just couldn't help but start shouten' and praisen' the Lord. That was the first time I have ever shouted."

Bea shouted many times after that and what a blessing she was to our church. Her radiant countenance, her love and exuberant praises were always welcome.

We had a wonderful evening talking about the Bible and the time just flew by. Before we realized it, it was two-thirty in the morning. Robert and Richard had fallen to sleep a long time ago. They had gotten pillows off the couch and were lying on the floor listening to us. Bea also joined in on what was to become our regular Bible Study. Barbara and her band were leaving for their tour early in the morning so she had very little time to get ready.

We really enjoyed studying the Bible with her. She had a never ending supply of questions. When studying The Book of Revelation she was held captive by the wonderful truths and prophecy. She had tapes on Revelation, she had books on Revelation, she had everything she could find on Revelation stuffed in her big Bible which she carried all the time.

Each night after we had eaten she had her notebook ready and we would spend the entire evening discussing the 'end-time' scriptures from Daniel, Zachariah, H Thessalonians as well as other references. Over and over she would say, "I just love talken' and learnen' bout Jesus, don't you?"

One night Billy asked if we could take these tapes with us. She said. "Sure, keep them as long as you want to." We knew how much they meant to her so we listened to them and took them back in a couple of weeks. There were many complicated and difficult questions that we did not know the answer. I would write them down and take them to my Dad who had made an in depth study of The Book of Revelation and had given seminars explaining the scriptures.

We had a weekly radio program with a segment for Bible questions and dad would answer them. He had been in the ministry for sixty years and was a Bible scholar. During our program most of the questions were about 'tend time'. I was glad to be the one asking the questions instead of the one answering the questions.

Billy loved to hear her sing, 'The Night They Baptized Jessee Taylor.' Many nights, especially on Wednesday, following Prayer Meeting she would say to Billy, and I can still see her and hear her saying, "Brother Langford, I would like to go down front and kneel at the altar. Would you go with me? I just feel like I need to kneel at the altar." They would pray very quietly and then in a few minutes she would come to me in the choir and give me a big hug and kiss and out the door she would rush carrying her big Bible with her purse slung over her shoulder.

Billy dedicated her beautiful little girls, Tara and Randina. Her son Randy was born after she moved. Bea was very faithful to bring them to church when Barbara was out on the road. They did not give her any trouble or misbehave during church.

Barbara was attending our church when she recorded "The Teddy Bear Song." Excitedly together we watched it climb up the charts and were thrilled when it became a number one hit.

A wonderful thing happened one night when Melba, a friend of Barbara's came to visit her from St. Louis. Melba could not walk. Barbara invited us out to her house and when we arrived we were in for a surprise. As we were walking into the den she said, "A friend of mine is here and she needs to be healed. I want you all to pray for her." Barbara pointed toward the living room. We turned to walk in the room we saw Melba sitting on the couch. Barbara introduced us and continued, "Brother Langford is going to pray for your healing." Melba had a very sweet smile. She reached out her hand to Billy. He took her hand and held it and said, "What about our praying right now." She replied, "Please do." Barbara and the boys and I knelt at the couch. She had been injured while working in a hospital by lifting a patient and had not walked in over a year.

Following the prayer Barbara said, "Come on Brother Langford Bea has your supper ready." She was a wonderful cook and she had prepared a delicious meal. Melba had made her way to the table using her crutches but she didn't eat much and excused herself from the table. We all watched her as she drug herself up the stairs. There was a feeling of disappointment in the air though none of us said anything. We left around midnight and Billy told Barbara, "You tell Melba we will continue to pray for her to be healed."

The phone was ringing when we got home. Billy rushed in to answer it. We wondered who would be calling at this time of the night. But when I saw Billy smile and heard him say, "Praise the Lord," I sighed with relief and thought at least it is good news. Billy came up the stairs calling me. "Honey, Honey guess what? That was Barbara on the phone. She said, Melba is walking. God has healed her."

Barbara said that she had gone into the kitchen to talk to Bea after we left when Melba came walking into the room and she was laughing and crying at the same time. Melba said, "I sat up in bed and my feet were on the floor before I realized what I doing." She continued, "Earlier today when we were praying in the living room I thought I had a different feeling in my legs but I was afraid to try to walk."

Barbara said Bea was afraid Melba would fall so she ran over to her and said, "Child, be careful. Your legs are bound to be weak." Melba said, "No, they feel strong. God has healed me and I can walk."

The next Wednesday night during our Prayer Meeting, Barbara and Melba came walking through the door. Billy said it was one of the greatest experiences that he had ever had to look up and see Melba walking down the church aisle, smiling and waving her hand at him. Oh, what a feeling of excitement there was. Billy asked her to come down front to share with the people what God had done for her. Barbara also gave her testimony on our radio program the following Saturday and said, "Doctors take care of us but God heals us." When we listen to the tape the excitement of that night is still very evident. How thankful we are that we have the assurance that God answers our prayer,

We were walking through and showing some friends, Roy and Nettie Talbert, from Kingsport, Tennessee the beautiful Opry Land Hotel. On the billboard just inside the lobby were the words 'Barbara Fairchild performing in the Stage Door Lounge on the second floor.' We walked up the beautiful wide stairway and on around to the rear door. Billy knocked on the door and a young man came and stepped outside the lounge. Billy asked if Barbara was on stage. The young man said, "She has just sung and isn't scheduled to be on again until later," Billy asked, "Would you tell her someone wants to see her?" He smiled waved his arm and said, "I'll be glad to."

In just a couple of minutes Barbara pushed the door open. She looked absolutely radiant when she came through the door. She was wearing a beautiful plain snow white blouse with a big collar and puffy sleeves just above her elbow and a long flowing colorful skirt that came just above her ankles. Her long blond hair was so pretty. Her dark blue eyes just sparkled. She squealed so loud when she saw us - everybody upstairs, on the steps and downstairs looked at us.

She hugged us and asked, "Do you have time to come in?" There was a lot more of the hotel to see so Billy said, "We would if we had time but there is a lot of area to cover yet." She insisted that we come back by when she was on stage again. We said we would try to. We talked a little while longer. She took Billy by the hand and said, "Would you say a prayer for me before I go back on stage to sing"? Billy smiled his beautiful smile and said, "Sure we will. Let's all pray for Barbara." We all joined hands and made a circle and prayed at the back door of the Stage Door Lounge.

She hugged each one of us, turned with her skirt swishing around and rushed back through the door. She disappeared into the applause and sounds of merriment and into the life she loves and soon would be back on stage to make another appearance.

Barbara has been performing in Branson, Missouri. God is using Barbara in a wonderful ministry of sharing His Word and His Love in her theater in Branson, Missouri. She has ministered each Sunday Morning with her husband, Roy Morris. She first went to Branson in 1991 and then opened her theater in 1995.

An April 2, 1999 remembrance:

Last night while we were talking on the phone she mentioned again about her horrible experience of being raped when she was seventeen years old and how she had suffered for years with the terrible thoughts, the nagging fear and the stabbing pain in her heart. She said it had brought great mental anguish into her life. But she quickly continued with a calmness in her voice added, "God has done such a wonderful healing in my life and in me. I praise Him every day and you know, I just love talken' about Him." Feeling the warmth of the God's love that we have shared through the years thrilled my heart.

Placing the receiver back on the phone, I stood there and remembered all the times we had gone to her house and visited with her and how we always talked about Jesus and His love. Once again I felt the assurance of the fact that God takes good care of us.

Walking down the hall to my bedroom there was a smile on my face and joy bubbling in my heart. I know Barbara is doing what she loves best of all, and that's 'talken' about Jesus.

CARL AND PEARL BUTLER

◇◇◇◇◇◇◇

Junior Tullock, who played "Jake" on The Platt and Scruggs Show, attended the revival that Billy and I were holding in Knoxville in 1949. In later years he played the bass fiddle on the theme song for the Beverly Hillbillies.

During our revival Junior and His wife Mary attended every service. Following each service all the young people would meet in front of the church under the street light and talk for hours. The neighbors who were sitting on their porches didn't seem to mind our late night meetings sometimes they would even come and join us for a little while. We will always remember how we enjoyed the warm summer nights and feel the fresh cool breeze flowing gently from the tall mountains that surrounded us. We developed a warm friendship.

A few years after Billy and I moved to Nashville there was a knock at our door and when Billy opened the door there stood Junior and Mary. The Platt and Scruggs Show moved to Nashville to become more involved in Country Music.

Junior introduced us to Carl and Pearl Butler who worked with him in the same factory in Knoxville. They had also moved to Nashville and already, "If Teardrops Were Pennies" was on the charts and "Don't Let Me Cross Over" was named the number one song of the year in 1963. They toured with Roy Acuff and appeared in several concerts overseas. They also appeared in the movie "Second Fiddle to a Steel Guitar."

They joined the church and were always there if they were not on the road. We enjoyed being with them and shared many good casual times together. We would sit around the table following a wonderful meal and Carl would go into the other room get his guitar and come back to the table. Usually we would sing several church songs and then he would shyly say, "Now this is one I'm working on. See how you like it."

Pearl was a lot taller than I. She would usually pick me up as she hugged me and swing me around and say, "I sure do love you!"

We met Dolly Parton one Sunday afternoon after we had eaten dinner with them. She came by to check about some songs. She was recording a song that Carl had written and she wanted to ask him about another one that he was working on at the time. Carl and Pearl were coming to our house for supper. I was PTA President and was hurrying home from a Parent Teacher Association Meeting but had to stop by the grocery on the way home. We were not too well aquatinted with them yet and I was anxious about their coming. However, everything was prepared except the salad. I could not find the lettuce and I was sure I bought some when I stopped at the grocery.

Billy came in and rushed into the bathroom to freshen up before they arrived. He yelled so loud that it startled me, "Leta, what in the world is this lettuce doing on the back of the commode?" I ran in there and said, "Oh, you found my lettuce." He squinted his eyes and said, "What did you say?"

I went running down the hall as I was saying, "I knew I bought some lettuce." Billy was still standing at the sink in the bathroom as I went by him to get the lettuce. I was holding the lettuce with both hands when I passed back by him. He followed me into the kitchen, walked slowly to the refrigerator, opened the door and just stood there. Then he reached down and opened the crisper and there was the package of toilet tissue. He said, "Leta, since when did you start thinking that our toilet tissue needed to be refrigerated?"

He reached down and lifted the package slowly and put it under his arm then reached over and hugged me with his other arm. He squeezed me real tight, kissed me on the forehead and with a big smile said, "I'll put this in the bathroom, if you don't mind."

I gave him a little shove and said, "Hurry, I hear them driving in the driveway now." My salad was finished and on the table and just in time. I was afraid all during supper Billy would mention it but he didn't, at least not this time, however he has many time since then.

Before their records were hits Pearl worked in the meat department of the A&P grocery store on West End. I had a dream about Pearl and Carl on the Sunday night shortly after the store opened. On Monday morning I ran by to check on her and tell her about the dream. When she saw me enter the store she practically jumped over the meat counter. She ran and grabbed me lifting me off the floor. She said, "I'm lucky to be alive. You were praying, I know you were praying."

She continued speaking, hardly taking a breath, "As we started down the mountain from Crossville, an Esso gasoline truck had turned sideways on the ice-covered two lane highway. We were gaining speed all the time. There was nowhere for us to go on that narrow road. On one side was the mountain which went straight up, and the valley far below was on the other side."

She gripped my arm harder as she said, "Carl said he felt something take hold of the steering wheel and he even took his hands completely off and the car was guided up the mountain and around the truck and safely on the other side."

"He asked me, "Did you see that?"" "As soon as we could find a place to pull off the road we stopped and thanked God for saving our lives."

Placing my hand over hers I said, "I know, I even know what time that happened. It was between 3:30 and 3:45 this morning. I was awakened suddenly from my dream where there was smoke and fire all around a huge truck. You and Carl appeared just beyond the fire. There was a terrible fear surrounding you. After praying a while the fire seemed to die down and eventually went completely out and the terrible fear passed. I knew God had intervened some way and had protected you both. It was around four o'clock when the burden lifted."

Pearl said, "At four o'clock we stopped at a truck stop and were having coffee. We were trying to get our nerves settled down after having such a close call. We noticed the time because of my coming to work."

Carl's mother came to live with them in the later years. She did not want to miss church so when they were on the road, Billy or I would bring her to church. She was a wonderful cook and she liked to make pickles, relish and jelly. Each time we picked her up she would give us something she had made. She was so grateful and appreciative. She died several years ago in a Franklin hospital.

After they made it up the long hard climb in Country Music the many record sales paid off and their dream finally came true. They bought a beautiful farm with twenty-seven acres on Trinity Road near Franklin, Tennessee where they raised horses. They named it, "Cross Over Acres". They adopted two little girls, Carla and Robin. Carl collected clocks of all sizes, shapes and ages. Pearl had a collection of rare dolls and antique dishes.

Pearl fought hard to live but cancer took its toll and she died in 1988 at St. Thomas Hospital, here in Nashville. Soon after Pearl's death Carl's health began to fail also. He could not get over Pearl being gone. He died in 1992.

Thinking of them brings to mind many fond and precious memories as we use daily the beautiful gold plated silverware they gave us. As the years pass by the memories grow more priceless and gives us something to keep forever. How blessed we are to have God's blessings and protection.

GARY PAXTON

◇◇◇◇◇◇◇

Whenever you see Gary Paxton you can't help but notice the bulging five by seven notebook that he always carries with papers and notes sticking out of it. Each Sunday morning he entered the sanctuary and usually sat on the back pew. During the worship service he always had his notebook open, his pen in hand and his open Bible lying on the seat beside him.

I have often wondered how many and which of his beautiful songs were written while Richard was leading worship or Billy was preaching. Two of my favorites are "Jesus, It's All In One Word" and "He Was There All The Time".

Gary has also written songs with the Gaithers. He is very laid back and is an unassuming type of person. He says that sometimes he has prayed for hours for just the right word when writing a song.

RALPH SLOAN SQUARE DANCERS

◇◇◇◇◇◇◇

While attending the Grand Ole Opry one Saturday night the news came back stage that Ralph Sloan, who was the leader of the dancers, was in the hospital and had taken a turn for the worse. He was not expected to live through the night. Ralph's brother was taking over for him.

When the Square Dancers heard the news they went to pieces. One of the dancers, Tauna Seager, attended our church. Tauna knew that we were there as her guests. She came running out of their dressing room with tears streaming down her cheeks, almost screaming, "Brother Langford, where is Brother Langford"? We were sitting in the coffee room lounge and everyone heard her screaming and knew something dreadful had happened

Tauna saw Billy, ran to him and grabbed him by the arm. She said, "Ralph's going to die, please do something," Billy put his arm around her and together they rushed back down the hall into their dressing room. When the door opened the crying was so loud I'm sure you could hear it all the way to the stage.

Billy said that when he was finally able to talk to them they said, "We are not going on stage." Billy prayed with them and for Ralph. Then he told them, "Ralph would want you to go on stage. You will be doing this performance tonight especially for him. Keep your mind on the thought, "we'll do the square dance the best we ever have.'"

It was time for them to be on and they were wiping their eyes as they were coming down the hall and onto the stage. As they passed Billy each one of them gave him a thumbs up sign and a big smile. They all did beautifully. What a performance! Never have we seen anyone try harder than they did that Saturday night

Ralph did live through that night and several months longer. The dancers told him that they had prayed for him and had danced just for him. Tauna called and told Billy, "Ralph said he was so proud of us. We gave him the best gift we possibly could." And she continued, "I want to thank you for helping us so we could go on stage."

Tauna had often invited us to the Opry. I am so glad we chose that certain night to go. With her dark eyes sparkling and a big beautiful smile she would ask every Sunday, "Can you all come see me square dance this Saturday Night?" Billy said, he was glad that he had prepared his sermon early and was free on a Saturday night.

We are always amazed to see how God works in mysterious ways - His wonders to perform.

ROY ACUFF

◇◇◇◇◇◇◇

Billy was making a hospital call several years ago. He was walking down a long corridor when he noticed a lady all alone just outside one of the hospital rooms. She was leaning against the wall weeping very softly. He stopped and walked over to her and said, "I'm a minister making hospital calls is there anything I can do?"

Through her tears she responded, "My husband is very ill. Would you please come in and pray for him?" Billy and the lady entered the room. There were so many tubes and machines you could not get close to the bed. Billy squeezed between them and placed his hand on the gentleman's hand. He recognized that it was Roy Acuff as he leaned over the bed to tell him he was going to say a prayer.

For some reason the security guards had not yet been placed at his room. However as Billy was talking to his wife and getting ready to leave the room, two guards arrived and rushed in. They wanted to know what he was doing in the room. Mrs. Acuff spoke to them and pointed toward the door. They quickly stepped out of the room and stood at the door. As Billy left he introduced himself to them. One of them spoke up and said, "I'd like for you to say a prayer for me too." And the other guard joined in and said, "Me too." Billy said they probably didn't mean to pray right then and there but when they reached out to shake his hand he held their hand while he prayed for them.

Several years later our family was returning from a vacation in Florida and we were eating at Morrison's Cafeteria in Rivergate Shopping Mall when we saw Roy Acuff and his wife standing at the register getting ready to leave. Billy walked over toward them. His wife smiled and said, "I remember you, very well." She related to Roy about Billy stopping while walking down the hospital corridor.

Roy Acuff reached out to shake hands with Billy and said, "It must have worked. That's been several years ago and I've done a lot of appearances since being in the hospital. I want to thank you for your prayers."

We had finished eating and we all walked out together. Roy stooped over, pulled Kori, our eight year old granddaughter over to him and kissed her. Billy said, "We still have our camera with us. May we get a picture of you and my grand-daughter?" He smiled and nodded his head yes and said, "You sure can." He pulled her to him again and gave her another big hug and kissed her on the forehead. Kori has since graduated from Vanderbilt University and she is still proud of that picture.

BILLY BYRD

◇◇◇◇◇◇◇

Billy Byrd played the steel guitar and performed many years with the Ernest Tubb Show. If you ever listened to The Grand Ole Opry or heard his recordings on the radio you will remember hearing Ernest Tubb saying many times, "Play it Billy Boy."

At one of the last funerals that Billy conducted he met with the family to have prayer before the service. After the prayer one of the men stepped up to Billy and said, "Don't you remember me?" After a short pause, he continued, "You came to the VA hospital to have prayer with me. I was very sick. I had never accepted the Lord as my Savior."

He sighed deeply and said, "You knew that I felt uncomfortable talking in front of the other visitors at the hospital so you said, let's go outside if you feel strong enough. We went to your car and while sitting in the front seat, I accepted Christ as my Savior and asked Him to forgive me of my sins. I have never forgotten that visit or the prayer that you prayed for me."

Billy said he did remember the visit and the prayer. He said, "Billy Byrd, how could I ever forget? You made my day. Your daughter, Billy June, requested prayer for you at every service when you became ill."

Through the years Billy Byrd's family attended our church regularly and we cherish the close relationship that we have shared.

JERRY CHESTNUT

◇◇◇◇◇◇◇

Jerry and his lovely wife Pat were active in the church activities. Each week he and several men from the church participated in the Outreach Prison Ministry which included giving personal testimonies of God's goodness and grace and singing hymns.

Following a Prayer Meeting one night I mentioned to Jerry, who is a noted songwriter, among his songs are "Oney" recorded by Johnny Cash, "Good Year for the Roses" by George Strait and "T-R-O-U-B-L-E" by Travis Tritt. A long time before we met, we received a letter in October 1982 written on his stationery concerning him. He gave me permission to print the letter.

"Dear Brother Langford,

Several weeks ago I attended your church on Music Row, while living in a boarding house where people stole, drank, smoked pot. I was barely staying alive; I would work all week and not even have enough money to go to a movie. I went forward, if you recall, and asked God to take me out of that place. You prayed with me and God granted me the wish of a lifetime.

I'm now staying on the farm of a millionaire song writer north of Nashville.

I'm responsible for his estate while he's away. I hope to be like a son to him and express my appreciation by being a good Christian witness, and he can be the father image that I desperately need.

I'm so happy that I could cry, Again, I hope I can express my joy and appreciation by being a good Christian witness."

Leta Langford
February 25, 1999

2607 Tiffany Drive
Nashville, TN 37206
RE: Letter to W. C. Langford from Al Johnson
Dear Leta:
You have permission to print the letter you
received from Al Johnson in your forth coming book,
tentatively entitled "LIVING IN THE SHADOW OF
MUSIC ROW"

P.S. "When I attended your church I had holes in my
shoes. I'd put the church bulletin in there to protect my
feet, after the service."

COUNTRY MELODIES

◇◇◇◇◇◇◇

Minnie Pearl, Lefty Frizzell, Donna Stoneman, and Sergeant
York, the hero of World War I, are among many others that Billy had
the privilege to minister and to pray.

What a joy we have had to share the back stage experience with
country music people and become acquainted with those who have
given so much a part of themselves to their fans.

Our ministry has been enriched and made much fuller because our
lives have touched and become entwined with the thread of their music
and God's love. Henry Wadsworth Longfellow stated, "Music is the
universal language of mankind." In Nashville, Music City, U.S.A., you
are aware of this music blending into your life. It is heartfelt and real,
strong in spirit and always filled with feeling. You can easily identify
with the story it is telling and you feel comfortable with the simplicity
and "country way of life."

When you push back the closet door in our downstairs bedroom
you will see a big box crammed full of autographed 'demo' records
and tapes. If you listen closely I am sure you will hear country music
and familiar songs coming from the box, followed by many gentle

memories and much love. As you close the door the warm feeling of thankfulness and gratitude fills your heart.

Psalms 65:12-13 "The little hills rejoice on every side, the valleys shout for joy, they also sing."

CITY VIEW

◇◇◇◇◇◇◇

It was a very hot and humid Saturday morning in July. The youth group from our church was meeting at nine o'clock to clean and paint the upstairs of the Friedman Loan Building on lower Broadway. This is the place where we would have "The Open Door." The coffee house that was meant to help people on the streets and also those who were visiting Music City ended up changing our lives. This building adjoined the world famous Tootsie's Orchid Lounge, where country music singers came to make their dreams of being a country star come true.

Our plans of having a coffee house were becoming a reality. We had already decided on the name "The Open Door" taken from the scripture in Revelation chapter 3 verse 8. We were not aware of all the repairs that needed to be done to make it presentable as a neat, clean and restful place. We wanted the visitors to relax and feel the love of having fellowship of our young people.

To be at our coffee house on Broad Street was to be just above Tootsies' Purple Lounge. The door to the right went upstairs and the next door on the left was the door into the world famous "Tootsie's Orchid Lounge." We were frantically working trying to get the coffee house ready when City View made his first low-key entrance on that hot July morning around ten o'clock. We were privileged to come into contact and be very close to those working at Tootsie's. The stars would take a break at the lounge. They would pass our back door and could step through our upstairs window from the back porch which extended to the roof of Tootsies.

Friday and Saturday nights were exciting and the young people from our church and other churches in town were faithful and came each week bringing their exuberance and energy. We served hot buttered pop-corn, Kool-aide, lemon-aide, chocolate brownies and cookies. The ladies of the church would provide and prepare everything and we served it with joy and everyone seemed as though they were eating at a luxurious restaurant. We mopped the floor, painted the walls and cleaned the windows - everything had previously been painted black. We didn't know who had rented it before us or for what purpose they had used the building. We soon found out that black is a very hard color to cover. By the next weekend we had wanted to be ready to open our coffee house.

We had the name painted on the door with an arrow pointing upstairs to "The Open Door." The door to the left was the entrance to "Tootsie's Lounge." With a very limited budget it turned out pretty good. For tables we used empty cable wire wheels that the phone company gave us. We turned them on their side and painted them blue. For our chairs we used empty orange crates from the grocery store that was located on the corner of Division and Eighteenth Street. We painted them to match the tables. The walls and the floor were also painted a darker blue but lighter than the floor.

Then City View appeared. No one seemed to notice as City View who lived on the roof of Tootsies' would come climbing from the roof into and sometimes losing his footing would fall on the floor into our coffee house. City View first appeared on a hot July morning around ten o'clock as we were frantically trying to get the coffee house ready for next Friday night. What a sight City View must have seen when he saw me, a pastor's wife wearing old blue jeans and a shirt that was way too big and a ball cap, to keep the paint out of my hair, painting the window frame when his big foot stepped on the window sill. I stepped back and a tall thin white man with dark brown hair and squinted eyes stooped down to step into our building. Every one stopped their work and ran over to the window not believing their eyes. He looked at the ten of us as though we had invaded his territory. We later found out, that was just what we had done. This nice looking but ill-kept dressed man smiled, stuck out his hand to shake hands. After shaking each person's hand he said, "My name is City View. See the roof of that building next door? I live there. That is the roof of Tootsie's and she lets me live there. Someone asked him how long had he lived there? He said, "Oh, 'bout ten years." Over next to the chimney, which kept him warm during the cold winter, was City View's home. The overhang from the roof of our building was his shelter when it rained.

He wanted to know what we were doing there and then after looking the place over he said, "Can I help ?" Each Friday and Saturday night around ten o'clock he just seemed to appear in the coffee house mingling around with the visitors. Usually he would have a glass of lemon-aide and after a while he would disappear. One night after he had gotten acquainted with us he said, "I'm not going anywhere tonight. I'm staying and I'm helping you guys." On a Friday night several weeks later he said, "Before you'all close up, if you will watch your step, you can come over to my house for a little while." So after we locked up and all the visitors were gone he helped each of us step out of our window onto his roof. You could understand how he got his name "City View." What a beautiful view of lower Broadway, the Ryman and across the river into East Nashville.

While we stood there getting an unbelievable beautiful aerial view of part of the Music City, City View cleared his throat and with pride and respect for where he had chosen to live said, "I'll tell you my name, if you want me to," he didn't wait for an answer. Then he continued, "It's Dave well really it's David but just call me City View."

Linebaugh's restaurant was just across the street and my husband, Billy would often ask him to eat supper with him. We ate there on Sundays and if we could find City View we would ask him to join us. He was always courteous and quiet and always seemed very grateful.

The country stars were all acquainted with City View and would give him money and he would join them at their table sometimes.

We lost touch with City View except every once in a while he would show up at church for the Sunday morning worship and maybe go eat with us.

Our back door and Tootsie's back door shared the same back porch. I can still remember seeing City View sitting on these steps which entered into the alley. The steps led to the back door of the Ryman Auditorium, home of the Grand Ole Opry. These back steps of the Opry are still a resting place for the stars between performances. Each weekend we had country stars drop in at the "Open Door." Some of these people became regular guests.

Our young people who oversaw the Open Door Coffee House went away to college and eventually the lease with Friedman's Loan

Company couldn't be renewed because they were going to sell the building.

CHAPTER FOUR

TINSEL LOVE

(some names have been changed)

It was five a.m. on a beautiful all morning in September. The aroma of the freshly brewed coffee filled the kitchen and filtered down the hall to the bedroom. There was just a slight hint of the sun appearing through the kitchen window. Our usual breakfast of orange juice, scrambled eggs, crisp bacon and toast was prepared and on the table. My heart was pounding with anticipation as I hurried to the bedroom to awaken Billy. I could wait no longer to tell him who came to our house last night.

My encounter with the unexpected visitor was still vivid in my mind and my thoughts were spinning over and over in my head remembering every word that was said. But the most amazing thing about the visit was the awareness of His presence that could still be felt.

Billy walked slowly down the hall and into the kitchen. He squinted his eyes as he looked at the clock. Taking a second look he said, "What time is it?" then added, "Honey, is everything okay? It is only five after five." Glancing out the window he pulled the curtain back and looked up at the beautiful sky with the sun just beginning to rise. He pulled his chair back and sat down. He didn't say anything but had a bewildered look in his eyes and was looking straight at me as he stirred his coffee,

Nodding my head yes, I said, "Last night something very unexpected, unusual and exciting happened."

Billy, still half asleep, asked the blessing for our meal. The experience was overwhelming and filled me with awe that left me speechless much less able to eat. He said, "What in the world happened and who came over last night? He smiled his familiar, beautiful smile and continued, "Honey, tell me what happened."

Electrified with the warmth of Jesus' love, I smiled at him and answered softly, "I'll have to tell you later." Billy didn't question me further. He reached over and put his hand on mine. Finishing his last cup of coffee and breaking the silence said, "I don't have a heavy schedule today. I can stay with you if you want me to." He also became aware of an omnipotent presence. The warmth filled the house. He pushed his chair back from the table and walked over and stood behind my chair. He put his hands on my shoulders and said, "I don't know what happened here last night, but your face is absolutely radiant. Whatever it was it must have been phenomenal."

He put his arm around my waist and we slowly walked into the living room. We sat quietly on the couch for a few minutes. The aura of the presence of Jesus was so evident and forceful we did not want to intrude on the wonderful presence and power of God.

In my mind I could vividly see Jesus and hear every word that Jesus had spoken. I said, "Let me start at the beginning." Following a deep sigh I continued, "Honey, I had a visitor last night."

With a questioning expression, Billy interrupted me and said, "I didn't know Robert or Richard (our sons) were coming by."

I smiled as I answered, "They didn't". Then his expression turned to one of surprise as he asked, "If they didn't come by then who did?" "Well let me tell you what happened. You know we have been concerned about our church moving from the downtown activities on Music Row to a more laid back suburb community of Oak Hill on Franklin Road with the big beautiful colonial homes situated on sprawling yards and perfectly manicured lawns next to it. Last night I kept tossing and turning unable to sleep with questions spinning in my mind. It was three o'clock and I decided to get my pillow and go in the other bedroom to keep from disturbing you. I picked up the Bible on the bed-side table and thought I would read for a while then finally decided to try to go asleep again. Under my breath in just a whisper as I turned over and I prayed 'Lord, help us and give us direction as we build our new church and help us reach the people who need you most.' I pulled the sheet and blanket over my shoulder and was confident God was in control. Suddenly my room was illuminated. I blinked my eyes in astonishment and sat straight up in bed. Someone was coming through the door and entering my bedroom. First, I saw two feet with sandals on walking through the doorway and then the bottom of a long white robe. The robe was tied at the waist with a long white sash. The robe had long full sleeves. His arms were in a relaxed position at his side. He took four small steps and stood at the foot of my bed.

He stopped and slowly turned toward me. There was a faint shadow across His face, yet His features were very clear. I could see His mouth and His eyes and as He faced me I could see His entire face. His beautiful medium brown shoulder length hair was not in the shadow.

My heart began to pound and I held my breath. I thought 'This is Jesus and He is going to answer my prayer. He will tell me what to tell Billy or Richard should do in their ministry to help in the building of our new church.'

Jesus was in full view. He stood silently as he looked directly into my eyes for a few seconds. My mind was racing, wondering what He was going to say. He raised his right arm in front of him not quite even with his shoulder and turned His hand up with the palm of His hand open toward me.

In a very gentle, yet serious tone of voice said, 'I want you to tell my sheep that I love them. My love is durable, solid and genuine. My love is not a tinsel, breakable love.' Jesus slowly lowered his arm to his side.

I wasn't panic stricken or scared but was extremely anxious. He stood motionless but did not take his eyes off mine. It was difficult to speak but I finally said, "You want me to tell Billy and Richard to tell people that you love them." He turned and took a step toward the window. I called out to him, 'Jesus, wait please wait, you mean that you want me to tell the people that you love them?'

Every nerve in my body was surging with the desire to respond to His call and yet feeling so inadequate. I exclaimed, "Lord, I have no idea what to do. I'm not a minister. Who will I tell? How will I do it? When will I have a chance to tell anyone? Lord, I would do it if I could."

Without moving his body, he turned his head and looked at me over His shoulder. His dark eyes were filled with an unbelievable love and tenderness. I quickly continued, "Billy or Richard could tell them when they preach."

He turned facing me and raised his right arm just as he did before but this time he pointed His forefinger at me and very distinctly said, "I want you to tell them." Continuing He said, "Tell my sheep who are discouraged and hurting that I love them with a pure, solid, genuine unbreakable love. Not with a tinsel ornament breakable kind of love." He paused then with sadness in his voice and added, "You see the outside of the person, and the smile. You hear the laughter and you see the well-groomed person but I see their bruised and broken heart. I see their hurt and pain and their disappointments. I see their longing for true love. I want you to tell them that I love them." He dropped His arm slowly and gently down at His side.

My eyes were fixed on Him, however finally the words came, "I can't do that. I just can't." With the words hardly out of my mouth Jesus turned back around and without saying a word took a few steps away from the bed and started walking toward the window. "Jesus, don't go please wait. If you will tell me what to say and who to say it to I will try!"

Prayerfully, I began to plead with Jesus, "Lord, you will have to help me and baptize me in your love." Even having been in the ministry all these years, I don't remember of ever hearing or knowing anyone who had ever prayed or asked to be baptized in Jesus' love. Over and over pouring out of my anxious pounding heart was the feeling and warm sensation of Jesus' love. As I looked into His eyes I felt the strong desire and hunger in my spirit to reach out to Him. Baptize me in your love Jesus; baptize me in your love.

His masculine voice was firm yet so tender and every word was distinct. He emphasized each word. The warmth of His love filled and radiated through the entire room. It penetrated and felt like warm sun rays on me. "Jesus, how will I know who to tell?"

Bending his arm at the elbow, He extended His hand gently and said, "I will tell you who and I will tell you when, just obey Me. When you feel the gentle tug in your heart and feel the warmth of My spirit, you need not be afraid."

Relaxed and in breathless surrender I said, "Lord, I'll do my best." The most bountiful peace came into my heart. It was as though a raging storm had just been calmed. Jesus dropped His arm to His side." He turned and walked out of the room going through my upstairs bedroom wall by the window! "This was the most unbelievable and awesome thing that I have ever seen. Joy and peace were all mixed together. Hot tears were running down my face and dripping on my bed. I was overwhelmed and filled with astonishment and unable to move for several minutes. While sitting in the darkness and still thinking about what Jesus said I began to wonder. Why did Jesus use the word sheep?

Living in the city all my life, I am unfamiliar with farming and the responsibility of raising livestock, knowing even less about the relationship of a shepherd to his sheep. Then immediately coming to mind was the familiar Twenty-Third Psalm. "The Lord is my shepherd."

Grabbing my robe and slipping into my house shoes I ran downstairs to the office and started looking for <u>Strong's Concordance.</u> It was on the desk. The rest of the night was spent down there. I was amazed at all the references concerning 'sheep' and 'shepherd.' My confidence and courage grew with the confirmation of the Holy Spirit through the established Word of God.

Almost the entire tenth chapter of St. John is concerning 'sheep' and the 'shepherd.' Hebrews thirteen verse twenty mentions "Jesus, the great shepherd of the sheep." I Peter chapter two verse twenty five, and chapter five, verse four says,

"When the chief shepherd shall appear."

Even in Revelation, the very last book of the Bible, there it was Revelation seven verse seventeen , "For the lamb at the center of the throne will be their shepherd: He will lead them to springs of living water and God will wipe away every tear from their eyes."

Billy had listened very intently and hardly moved while I was telling him of this wonderful unexpected experience. He reached over, put his arms around me and pulled me over to him and held me a few minutes. He said, "I've never experienced anything like this honey. Your face is absolutely radiant and this will probably become a consuming passion for you with tremendous results."

As I pulled away from him and looked into his beautiful sparking blue eyes I asked him, "After we get dressed would you drive with me to see Jerry Jackson? I must tell him today that Jesus loves him."

Billy questioned, "Do you think he will be home during the day? Won't he be at work?"

"He might not be home but let's go see." We had not seen him or his family since they had joined another church when they moved from our area of town. When we arrived at his house we kept knocking on his door but no one answered. We turned and started to walk off the porch but before we reached the steps he barely cracked the front door open. I turned and ran but before I could say anything he said, "I'm just leaving. I have to go pick up my wife from work."

He tried to push the door shut. Billy came back and held the door open. I said, "Jerry, I have to tell you something. Last night I had an encounter with Jesus and He told me to come tell you this, "He loves you. His love is pure, strong, and unbreakable. It is not a tinsel ornament breakable love. He loves you enough that He sent me here to tell you."

Jerry opened door to where it hit against the wall. "How did you know to come here?" Before I could step back he grabbed me by my arm and said, "I'm taking you into the kitchen." He gently pulled me through the living room and on through the dining room. From the doorway as we entered the kitchen, while still holding my arm, he pointed to the counter. There were several packs of beer stacked there. He continued, "I wasn't going after my wife. I had decided that I was going to drink until I didn't hurt anymore. Everything has gone wrong."

Without letting go of my arm he led me back into the living room. He gently pulled me over to a chair and said, "Please, sit down here and don't leave. I need to talk to you. I needed so badly to hear what you just told me. I am at the end of my road. Thank you, thank you for coming."

Billy had walked quietly behind us. He was sitting on the couch in the other corner of the room. I kept glancing over at him and watched the big tears roll down his face. After two and a half hours we left.

Since that day I have told many people, some I know, but most of them I do not know, "Jesus loves you!" Without exception, everyone accepts it, gladly and warmly. What a thrill to see in their previously sad eyes an exciting sparkle come to life as they truly experience the warmth of Jesus' love.

BEAUTIFUL LADY IN BLACK

◇◇◇◇◇◇◇

My attention was drawn to the beautiful lady dressed in black sitting at the table near the front of O'Charley's restaurant which is located on 21st Avenue across the street from Vanderbilt University. This was the first time I felt the gentle tug in my heart to tell of Jesus' love to someone I didn't know. Sitting three tables in front of our table was a nice looking well-dressed man in a business suit and a beautiful lady wearing an off-the-shoulder elegant black street-length dress trimmed with black lace. The sparkling necklace that she was wearing matched the beautiful earrings that hung down almost to her bare shoulders. Her dark hair and dark eyes with that black dress were absolutely gorgeous.

We were guests of friends and were enjoying our delicious meal when I looked up and noticed this lovely lady. The Lord spoke to my heart and said, "Tell her I love her." I could hardly swallow my food. "Lord, are you sure?" I asked, along with other questions that would be asked quite often. "How?" "When?" "Now?"

Our friends became aware of my not conversing with them and said, "My, you sure have gotten quiet." I managed only a half-smile while keeping my eye on this lady. She was getting up from the table, "Lord, if she goes into the ladies' lounge I will follow her." I excused myself from our table and was only a few steps behind her as she entered the lounge. The door closed behind us.

Very timidly I mustered a weak, "Hello." She replied very sweetly, "Hello." She had brought her champagne glass with her. She was holding it in one hand and straightening her hair with the other, looking into the large mirror. I walked over and also looked into the mirror then I turned to her and said, "I would like to tell you something. Jesus loves you so much. He wanted me to tell you that He loves you with an unbreakable, pure love and not with an ornament tinsel kind of love. He knows when you are hurting and He cares for you. Jesus loves you!"

She startled me by throwing her glass into the sink. It broke and exploded into a million tiny pieces. It was all over the counter and on the beautiful matching tile floor. She grabbed me by my shoulders and started shaking me.

I was terrified, wondering what was she doing to do to me. She pushed me back from her while still holding my shoulders very firmly. She looked straight into my eyes and shouted, "Don't you ever quit telling people this. I am so thankful you told me. Oh, I feel so unworthy that Jesus loves me so much that he would do this. Now, who did you say you were?"

I answered, "I didn't say." Quickly following with her next question, "What is your name?" I replied, "That's not important. Just remember, Jesus loves you!"

She slowly let go of the firm grip that she had on my shoulders, pulled me to her and embraced me and held me for what seemed to be a very long time. The bond of love that I felt was so strong it was unbelievable. Only the Holy Spirit could do this for perfect strangers. We walked out of the lounge together. As I went to join my friends again my feet were walking on the floor but my spirit was soaring high into the heavens saying, "thank you" with every step I took. I truly believe she walked back to her table doing the same thing.

We were finishing our meal and the restaurant was very crowded. I did not realize that she had gotten up from her table. Neither did I notice that someone was standing behind my chair. It startled me when I felt a gentle pat on my shoulder. I looked up and back over my shoulder and there stood this beautiful lady in black standing next to me. She said, "Thank you. Thank you so much." She turned and walked towards the door with the gentleman. As she was walking through the door she turned back around and smiled a beautiful smile.

Our friends had a puzzled look on their faces, "If we may ask, what was she thanking you for?" I said, "Something very special." I looked at Billy sitting across the table from me and winked. My heart was filled and running over with joy as I obeyed the command of Jesus to share His love.

BRAD

◇◇◇◇◇◇◇

One cool crisp morning about ten o'clock while working in the church office the familiar voice spoke to my heart. Our new sanctuary was being built and the contractor worked with a father and two sons from Fayetteville to build the pews and pulpit furniture. There were other workers also in the building. As I walked down the unfinished isle I prayed under my breath, "Lord, which of these workers do I tell?" I felt impressed to tell which ever boy was down front. A young boy was installing the altar and another young man whom I found out later was his brother was carrying some boards outside.

Stepping over boards and in between tools I made my way over to him and said, "Hi, I'm Leta." He looked up with his beautiful dark eyes sparkling. While still holding his saw a beautiful smile came shining through all the sawdust on his face. He said, "Well, hello. I'm Brad."

"I was just wondering. You are not too busy for me to tell you something, are you?"

He laid his saw on the floor, took his ball cap off and wiping his forehead with his arm he ran his hand through his long brown hair. He raised his leg and rested his foot on the front part of the pew that he was working.

He said, "I guess not."

I breathed deeply and said, "Brad, Jesus came into my room several weeks ago and told me to tell people that He loved them, and this morning, I am to tell you. Jesus loves you with a strong, unbreakable, pure, genuine love not a tinsel breakable love."

His smile turned into a serious expression and his beautiful eyes squinted as he looked toward the opening that was to become a door. I said, "Brad, have you ever prayed the sinner's prayer, asking God into your heart to become part of your life?"

Still gazing out the door he replied, "No, I have never thought about it."

I asked him, "Do you mind if we do? And would you say it with me?"

He took his cap off again and laid it on his knee then looked back at me and said, "I sure will."

With a simple prayer we both got back to work. He worked another week before the pews and furniture was completed. They did a magnificent job. Visitors attending our church had commented on the beautiful pews and platform furniture. The furniture was white trimmed in dark mahogany with medium blue padded seats. Our sanctuary was used by many outside of our membership for weddings because of the elegant colonial style and beauty of it. Brad's family not only installed the furniture but their family had a wood shop and they built all the furniture, including the pews, communion altar, the front altar and the pulpit and pulpit chairs. Their father had started the business and as the boys grew older they continued to carry on the family business.

In the fall of 1984, about a year after Brad and I had talked, Brad's mother and father came by the church to see the work their sons had done. As we entered the sanctuary, Brad's mother began to cry. She said, "Brad wanted us to come and attend a church service with him. He wanted us to see this before they took the job in Florida. Of all the work they had done in churches, he said, you were the only person that had ever asked him about Jesus. We had planned to attend but just never got around to it. He talked of this church every once in a while."

"The next big job we received for installing and building church furniture was in Florida. On the way to that big job the van turned over and Brad was killed instantly. One of my first thoughts was we didn't go see his last job in Nashville that he had mentioned so many times. I just had to come see it and I wanted to meet you."

We were all crying. I tried to get my composure. She sighed a big deep sigh and stood motionless for a minute or two. Then she slowly started walking down the beautifully blue carpeted sanctuary. Her husband, Billy and I followed closely behind her without saying anything. She touched and gently rubbed each arm of the pew as we walked by. Standing for a while looking all around and even looking up at the ceiling for a while before walking.

We reached the front of the church and while standing there at the altar I don't know what they were thinking about but my heart was pounding as my mind recalled that day.

How thankful I am that Jesus stopped by our house. Feeling the warmth of His love once again, just like that night. I stood almost overwhelmed in the awe of His tenderness and understanding. Praying as sincerely as I have ever prayed, "Jesus, please don't let me fail you. Help me to always be obedient to your voice."

We walked behind Brad's mom and dad as they very slowly and quietly turned to go back up the aisle and stopped at the sanctuary entrance. His mom had tears streaming down her face as she reached out to hug me. She held me so tight. With her head leaning on my head she whispered over and over, "Thank you, thank you." Then they left.

We stood in silence as we watched Brad's mom and dad walk out the sanctuary doors, down the walk and get into their car. Billy put his arm around my waist and pulled me close to him as we felt the strong mixed emotions of unspeakable joy and a deep piercing heartache. This meeting may never to be forgotten.

SAM RUST /TRUCK DRIVER

◇◇◇◇◇◇

On Wednesday night, October 24, 1985 it was pouring down rain. It had rained all day with no let up at all. Of all times, we had announced that we were having a special treat for this Wednesday night prayer meeting. The trucker who drove his 18 wheeler for Jesus, Sam Rust, was coming to speak. We knew the attendance would be down with this torrential rain.

While Brother Rust was speaking, the Lord spoke to my heart, "Tell him, Jesus loves him. I said, "Lord, he travels full time sharing the message of Jesus with his trucker friends. He goes to truck stops all over America. He has made a chapel in his truck and he does this as a full time ministry. Why should I tell him? I don't know why but I will."

Following the service he invited the people to go out and see his chapel while he explained his mission. I stayed inside the church. Everyone had gone but Billy and me. Sam walked back into the sanctuary getting the rest of his material before leaving. I walked over to him and said, "Brother Sam, may I tell you something? You probably don't need me to but I want to tell you about an experience that I had and to tell you that Jesus loves you and He knows when you are hurting. He loves you with a pure, solid, genuine, unbreakable love, not an ornament tinsel kind of love."

He grabbed my hand and led me out into the pouring down rain and said, "I've got to have you see something. You need to see it." I couldn't imagine what he was talking about and what in the world did he want me to see? I was trying to hold the umbrella that Billy handed us as we walked into the rain. He reached into an overhead compartment in the truck and pulled out a big broken Yale lock. He took my hand and put the lock in it closed his hand over mine and said, "As I broke this lock tonight I said, this will be my last service. I am so discouraged and so tired. It gets so lonely on the road. I called my wife before I got here tonight to tell her I am coming home. I am quitting this traveling; no one knows how it is anyway. The going gets so rough and I get so tired. Tonight this lock was stuck, it was pouring down rain and I was getting soaking wet. Did you notice that my clothes were wet when I was up front tonight? I couldn't get the lock open to get into my truck so I said, I've had it. This is my last service. But since you told me that, I'm gonna call my wife and tell her what has happened and I think I can make it now."

He took his big hand off of my hand and said, "You keep this lock; I want it to be a reminder to you to never stop telling people about the wonderful genuine, unbreakable love of Jesus. By this time he had led me into the trailer. You could hear the big drops of rain falling hard on the roof and hear it running down the sides. Billy had been inside the trailer all the time listening to Brother Sam, I reached up to hug Brother Sam. The three of us were crying tears as large as the rain drops that were falling. We didn't mind the tears or the rain.

I received a letter and picture from him with permission to use them. His picture and his rig was in an article from the Frontline Report in the Pentecostal Evangel, August 22, 1999 (permission to use). By the way, I still have that broken lock and I still remember for what it stands.

ANOTHER LONELY TRUCKER

◇◇◇◇◇◇

This was the only Easter Sunday that I can remember when Billy and I were eating dinner alone. It was a beautiful picture perfect Easter Sunday with a record attendance for the worship service as well as the sunrise service. Easter Sunday is my very favorite day and it is always a very special occasion as we observe the Resurrection of our Lord.

We decided to go to the Shoney's in Brentwood which is a couple of miles from the church. By the time we got there the noon rush was over and no one was waiting. The hostess seated us and because of all the activities of the morning we were exhausted and it felt good to sit down and relax a bit. After placing our order I reached across the booth and took Billy's hand and breathed deeply and said, "It's been a good day." Having said this I looked across the aisle and sitting alone was a large muscular good looking young man. He looked clean and well—kempt. His light brown hair was shining clean. But his beautiful light brown eyes were staring at the floor. He looked to be in his middle to late thirties. His sport shirt sleeve was torn and his jeans were torn and had mud on them and there was so much dirt and mud on his boots you could hardly see what color they were. He was drinking a cup of coffee. Billy and I continued our conversation.

There was a gentle tug on my heart saying, "Tell him I love him." I hesitated to go to a man when he is alone, but I must as I remember the words, "not a man or a woman, no make-up, no beautiful attire, no fashion statement; only a heart wanting to hear words and the warmth of love from the gentle shepherd, "Tell him My love is true, solid, genuine, unbreakable. Not a tinsel ornament love. And He knows how your heart is hurting."

By this time I was standing by his booth and said, "Do you mind if I sit down here with you for just a minute and tell you something?"

He extended his hand toward the seat across from him and said, "No, not at all."

"I just wanted to tell you that Jesus loves you. He loves you with a strong, unbreakable, genuine not tinsel love and He knows when you are discouraged and your heart is hurting."

He reached across the booth and took my hands. He put one of his big hands under and the other hand over mine. He held them in his big hands as we talked. "This has been the loneliest Easter I have ever had. My rig is up there on the interstate with a burned-out clutch. I had to leave my family before we could eat dinner together. My dad is on his way to get me and we are going to try to tow the truck back home. I couldn't get anyone to stop and help me I had to climb over the big eight foot fence and come through the field to get here." He looked down at his dirty boots and torn shirt and pants, and continued, "That's why I am so dirty and look so ragged"

Then he looked up at me and said, "Thanks ma'am, you have made my day." He let go of my hands and ran his hands through his hair and leaned back against the back of the booth. A beautiful smile came on his lips and a happy contented face replaced the worried sad look. What a transformation! His eyes sparkled and he repeated, "Thanks again, ma'am." I invited him to join Billy and me and eat with us at our table but he replied, "Ma'am, I would just like to sit here and think awhile, if you don't mind."

Billy was about through with his dinner. He gave me his beautiful, understanding smile and without further conversation we finished our dinner. As we were leaving Billy walked to the cash register and I looked back and waved at him. He raised his arm all the way up, stood with one foot on the seat and with a big smile from ear to ear said, loud enough for everyone in the restaurant to hear, "Ma'am, thank you."

SUNSET BOULEVARD

◇◇◇◇◇◇◇

We arrived in Anaheim, California on a Saturday for the Assemblies of God General Council Meeting. We had been looking forward to coming to the wonderful land of California and being in the famous city of Hollywood. Billy was scheduled to be in conferences all day; Richard and I were free to go into town. Monday while standing at the corner of Vine and Hollywood he said, "Mom, I think I'll try to get on the "Wheel of Fortune" game show." The studio was just down the street.

Knowing he didn't have a chance I said, "Sure. Why not?"

Stepping just inside the door was the notice: Try-outs for the "Wheel of Fortune" game show straight ahead."

Richard turned his head and nodded 'yes' and disappeared down the hall. A lounge just inside the door offered coffee. After visiting with those in the lounge and drinking several cups of coffee I stepped back out on the sidewalk and joined the mother of a young lady who had also gone inside. We introduced ourselves and after a few minutes we started walking slowly up to the corner. We talked and were having a friendly light conversation about the weather, country music and our kids.

We were watching the traffic pass by and had walked back and forth several times in fact it had been almost an hour. The weather was warm but the breeze made it very comfortable and pleasant.

Coming again to the corner of Sunset and Vine the Holy Spirit spoke to my heart, "Tell Lynn, Jesus loves her." I bit my lip as I sighed and prayed silently, "Lord please help me to say what I should and must say."

Carefully explaining the events that led up to my telling her this I was wondering how she would accept it. So here goes. "Lynn, Jesus told me to tell you that he loves you with a pure, genuine, unbreakable love, not a tinsel-like fragile love. He knows when you are lonely and hurting."

She stopped and turned, facing me and looking directly into my eyes. She did not move or take another step while I was saying this to her. She squinted her pretty, deep blue eyes and pulled her lips together. Still without moving she slowly parted her lips and opened her eyes wide and kept her eyes fastened on mine. It was as though she were looking clear through me. My heart was pounding with anticipation.

Slowly her expression changed. She had a beautiful grin then a big smile showing her perfect white teeth. Her eyes were sparkling. She reached her hand out and put it on my arm just below my shoulder and held it as she said, "That is so strange that you should tell me this." She squeezed my arm hard then patted me on my shoulder.

She turned around and we continued our walk with very little conversation. In fact our conversation was over. She was in deep thought and concentration. As we reached the door it flew open and out rushed the contestant hopefuls.

Richard and I hurried to the parking lot for our car. We had to rush to get back to Anaheim for the evening service at the convention center. The late afternoon traffic was terrible. Richard explained the interesting rules of the game. He had made it through the present contestants but it would be necessary to stay over the week end to enter the game.

He was scheduled to preach on Sunday and so was Billy. We were scheduled to fly home on Friday. He told the T.V. producer that he could not stay.

The convention was over and settling back in the seat on the plane we were talking about all the happenings of the week. Billy was excited about attending the convention and renewing friendships. Richard just as excited about his experience at the "Wheel of Fortune" and me sharing the love of Jesus on the corner of Hollywood and Vine and thrilled to be telling a hurting or discouraged lamb about the genuine, unbreakable love of our Shepherd.

UCROSS, WYOMING

◇◇◇◇◇◇◇

We were enjoying the vacation of a life time with our friends, Jim and Frances Sterritt. Western movies are Billy's favorite and he has always wanted to go out west but we neither had the time nor the money to take such a long vacation. Even though we have wanted to see and visit the many wonderful points of interest that we have read about.

Jim and Frances went to Sheridan, Wyoming every year to check on property they have there. They had invited us many times to take the trip with them but Billy felt that he could not be away from the church so many Sundays so we always declined their invitations.

In the summer of 1988 Jim really insisted that we go, reminding us, in love of course, "You are not getting any younger, you know. You need to take this trip while you feel like traveling." Realizing this was true, Billy was persuaded to go. Richard, our son was associate pastor and assured his dad that everything would be fine at the church.

What a trip! We traveled 5,652 miles from June 22 to July 15. I didn't know Sheridan, Wyoming was so far from Nashville, Tennessee. In South Dakota it included the Corn Palace, the beautiful and meaningful lighting ceremony at Mt. Rushmore, Wall Drug Store and Deadwood, in Wyoming. We also visited Sundance, Badlands and Devil's Tower before arriving at our destination.

We visited everything in and around Sheridan for miles and on the Fourth of July we attended a picnic held in U Cross, Wyoming. Written on the marker at the edge of town was Ucross, Wyoming (population 25). We had heard the local people talking about last year's attendance when at least two thousand attended and they expected many more this year. We just passed the marker and suddenly there were people everywhere. The exuberance and electricity from the sound of music filled the air and was coming from the big white house sitting on the hill.

A band was playing on the front porch of the big two story house. Upstairs an outside balcony was above the front and back porch. The huge green sprawling lawn was filled with children playing games that had been set up for them. The entire back area was covered with lawn chairs which had been brought by those attending the festivities.

Over to the left side were two big open pits with smoke coming from them. A big pig held by his feet fastened to a pole was roasting over each of them. There was a huge tent set up with tables for the food. There were two long serving lines and it took three hours for everyone to be served. It was worth waiting for!

Shortly after we arrived, Billy and a newfound friend from Sheridan, Al Slicker, were pitching horse shoes on a beautiful shaded area across a little creek. Several games were going on at the same time. Billy and Al took on anybody that would play. Late in the afternoon the horseshoe game came down to the winners of the separate games. It ended up with Billy and Al throwing against two fellows living on a ranch nearby; only to find out after the final game they were originally from Tennessee. Billy and Al were the champions. Everyone was really surprised when Jim announced to them that Billy was a preacher from Nashville, Tennessee and he had beaten all the ranchers.

The entire setting of the picnic was picturesque. The gorgeous evening with the sun slowly going down in the western sky was absolutely magnificent and the most beautiful sunset ever. The visitors were turning their lawn chairs and gathering on the slope of the freshly mowed lawn, to be able to see the fireworks better. The children were running ahead of their parents and some got too close and had to be moved back from the fireworks stand.

The band was still playing and the children continued to play on the lawn. Others were making their way to their cars. Before you hardly knew it the blue sky had grown dark and the bright stars were coming into view. What a beautiful open, western sky that extended forever that we admired on our drive back to Sheridan and what a way to celebrate the Fourth of July. After a long time of silence Jim said, "Leta, you didn't do your thing today." Followed by a deep sigh as I thought back and answered, "I know." He didn't question me further.

CODY, WYOMING

◇◇◇◇◇◇◇

Unable to convince Jim, Frances, or Billy that a day of rest was needed following such a full day of activities, we were up, dressed, in the van, and on our way to Cody, Wyoming and Yellowstone National Park before 6:30 a.m.

We arrived in Cody around noon and headed straight for the Cody Museum which we heard about all the way there. Bobby Bridger was to be appearing there and was presenting a spectacular program in the afternoon. We were looking forward to enjoying the songs with him and singing the ballads he had written. They tell the stories of a famous western mountain man and scout, Jim Bridger. Bobby is a descendant of Jim Bridger.

Bobby Bridger, according to the Sheridan Scene Newspaper, began touring and listening to balladeers when he was eighteen years and has performed his ballads around the country.

We had traveled much of the route of the Bozeman Trail. While he was performing one of his ballads, the Lord spoke to my heart, "Tell him, Jesus loves you." Immediately following the gentle tug and feeling the warmth of the Holy Spirit from my head to my toes was a deep and silent cry from my heart for help.

As soon as their performance was over I began making my way toward the front of the auditorium with Billy right behind me. Many others were coming down also. I waited until he had finished signing autographs and everyone had talked with him before I walked up closer to the edge of the stage. He knelt down and shook my hand.

As a way of introduction I said, "Hi, I'm from Nashville, Tennessee." While still holding my hand he inquired, "Do you know any of the country music people? Did you know Marty Robbins?"

"We sure do." I pointed to Billy who was sitting on the stage steps with Jim and Frances and said, "My husband conducted Marty's Memorial Service. Marty and his wife, Marizona attended our church. Billy also performed the wedding of his daughter, Janet and his son Ronnie. Our friendship goes back a lot of years. Marizona and I have remained very close friends.

Billy has been the pastor of a church in Nashville for thirty-eight years. He has built a beautiful colonial church on Franklin Road. We have had the privilege to meet and minister to many of the country music people."

Bobby looked over at Billy and motioned with his other hand for him to join us. He had his big beautiful smile as he walked over to us. I said, "Bobby, I want you to meet my husband." After the introduction, Billy took a couple steps back. He knew why I had gone down to the stage.

"Bobby, I know you have a heavy schedule and another show to do right away but I just want to tell you something. Jesus loves you with a strong, true, genuine, gentle love and not a breakable, tinsel love."

Instantly he threw his legs over the stage and sat down and leaned forward toward me and said, "Tell me that again. I want you to say exactly word for word what you just said to me."

Noticing his interest in our conversation his manager, Jackson Whitney, came over and knelt down and began listening just as I said, "Jesus loves you with a strong, true, genuine, gentle, not a breakable, tinsel love."

Bobby said, "Would you please say that one more time?"

Before I could say anything Mr. Whitney said, "Why didn't you come up to tell me that?" I replied, "The Lord didn't tell me to, however," and before finishing my statement he said, "Can you say that to me anyway?" I replied, "I sure can. Jackson Whitney, Jesus loves you with a strong, true, genuine, gentle love not a breakable, tinsel love." He and Bobby jumped off the stage at the same. Each one gave me a big bear hug and kissed me on my forehead and both were saying, "With their faces beaming they said, "thank you for taking time to come up to the stage to tell us and to remind us that Jesus loves us."

The feeling of excitement filled the air. My heart was bubbling over with joy as we walked out of that auditorium and so thankful, yet so humbled and so privileged to see how God had spoken and proven His love once again.

ROOSEVELT LODGE

◇◇◇◇◇◇◇

Visiting Yellowstone National Park with its beauty, splendor and magnificence was a great experience and another highlight of our vacation. We read about Roosevelt Lodge and wanted to make it there by lunch time. Traveling steady and no extra stopping we made it by 12:30. The beauty and grandeur of this rustic lodge made of logs nestled among the trees was much greater than it looked on the pamphlet.

We climbed the steps slowly, gazing at this magnificent structure and talking about the architect that built it. Just inside the entrance was a spacious dining room. To the left of the dining area was an old upright piano. On top of the tall black piano was a picture frame with an index card under the glass with the words, "We invite you to play the piano for your enjoyment and the enjoyment of our guests. We thank you. Roosevelt Lodge Staff"

We were seated at a table near a window. The view was almost breathtaking. Following our delicious meal I walked over to the piano, sat down and started playing. The guests and the waitresses came over and asked me to play their favorite songs. Time passed quickly and without realizing it over an hour had passed.

We needed to be on our way to reach the Travelers Inn in West Yellowstone, Montana before 6:00 p.m. I thanked the guests and the staff for singing along as I played. The staff bowed to me and the other guests with a gesture of opening their arms. They said "When somebody plays the piano it always makes our day."

We were rushing down the steps when a gentleman just in front of me fell when he was three steps from the bottom. His wife knelt down beside him and started fanning him. Everyone just backed away. No one was able to help him as he was struggling to get his breath.

I stood and waited a few moments then walked over. Praying quietly to myself asking God to give me wisdom for what I should say to the lady. She was so upset. I knelt beside her and asked, "Do you mind if I say a prayer for him?" She responded by reaching her hand toward me and took my hand. Still looking at her husband she said, "Oh, please do. I know God put you here when I heard you whisper the name of Jesus as you knelt down by me." We bowed our heads and after a short prayer she said, "My husband has epileptic seizures. The medication usually takes care of the problem but since we have been on vacation we have been on the go constantly and he is so tired and needs to rest more. Thank you for being here."

We had been kneeling for several minutes so we helped each other to stand. Someone inside the lodge brought a glass of water for him to drink. Some of the waitresses helped him to his feet. He leaned up against the wall by the steps until he regained enough strength to walk.

The pretty lady stepped closer to me and said, "My name is Agnes. Please keep my husband and me in your prayers." Feeling the familiar tug and warmth of Jesus' love I replied, "I want to tell you something very special. Jesus loves you with a true, solid, genuine, gentle love and not a tinsel love. He knows you when you are hurting. Each day Jesus will give you strength."

A big beautiful smile came across her face and she sighed a sigh of relief as she said, "Oh, thank you. May I give you a hug?" I said, "Sure you can." Her husband had taken a couple of steps and was standing by her side. With a look of embarrassment he shyly smiled and said, "Thank you for caring." Placing his still trembling hand on my arm he gave me a gentle pat.

Everyone was in their cars. The tour bus was waiting for the couple to get inside. I watched them climb aboard the bus. They turned around and waved to me giving me a big smile and soon they disappeared into the bus behind the darkened windows

What a wonderful feeling of being at the right place and sharing the love of Jesus to the right person at the right time. Walking over to our car I was lost in my thoughts, unaware of the questions from Billy, Jim and Frances. "Are you going to stand here gazing at the lodge all day?" I sighed a big sigh and felt the warmth of Jesus' love surround me and penetrating inside of me. I was unable to move, standing in complete amazement and awe; it was almost overwhelming to see the stately picturesque rustic Roosevelt Lodge nestled amid the wonder of God's creative handiwork. The beautiful clear deep blue sky above and over to the right the sound of the small bubbling geyser is what I could see. And to think, God had chosen such a place of such grandeur to speak with the still small voice and give the gentle tug of the Holy Spirit and share His love.

COPORATE AMERICA

◇◇◇◇◇◇

On a beautiful Sunday just following lunch, the phone rang. It was Bob. He said, "Mom, can you come back to church? I need to talk over something with you." I said, "Sure, I'll be right there."

I turned and drove into the church parking lot and there were two other cars there next to Bob's. I entered the Fellowship Hall and hurried down the hall into the Sanctuary. Bob who was COO of a restaurant and hospitality company and two other executives from that company were sitting in the back on the very last pew. Their expressions let me know they were very apprehensive about something and were well aware of a serious situation.

Bob met me, gave me a hug and kissed me on the forehead and said, "Mom, we have had a meeting at the office. We were made aware of someone who has cancer; who is very sick. We had prayer for her then we decided it would be great if someone could go see her and maybe have prayer with her at her home. We decided that you should be the one to go."

After a few moments and a lot of questions flooding my mind, I asked, "Who is she, do I know her?"

Bob shook his head and said, "No I don't think you have met her." Quickly adding, "but she really needs you." I asked, "When should I go?" The three of them answered at the same time, "Now!" Bob handed me a map that he had drawn and showed me the different landmarks to look for on the way to her house.

Many questions flashed through my mind as I was driving to her house. "Lord, what do I need to say? Will she accept me and will she accept what I have to say? Lord, tell me what to say." A very firm, but gentle voice within me said, "Tell her, 'Jesus loves you.'" I thought, of course, why was I so frustrated and afraid?

I drove into her long driveway and looked at a very beautiful sprawling ranch style home. The lawn was meticulously manicured. The houses are so much larger in this neighborhood than in mine. The flower gardens were gorgeous and so perfect you wanted to feel them to make sure they were not molded and placed so neatly. I sighed as I pulled into the driveway. When I turned the motor off I just kept holding the keys in the ignition, "Lord, direct me. Please."

When I reached the door before I could ring the doorbell a beautiful lady opened the door and said, "Hello, Bob called and said that you were on your way and would be here shortly. Please come in." What a relief, she was so receptive and easy to talk with. Walking into the lovely spacious den that overlooks the lawn she asked, "Would you like something cold to drink?" "Oh yes. Thank you I would." I was glad that I did because it seemed to help my nervousness to hold the pretty fragile crystal glass as we talked. The lawn looked like a dark green velvet carpet. We sat on a beautiful light beige couch with pale, yet colorful throw pillows. You could see the entire backyard when sitting here.

My host was a small, beautiful lady with a very gracious and charming attitude and lovely smile. She was wearing a white and floral casual summer dress and white sandals. We had small talk for about thirty minutes. Then I said to her, "Before I go I would like to tell you of an encounter I had with Jesus." She opened her eyes wider and didn't take them off of my eyes. She hardly blinked her eyes while I was telling her of the experience. On the way over to your house, I was wondering what to say to you. Jesus spoke to me and said, "Tell her, Jesus loves you. He loves you with a genuine, true, gentle love not a breakable tinsel love."

She reached over and took my left hand holding it with one hand and covered it with her other hand. We sat quietly looking out the window for several minutes. I was praying silently. She was lost in her thoughts. She slowly turned her head and looked back at me with a big smile. She continued to hold my hand. I asked, "Would you mind if I anoint you with oil and pray and ask the Lord to heal you?"

"Oh no, that would be fine." My purse was lying next to me on the couch. I reached into it to get my billfold. In the change purse I always carry a tiny perfume bottle filled with olive oil, I put a tiny bit of oil on my finger and touched her forehead and prayed a very simple prayer of faith. She hugged me and held me when I started to leave. We both had tears of love and happiness in our eyes.

When I returned back to the church, it was almost service time. When Bob got there he came directly over to the piano and said, "Mom, how'd it go?" With a smile on my face and a bigger smile in my heart, I replied, "Great. Jesus met us there."

In the late fall, on October 13, 1983, I received this lovely thank you note:

Dear Mrs. Langford,

There are no words to tell you how much your prayers and concern mean to me and to my husband. Your visit that Sunday afternoon brought me the first ray of hope I felt after Learning about my illness. You set me on the road to a peace I couldn't have found without your prayers. I have started treatment which, with God's help will cure me.

With love and gratitude.

Your New Friend

While attending a social event later that year at Bob's home, I thought I recognized a lovely lady and her husband as they passed through another room. I motioned for Bob when he came over I asked, "Do I know that couple?"

He smiled, pulled me up close to him and said, "Well mom, you should. That's 'your new friend'" How my heart leapt with joy. She had turned and was coming toward me, She said, "I thought I recognized you and when I saw Bob come over and hug you then 1 knew for sure you were who I thought you were." We embraced and held each other feeling again the warmth and love of the Holy Spirit that we felt that Sunday afternoon. She said, "I'm so glad to see you. I'll never forget that Sunday afternoon that you came to my house. I want to say thank you, again."

SAM/ MY HAIR DRESSER

◇◇◇◇◇◇

Sam was running behind in her schedule this afternoon. When I entered the shop she came over and said, "Leta, do you mind if I finish with this customer before you get your shampoo? If you are in a hurry I will finish her later because she wasn't really scheduled for me." I assured her, there was no reason for her to rush. This Friday was unusual. I had absolutely nothing planned. It was good to just sit down, get a magazine and relax for a few minutes. The shop was relatively quiet. The other hair dressers were already gone.

Sam had to call to me when she had finished with the customer. Sam said, "Well, we got the place to ourselves. It sure is nice and quiet isn't it?" While she was shampooing my hair I felt the gentle tug on my heart that today is the day to tell her. Sam has done my hair for years and I had talked to her about the Lord and had invited her to attend church many times.

She was drying my hair. I raised my arm up and took hold of her hand that was holding the dryer. With a puzzled expression she looked down at me. I said, "Sam, I want to tell you something very special that Jesus told me to tell you today." She turned my chair so it was facing her. "Sam, Jesus loves you with a strong, unbreakable, gentle love and not an ornament tinsel breakable kind of love."

She leaned over toward me so fast her pretty long blond hair almost brushed my face and her expression changed to astonishment. Her beautiful big blue eyes opened wide and she did not even blink them. She was looking clear through me. She bit her bottom lip and exclaimed in a loud whisper, "Leta, I can't believe that you just said that. Today of all days."

She raised her head and stood straight as she continued, "I have not told anybody this but I am not staying at home. My husband said I should leave so we could have some time apart. We have been married seventeen years and I don't know what is happening."

"Sam, God can let you know exactly what is happening and what you should do. What about our praying and asking God for his guidance, protection and healing."

She finished my hair and as she was closing and locking the door to the shop she leaned over toward me and said, "I'm sure glad it worked out that you were my last customer. I feel so much better."

The next Friday she was looking toward the door when I opened it to go inside the busy shop. She was smiling as she almost ran, dodging the customers to get to me.

Exclaiming, "You know what? God answered our prayers. I'll tell you about it later."

Richard, the owner of the shop, came over to where I was sitting and sat down by me and said, "Tell me what you told Sam last Friday. She has been like a different person."

While he was talking to me I looked over at Sam and she was looking at me. I smiled and winked at her. She gave me a pretty smile and winked back.

Richard seemed not to be aware of his shop filled with customers. In a teasing tone of voice I said, "I guess I can tell you." He moved over a little closer to me. I related to him about the visitor that came to my house and what he had told me to do. His hand was resting on my chair arm. I put my hand on his arm and said, "Richard, Jesus loves you with a strong, true, genuine, gentle love not a breakable, tinsel love."

He listened intently with his brown eyes fixed on mine. He didn't move and sat there a few minutes looking out into space then he reached over, hugged me and kissed me on the forehead and said, "You have made my day."

Sam started attending our church. She met a wonderful Christian man there. Billy performed their beautiful church wedding. They have a lovely home on Franklin Road in Oak Hill and have a beautiful daughter, (by the way, the doctor had stated Sam could never have children.)

SHERRIE

◇◇◇◇◇◇

I shall never forget Sherrie and the scare she gave me. She was the young housekeeper who was running down the long hall at the Marriott loudly calling, "Wait, Ma'am. Wait." I was standing alone and waiting in front of the elevator on the ninth floor. She startled me and I couldn't imagine why she was running and telling me to wait about getting on the elevator. So when it stopped I didn't get on. She breathlessly said, "Oh I'm so glad I caught you. I have been watching for you. Tell me what you told me yesterday."

I took her hands and put them inside of mine and said, "Sherri, Jesus loves you with a genuine, true, strong, gentle love, not a breakable, tinsel love." She gave me a hug and with big tears rolling down her pretty thin face she smiled and said, "Oh, thank you. Thank you so much." The elevator had returned and the door opened. I gave her a little squeeze and stepped onto the elevator. As the door was closing she was still standing next to the wall. She raised her hand toward me then wiped her tears away, saying in a whisper, "Thank you, thank you, thank you." The door closed before she finished saying her last, "thank you."

When the elevator stopped and the door opened on the first floor, my heart was over flowing with joy and so very much aware of the fact that I had just experienced the feeling of the warmth of the gentle, genuine, unbreakable love of Jesus.

PHONE CALL

◇◇◇◇◇◇

In March several years ago, I received a telephone call at 10:30 in the morning, The lady said, "Would you please tell me again today what you told me ten years ago?" I questioned, "Who is this?"

This is Lori, "I was going through one of the most difficult times in my life. You called my office and told me that you felt you should call me and tell me, Jesus loves you. You will never know the strength that I received from those words. Many times I have thought of them since that day. But today I really need to hear them again. I read the Bible and I know Jesus loves me but I would like to hear it again. Would you have time to tell me that again just like you told me at the office?"

"That would be my privilege. Lori, Jesus loves you with a true, genuine, strong yet gentle love and not a breakable, tinsel love." Before I could say anything else she said, "Thank you." and hung up the phone.

OVERFLOWING LOVE

"Jesus Loves Me, This I Know" is one of the first songs we learned as a child. Today the strength, the power and the direction we receive from these words gives us faith to believe in God and in ourselves.

Like Sherri, the young housekeeper running down the corridor at the Marriott and the many others we all reach out for love, desperately and anxiously, and we long for that pure, solid, genuine, gentle love and not a breakable, tinsel ornament love.

Words that are so simple yet always so welcome. Love dissolves loneliness. In the midst of pain and heartache there is healing power in love. There is a wonderful fellowship with Jesus because of obedience to Him. "God, who is the Lawgiver and Judge," Isaiah 33:22 also wants us to know that He has given us a shepherd who loves us. Just to know the characteristics, the motivation and sacrificial love of a shepherd quickens the spirit as we learn the similar behavior of sheep and people.

Obedience to God is the door to blessing and an intimate relationship with our Lord and Savior Jesus Christ and it is the bottom line in Christian living and service. Looking at the person and feeling that gentle tug to tell of Jesus' love is so special. I see no beautiful attire, no make-up, no jewelry, no fashion statement of any kind, not a man not an woman; only a heart wanting to hear the words from the loving and gentle Shepherd and again feel the warmth of His true, genuine, unbreakable love,

At any time, someone with a hurting heart may be sitting at a table or booth in a restaurant, walking or shuffling down the aisle of the grocery or department store, waiting at the doctor's office, walking in the mall or maybe even knocking at your door.

It only takes a few minutes and it is so simple to offer encouragement as you open your heart to someone. The feeling of joy is beyond description. The results are incredible. These words have been accepted warmly, without exception. They were never rejected nor have I ever been embarrassed as I presented the gift of Jesus' love.

In my Bible on the back pages are written names, dates and just a word or two as a reminder of a unique story for each name. Several pages are filled and it is a special thrill and joy beyond words when I find a name written on a folded napkin or crumpled piece of paper in my pocket or purse to add to the list.

Everyday living changed for me that night when life brought a new reaching out and a new resurrection of love. It is exciting each day to stand on the tiptoe of expectancy waiting to feel the gentle tug and hear the still, small voice speak and become a channel through which His love can flow.

Today will be a very special day with the challenge and awesome responsibility to share Divine Love once again. There will be an appointed time and an appointed place and best of all there will be an appointed person to hear these words: "JESUS LOVES YOU!"

CHAPTER FIVE

CASTAWAYS

To our congregation attending church on Music Row and to many of our friends, our house has become known as "The Langford Lodge." Often when talking about our house they will add, "No reservations needed."

The quiet tranquility of home life is something we have read about and heard about, but it is not to be found in our home. Privacy is a luxury usually not obtainable. When our friends who live out of town are planning to come to see us, they always call before coming and ask, "Who's at your house? Do you have room for us?" I remember one night we had three beds filled. Someone was sleeping on the couch and Robert and Richard were put to bed on quilts on the floor in our bedroom. Even then we had to bring the chaise lounge in from outside to use as an extra bed in the kitchen.

When we return home, push the den door open, and step inside the house, one of us or all of us together will say, "Hey, who's here?" We are not surprised but I still feel a bit anxious, apprehensive and perplexed to see a suitcase setting under the ping-pong table, or maybe a brown grocery bag stuffed with clothes and a toy or two sticking out of it or lying beside it.

Seeing an old tattered suitcase tied with a belt or rope to keep it closed or a brand new set of luggage lets us know without a word being said some of the circumstances that are involved with our new house guest. Sometimes the clothes are all new with price tags still on them. Other times they are so worn and are either too large or too small.

Billy and I look at each other, and in our minds we are asking questions and wondering, "Who is here this time and for what reason?

How did they get here? How did they know about us? How long have they been here and how long will they stay?" We have become part of a situation which we know nothing about. For a short while we become responsible for the lives God has entrusted in our care.

At times we have found children sitting on the couch in the den, on the steps in the foyer, or upstairs in the living room, sitting on the floor staring at a blank television screen. They have pretended as if they haven't heard us come in.

There have been expressions in the eyes of these children that are different. There are looks of terror, fear, distrust, and the feeling of suspicion. They have usually been withdrawn, quiet, and desperately hungry for love. After talking to them a little while, we will ask, "Are you hungry?" Following with the question, "How about our going to the kitchen?" Then we would say, "Let's go into the kitchen and see what we can find to eat."

Often the children say they are not hungry but they are always willing to follow us into the kitchen. That always seems to break down the first barrier. Most of the children do not want to be touched, but it is hard to refrain from hugging these frightened, hurting little ones.

They are dubious of us. Usually after eating, sometimes a lot and sometimes just a bite or two, they will at least look at us, not in the eyes, but in our direction. If they do look at us in the eyes, it is a very quick glance and then they look away. It is unbelievable to see the hurt, distrust, emptiness, and fear so evident in their facial expressions, much less in their body language.

Billy and I will carry on a light conversation about the weather, the furniture, or anything we can think of, so they don't feel that we are looking at them, or watching them. Yet all the while they will be looking at us with very watchful, even squinting, eyes.

They will be biting their lips and fooling with their hair, making a curl around their finger. There is no doubt, and their expression lets us know, that they are not the least bit interested in the conversation.

Billy will take them on a tour of the house, and last of all he will show them the room where they will be sleeping. (Robert and Richard alternately gave up their room so the children could have a place of their own and feel more secure.) About this time the children seem to get over being so frightened of us, strangers whom they have never seen.

Billy is absolutely the greatest when it comes to making the children feel comfortable and at ease, even if it means his losing sleep and staying up late into the night. Often they have trouble falling asleep. If they are very young, Billy and I will lie down across the bed with them until they are asleep. We have seen the dawn break when it was impossible for them to get quiet enough to fall asleep.

Now our pain starts, as we try to get settled for the night. Our hearts are heavy and sad because we know life has dealt a devastating blow and another heartache has taken its toll on someone. Tragedy has come to another home and the children are feeling the results. Someone has sought shelter and safety in our home once again.

RUTHANNE

◇◇◇◇◇◇

In the late afternoon of a beautiful fall day, a truck pulled into the church parking lot. It was not a new truck but it was clean. Billy and I were just leaving the church office for the day.

The man stopped his truck in the middle of the lot and got out. He was motioning for us to get out of our car. Billy drove the car back into the church lot, got out of our car and walked over to the man. He was nice looking, well dressed, his sport coat and pants were pressed. He looked awfully tall standing next to Billy, who is 5 feet 8 inches tall. He appeared to be in his early thirties.

I could hear their conversation while I was sitting in the car. He was asking Billy if the little girl could stay with us for a day or two. Then he said, "You are the minister, aren't you?" Billy said, "Yes, I'm the minister and we will be glad to have your little girl." I sighed deeply; I knew what Billy would say before he answered.

The man turned and motioned for the little girl to get out of the truck. She jumped out and ran over to Billy and the man. Her hair was the same sandy blond as his. It was pulled in a pony-tail with the ribbon matching her little pants and top. She had white sandals and in her arms was a teddy bear. She called the teddy bear "Skippy."

The man put his hand on her head, sort of straightened her ribbon and said, "This is Ruthanne," and she joined in and said, "and I am eight years old." She and Billy started toward our car as the man went toward the truck, then Ruthanne turned, and ran toward the truck calling, "Wait daddy, my suitcase."

Ruthanne was not frightened and seemed to feel very comfortable with us. She talked all the way home. She asked, "What are we having for supper. Do you have any boys and girls? Where is your house? Do you have a big yard? Can I play outside?"

After we ate supper she helped me clear the dishes from the table. As we were washing the dishes she said, "I help my mommy at home." She played some games with Robert and Richard down in the den and I could hear them teaching her to play ping-pong.

When it was time for bed she went into the room that Billy had told her was hers. She came out in just a few minutes and asked me to help her get her suitcase open.

"May I show you what's in my suitcase?"

"Sure you can."

Ruthanne and I sat on the bed trying to get her suitcase opened. She had locked it and the key would not unlock it. She and I were pulling on it; finally it came loose. Records went all over the bed; a couple of them fell on the floor. They were the small singles, 45 rpm size. Records were the only thing that she had in her suitcase. I couldn't believe it. No clothes, no games, nothing but records.

"Have you got a record player?" She asked. "Sure we do and you are welcome to play any of these records that you want to." Our stereo is in the dining room. She and I carried all the records into the dining room and put them on the dining room table. I showed her how to turn the stereo on and set it to play the single records.

As I was doing this she kept looking through all the records over and over, turning them from one side to the other. I said, "Can I help you find one?" She would read each label very carefully, and then put it down. I started reading them with her. The labels read . . . Jim Reeves--Patsy Cline--Marty Robbins--Pearl & Carl Butler--Hawk Shaw Hawkins

--Ernest Tubbs--Cowboy Copas--George Morgan--all the records were made by country music artists.

She finally found the three she was looking for and held them up and said, "Here they are. I want to play these first. My mommy always cries when she plays them." It was Patsy Cline, singing "Crazy", "I Was So Wrong" and "I Fall To Pieces." I called Billy into the room to listen to the records with us.

Ruthanne did not say a word and hardly moved the entire time the records were playing. I wondered what she was thinking as she stared out the window into the darkness of the night. We told her she could play the records as long as she wanted to.

After listening to a few records Billy and I went across the hall into the living room. She would play other records but she played the first two records over and over. She played them for over an hour. Finally she turned off the stereo, gathered all the records in her little arms carried them back into her room and put them back into her suitcase. Then she put her suitcase on the floor at the foot of the bed.

I fixed all of us a glass of milk and cookies. Robert and Richard came up from the den. We sat around the table talking. Robert went to bed first, then Richard. I asked Ruthanne if she was ready for bed; she shook her head no. Her eyes were getting heavy and she could hardly hold them open. She was so sleepy.

Finally, I told her that Billy and I would come into her bedroom and sit on the bed and talk with her. Robert brought one of his tee shirts for her to sleep in. She didn't give me any trouble about sleeping in it. In just a few minutes she was sound asleep.

Billy and I had just gotten to sleep. Someone was knocking on our front door so loud, it sounded as if they were going to break it down. The light in the clock on the dresser was the only light in the room. When I could get my eyes open enough to focus on the numbers, I read 2:45 a.m. Billy looked out the bedroom window and said he could see car lights in the driveway but couldn't see the car clearly enough to recognize it.

We were asking each other, "Who could be here at this time of the morning?" Billy and I went down the stairs together. When Billy opened the door, there stood Ruthanne's father. Billy and I looked at each other, wondering, "How did he know where we lived?"

"Is Ruthanne here?" He asked.

"Yes," Billy answered, "but she's asleep." Then Billy added, "You are welcome to come in and spend the rest of the night with us."

"No, we won't be able to stay. We have to leave right now." Billy asked him to step inside into the foyer. I went back upstairs to get her.

There on the floor by the bed was laying a couple of her records that she had overlooked. I put them in her suitcase with the others and put her shirt and pants, sandals, and hair ribbon in the suitcase on top of the records and fastened it.

I was so sorry that I had to wake her. She was sleeping so soundly. She looked like a big doll with her long blond hair on the pillow. She was so little.

Laying my hand on her shoulder I prayed, "Lord, be with her. Protect her. Keep her in your care." Then I shook her to awaken her. "Your father has come to take you with him. He said you have to go now."

Sitting up in bed, she reached for me and hugged me real tight. Then she pulled away from me and rubbed her sleepy eyes. I helped her stand and get her balance. She picked up her teddy bear and her suitcase and looked down at Robert's tee shirt. "He won't mind if you keep his shirt."

Together we walked down the stairs. She dropped her teddy bear and it fell all the way to the bottom of the stairs, into the foyer where her father and Billy were waiting. She handed her father the suitcase and reached down for her teddy bear. I don't think he was aware of the fact that it only contained records.

Her father was anxious to go and there was no time to talk about anything, including Ruthanne. "Thanks for your help with Ruthanne, I really appreciate it."

We couldn't see if there was anyone else in the truck, but she ran to it, opened the door on the driver's side and climbed in. Her father was carrying her suitcase. Billy and I walked toward the truck.

Ruthanne smiled and said, "I'll see you later." Her big eyes were sparkling even though she had just been awakened. Ruthanne stayed only a few hours in our home and we don't even know her last name, but I still think of her. I will always remember seeing the lights of the pick-up truck as they drove up the hill and turned back toward town and into the darkness of the night.

Billy put his arm around me and pulled me close to him. I put my head on his shoulder with hot tears falling on his neck. We stood under the tree in the front yard for a few minutes, neither of us saying anything, but being aware of an uneasy and restless feeling in the quiet and dark of the night.

Feeling a deep ache in our heart, we slowly walked back into the house. We wondered, where will Ruthanne spend the rest of the night? Why did they have to leave in such a hurry?

Today as I'm writing this, I wonder where Ruthanne is now and does she remember those few hours she spent with us in our home.

UNEXPECTED CHRISTMAS GUESTS

◇◇◇◇◇◇◇

It was 1:45 p.m. on Christmas Day and our Christmas dinner was just about ready. The Christmas tree looked bare with all the packages taken out from under it. The presents were in four separate stacks. My gifts were at one end of the couch; Billy's were at the other end. Robert had his in the platform rocker and Richard had his gifts in the chair by the television.

Robert and Richard were putting the pretty green and red ribbons and bows in a box, and neatly folding and putting the paper that was large enough for use next year into another box.

In all the excitement of opening our packages the Nativity Scene had been knocked over. Billy knelt down and straightened out the white sheet and was placing the animals, Mary and Joseph back in place.

As I stepped to the door to tell them dinner was ready, the phone rang. I answered, thinking someone from the church was probably calling to wish us a Merry Christmas.

Instead the operator said, "I have a long distance call from Arizona for Reverend Langford." I handed the phone to Billy and asked the boys, "Who do we know in Arizona?"

When Billy came to the phone he said, "This is Reverend Langford." He listened attentively, then asked, "What time did you say the plane would arrive?"

We couldn't imagine who was coming to see us this Christmas. When Billy hung up the receiver he walked into the dining room where we were putting the finishing touches to the festive table.

"Honey, add two plates. We are having company for dinner. I am going to have to hurry to the airport to meet a plane. Two little girls will be getting off here in Nashville in just a few minutes. If I don't meet them the lady on the phone said to call the police and have them meet them. She was sending them to Nashville. The lady said she was their mother and she was sending them here to their father."

"Billy, what about dinner? Everything will be cold. I have planned a special dinner for us." As Billy was getting his coat out of the closet he said, "If we don't have enough I am sure something will be open and I will pick up some other food."

"No, that's not it," I said. "I just wasn't expecting anyone else. I know, the spirit of Christmas is giving, reach out in love at Christmas, share the joy of Christmas. I know them well because I have heard them all of my life, but does that mean having uninvited guests for Christmas dinner and being happy about it?"

Billy said, "I will tell you what, let's just all ride out to the airport and I'll tell you what else the lady on the phone said. We'll warm everything up when we get back." As we were getting in the car, we were all asking Billy questions at the same time. He said, "I'll start from the beginning of the conversation on the phone. The lady said she was in Arizona. She had gotten our name from the phone information operator. (Our name and church location is listed in the yellow pages. Following the street address is "On Music Row.") The lady did not give her name but gave the children's names. Billy said she thought her husband was in Nashville trying to get some songs published, maybe trying to get a job singing. She wasn't sure whether he had arrived here or not. They had been separated several months.

She said, "If you are not able to meet the girls at the airport, call the police department and have them meet the girls and keep them. She has told the little girls that a minister or a policeman would be waiting for them."

It was a beautiful Christmas Day and very, very cold. We walked briskly almost in a run from the airport parking lot. Billy had the name of the airline and the flight number. Walking down the long corridor to the gate, you could hear Christmas songs being played over the intercom, interrupted only by the announcement of plane arrivals and departures. With the beautiful Christmas music and bustle of people carrying packages, some still wrapped and others with gifts, crumpled paper and ribbon tumbling from a shopping bag, even the airport had the atmosphere and excitement of Christmas.

We reached the gate and had just sat down as the announcement was made. The plane from Tucson, Arizona is arriving on time. We breathlessly waited for the people to start coming through the door. Finally they did. We scanned everyone especially the children.

We were surprised that there were so many children traveling on that flight but they always ended up with an adult coming right behind them. Then there they were, two beautiful little girls, holding hands and each clutching a doll.

The girls came bouncing down the walkway stretching their necks, looking at everyone in the waiting area. Their dresses had ruffles of white lace on them. The smaller girl's dress was red and the larger girl's dress was wine colored. Underneath you could see ruffled petticoats with lots of lace, making the dresses stand out so pretty. They had black patent slippers with socks that matched their dresses. Both girls had their hair pulled back on each side with barrettes. Their short dark hair and dark eyes made their complexion look just like a doll's.

Behind them was the flight attendant carrying a shopping bag. This contained everything their mother had sent with them. Billy went to the flight attendant and told her who he was and about the call he had received. "I'm glad you are here," she said as she handed Billy the shopping bag. The girls looked back at the attendant and threw her a kiss. She threw a kiss at them as she smiled a big smile and looked over at me and the boys standing just behind Billy.

Billy motioned for all of us to step over to the chairs in the waiting area. We sat down for just a few minutes. Billy introduced himself, Robert, Richard and me to the girls. The older girl said her name was Lorrie and the younger girl looked away as Lorrie said, "My sister's name is Patricia, but we call her Patty." They didn't tell us what their last name was. Lorrie quickly added, "I'm older than she is. I am almost 12 years old and Patty is only 5 years old" (Lorrie could have said she was 12 years old going on 17 years old.)

I asked Billy if I could see the shopping bag, thinking that it probably contained some warm clothes; maybe sweaters or jackets or at least something with long sleeves to put on them. Everyone in the waiting area had gone. I pulled out everything that was in bag and laid it on the chair next to us. To my surprise there were only six tank tops and short sets and six pairs of panties, three for each little girl. Could this be all? Not even an extra pair of socks!

While Billy was talking to the girls, I motioned for Robert to come over to me. I whispered and asked him. "Do you have a sweater on under your coat?" He nodded his head "Yes." "Do you think Richard has one on?" He went over and asked Richard and he nodded "Yes."

"What about you both allowing the girls wear your sweaters until we get home?"

They both hesitated then said, "Well okay." We realized why the hesitation; they were both wearing their new sweaters that they had just received for Christmas. Realizing too, the sweaters were one of the better gifts they had received.

"Just as soon as we get home, you can put them back on." Billy had taken his overcoat off and was placing it over the shoulders of the larger girl but she shrugged her shoulders and pushed it off.

He said, "You all wait for me. I'll get the car and bring it around as close as I can to the door."

Looking at the little girls dressed in their summer dresses with nothing else in their shopping bag, I was thinking..." I know what we will be doing tomorrow. There goes our Christmas money that the church had given us." With the money that we had saved and the Christmas money we had enough to buy a much needed couch for the living room.

The springs in our old one showed unless the cushions were turned just a certain way. The professional cleaning service that we had called stated, "It's really not worth cleaning. It is really worn." We had already picked out the couch that would have been perfect. It was beautiful. I sighed a big sigh and said to myself, "There goes the couch." And there it went!

The second day they were here we did go shopping and we did buy sweaters, shoes, socks, warm pants and tops and two winter coats. It took all day. There were only a few small shopping centers. After shopping at these we had to go downtown to the different department stores. Lorrie was very hard to please.

When I think of them I still have an overwhelming feeling of anxiety and remember the total lack of ability to handle what was to happen in the coming days which became the coming weeks and eventually the coming months. The situation became more difficult as the time drug by. Some days I felt I would suffocate.

For the next five months, January to July, we were to be in for quite an experience. On the way home from the airport and all through dinner they chatted about their Christmas day morning, what each liked to do and what they wanted to do while they "lived" with us. They wanted to know if Robert and Richard had games they could play with when we got through with dinner.

With the warmed-up dinner over and everything cleared off the dining room table we went into the living room. Billy asked the girls, "What is your last name? I want to call your mother and let her know that you are here with us and you are okay."

Billy went into the other room to make the call. He was gone for quite a while and I figured that he was telling her about the girls. Maybe she was telling him about the reason she had sent them here.

When he came back into the room his expression told me, something was not right. Then he told the girls, "The phone number you gave me has been disconnected. Do you have another place that your mother might be?" They both shrugged their shoulders and said nothing.

They went downstairs to play ping-pong. Billy said, "I'll try in the morning to make contact with someone."

As soon as breakfast was over Billy started calling. He continued to make inquiries all day. Finally around bedtime someone did return a call with some information concerning their mother. Their mother and older sister had moved, with no forwarding address. After only a few days Lorrie began to be difficult. Her attitude was terrible, she treated little Patty so meanly. When she and Patty fought she would break the few things that we bought for Patty. She would break anything she could find. We really had a problem. We felt that with prayer and understanding we could turn things around.

Billy said, "Honey maybe the Lord is teaching us to be patient and I've heard that a little suffering helps keep us humble." I failed miserably. No matter how I tried, what I tried, or when I tried, things did not go well. I was far too strict and far too impatient for the life style to which she had been accustomed.

In the downstairs bathroom, that they were using, she broke the edge of the tile around the sink. Patty said Lorrie broke it with her shoe heel. She broke the vacuum cleaner by pulling the wires and cutting the electric cord. She said I should not have asked her to vacuum the bath powder she spilled on the den floor. She broke drinking glasses and dishes. She got into my jewelry which was not all that much and certainly not expensive. Some pieces were given to me and had sentimental value such as my PTA Presidents pin. She would break the chains of my necklaces and say that Patty did it.

We finally had my bed room carpeted with a beautiful medium blue carpet to match the other rooms which had been carpeted a couple of years earlier. She spilled a whole bottle of Mercurochrome on it. The spot would never come out.

Ten years later for our Christmas gift Robert carpeted our upstairs for us. The Mercurochrome stain was finally gone.

After all these years we don't have to have an extra throw rug in my room.

Wendy, a young girl attending Scarritt College was staying in the other downstairs bedroom. Lorrie poured out her perfume from a brand new bottle. She spilled her fingernail polish on the dresser. Windy had received a gray silver mink collar for her coat from her parents for Christmas. Lorrie cut it up into strips. She went back into Wendy's room; took her pretty lacy things and cut the lace off.

When Billy asked her about it, she said, "I was only making some doll clothes for Patty." She blamed Patty for making her get into trouble every time.

We knew a change had to be made some way or another. But there was still no word from their mother. Lorrie became so defiant to me and to Billy.

Marie, a lady attending our church realized our dilemma. She said, "I think I can handle the problem." She had a daughter about the same age as Lorrie and maybe Patty would settle down if Lorrie had someone near her own age to play with. We told Marie that we would help buy the groceries if she could help in this situation. Patty was not a problem. Marie took both of the girls. However in a few days we brought Patty back to separate them.

Lorrie seemed to be doing much better with Marie. Marie was very strict, would not tolerate Lorrie's actions and Lorrie knew it. After a couple of weeks Lorrie called to ask if she could come back to our house. Then the calls came about twice a week. But I was physically sick by now. I was unable to handle the situation while still trying to continue my church activities. Marie entered Lorrie into school with her daughter. This worked for a week or two.

Marie called one day and said, "Leta, how did you ever put up with this child? She is unbelievable and very street wise. Lorrie has gone too far. Her resentment and her bitterness are destroying her. I don't know what we are going to do."

Marie said that we couldn't handle this alone and suggested that we take turns keeping her. I will forever be grateful to Marie for coming to our rescue. She and I still talk about that unforgettable episode. Marie is a dear friend until this day.

There was no word from her mother until around the middle of May. One day the phone rang and the voice on the other end of the phone said, "I know for sure Danny is in Nashville and know that he will be on Music Row."

Billy quickly asked, "Are you the mother of the girls?" "When do you plan to get them?" She responded, "I'll probably be in Nashville before too long." And with that she hung up.

Billy kept yelling, "Wait, wait, where are you calling from?"

One Sunday morning their father did attend church. He couldn't believe that sitting on the front row were his two little girls. As soon as church was over Patty ran to the back when she saw him. She hugged him around his knees, he picked her up and just kept hugging her; then asked, "Where is your mother?" Lorrie shrugged her shoulders and finally sidled up to him. Billy asked him to come to the church office in the back of the church to talk with him.

Billy asked him if he could take the girls but he said he was unable to take them with him because he did not have a place for them now, maybe later. He would not tell us where he lived as he said he was moving the next day or two. But he would get back with us as soon as he could and work out something with us about taking the girls. He said that he was busy every day trying to get his songs published and auditioning.

I kept reminding myself of the scripture, "Life consisteth not in the abundance of material things." That helped me deal with situations when things would get broken or misplaced. (Such as my high school class ring and PTA President pin)

One warm summer day the last of June, Billy said it would be a good day to be working in the yard at church; he wanted us to come and work with him. School was out so we decided to make a day of it. We pulled weeds, planted flowers and cleaned up around the church all day. Billy and I were just finishing up. Robert, Richard and Patty were playing in the shade under the big tree in the front yard.

A yellow car pulled up in the parking lot. It was packed to the top with clothes and boxes in the front and back. A pretty lady and a teenage girl got out. The lady was wearing bright pink pants and a halter top. She had long hair pulled back and tied by a pink ribbon. The girl was wearing faded jeans and a tight multicolor faded tank top with a blue shirt over it.

They were walking over to the tree. Patty saw them but kept on playing with the boys. The lady walked up to where they were and said, "Hi, Patty."

Patty jumped up and with dirt and weeds falling out of her little basket, she reached up to hug her. Patty had been very careful not to lose her flowers but she stepped on them when she got up.

She said, "Mommy." Patty smiled her pretty smile that we had seen and grown to love. When she smiled her nose sort of wrinkled and her dimples were prettier than ever. Patty stood there holding her mother's hand. The teenage girl stood just behind them.

Billy and I walked over to them and I said to myself, "So you finally decided to come get your little girls!" I wanted to say something to her but I dared not.

Billy introduced himself. She said, "Well, I am here to find their father.

The only thing I need is a place to stay."

I thought I would die. I cut my eyes to Billy hoping he would know, "There is no way we can do this, because that will mean Lorrie too." Billy said, "I'll tell you what, I'll help you find a place to stay. We cannot take the whole family."

He did find them an apartment and made arrangements for them so they did not have to put down a deposit for the rent. He also helped her find a job.

She and the girls attended every church service and one Sunday Danny came in. As soon as he did, Patty moved over and sat down by him. After service, he and their mother and girls talked for a long while. He said that he was going to move in with them the next day. He did, but that didn't work out.

The father called us the next week and said that he was filing for a divorce. His wife had not changed and she had been unfaithful to him. She was teaching the girls bad things and making them "street wise."

Lesa, the older teenage girl that had been with their mother, came to get Patty and her things. She stayed all afternoon waiting for her mother to come back to pick them up.

They moved from the first apartment; we did not know where they had moved. She stopped attending church. We didn't see them again before they left town, or their father. Danny later called and said that the children and their mother had moved to another state.

Months passed when one day while working at the church office, I heard a car drive up. I kept waiting for someone to knock on the door. When no one came to the door for a few minutes, I looked out the window.

Who should it be but JoAnn, the mother of the girls! She was standing at the back of the car with the trunk open getting something.

She was wearing a pair of dark dress pants and a beautiful white off the shoulder blouse and looked much younger than when she was here before. Her long dark hair was not pulled back in a ponytail but was loose around her face and really looked pretty; the high heels made her look even taller. She really looked gorgeous.

She put perfume on her wrists and behind her ears. She reached for a comb and combed through her hair; then she put on lipstick. She looked into the mirror; pulled the blouse farther down over her shoulders and then closed the trunk.

She walked across the parking lot up the back steps and into Billy's office. There was no way to tell Billy who she was; just hoped that he remembered her!

His office was located in the back of the house and my office was in the front. I buzzed him on the intercom. Then I realized he was having a conversation on the phone and I didn't want to interrupt him. The church offices were located in the house on the corner of Eighteenth and Grand across the driveway from the church.

JoAnn was in Billy's office just a few minutes when Billy came out front to my office and asked me to come in while he talked to someone. He had remembered her! He wasn't aware that I had already seen and recognized her. I have never told him that I saw her fixing up to see him.

Listening to her talk and tell her sad story, my heart went out to her. Lesa, the older sister had been killed in an automobile accident. Lorrie had run off with an older fellow. Little Patty had gone to live with her father's parents.

The emptiness of her life, home, and family was so evident. When JoAnn stood to leave Billy suggested, as he always does when he finishes counseling, that she commit all her problems and the rest of her life to God. She wept silently as Billy prayed aloud. In my heart I joined Billy and silently prayed that God would fill her with His love and joy, and give her peace. That was the last time we heard from her.

HELLO LITTLE STRANGER

◇◇◇◇◇◇

We were just finishing supper when we heard a car driving up the driveway into the backyard. Robert pulled back the kitchen curtain to look out the window. There was an old, dilapidated, faded blue Pontiac which looked as terrible as it sounded. The fender was dented and the headlight was wired on. We had never seen the car or the two people who were in the car. We had no idea who they were, why they had come or how they found our house.

The young man was getting out of his car just as Billy was going out the downstairs den door. He said to Billy, "I got your address out of the phone book, the gas station had a city map and I found your house without any trouble at all."

His clothes were clean and he was really very nice looking. The girl stayed in the car for a few minutes while Billy talked to them. The young man looked to be about 25 years old. When the girl got out of the car, we were surprised that she looked so young, maybe in her late teens.

As she was getting out of the car, she reached into the back seat and picked up what appeared to be a bundle of towels. She started around the car to where Billy and the young fellow were standing, talking.

Billy told them we were just finishing supper and would be glad to fix them something to eat if they had not eaten. They quickly accepted and said they appreciated our thoughtfulness.

The boys and I greeted them as they were coming up the stairs, wondering why she was carrying this bundle of towels. When she got to the top of the stairs, she pulled the top towel back and there was a beautiful, tiny baby, sound asleep. I told her she could lay the baby on Robert's bed because that bedroom was next to the kitchen. We could hear the baby when it cried.

As I was preparing their supper I prayed, "Lord, please stretch this food so that they will have enough to eat." He had done this before when unexpected people would arrive at meal time. And as usual, just like when the Lord fed the five thousand, with two fish and five loaves of bread, we always have enough food. They were really hungry and ate large portions and even had additional helpings.

After the couple had finished eating, we sat around the table talking about Nashville and anything that we could think of. Carol said that they were from Virginia. She didn't say what city. Dave was just as nondescriptive. Neither of them mentioned their last name even when Billy asked them two or three times, "Now what is your last name?"

Dave said that he had lost his job while working in a restaurant in Knoxville several weeks before. He had not been able to find another so they had decided to look for work in another location. Billy asked him if he had applied for a job here in Nashville. He said "No, not yet."

It seemed as if they were going to stay for a while so I suggested that we go into the living room where we would be more comfortable. As we were going into the living room, Dave said to Billy, "I really need some money to buy gas. We don't plan to stay in Nashville. We really do need to be on our way. We are going on farther south, maybe."

Billy said that he would take them to the gas station. They could follow him in their car. He would be glad to fill up their car. Dave said, "I'll go get the gas." Billy said that he would ride with him to the gas station.

While Dave and Billy were gone, Carol asked if I had a dish towel or wash cloth she could use for a diaper for the baby. I went to the bathroom and got a dish towel and handed it to her. She went into the bedroom and laid it on the bed next to the baby.

The baby was kicking and stretching and turning its head looking all around. What a beautiful baby, so tiny and yet so alert with bright sparkling eyes.

"What is the baby's name and how old is it?"

She replied, "We haven't really named her yet, we just call her 'Punkin'. She is two weeks old."

As we were talking, she pulled the baby to the side of the bed and started taking off the diaper. The name NOEL HOTEL was written on the wash cloth she was using for a diaper.

There was a hotel on Fourth Avenue and Church Street, downtown, by that name. (I still have the wash cloth.) Carol folded the small soft dish towel and used it for a diaper.

She then reached into the bundle of towels and pulled out an empty baby bottle. I reached for the bottle and said, "I'll wash the bottle for you."

I took it into the kitchen. There was no need to ask her if she had milk for the bottle,

I knew that she didn't.

While filling the bottle, I kept wondering, "How is this little thing going to make it? I wonder, do they realize what a wonderful little miracle they possess?" I was lost in my thoughts and stayed longer than I realized because this baby brought back my thoughts of Larry, our own 10 day old baby that God had taken home. We were so excited about his arrival and I've never understood why God took him. I still feel an ache in my heart for him.

I asked her. "Can I hold Punkin and give her the bottle?" She said, "Sure." When the baby had taken her bottle and fallen asleep, I laid her back on Robert's bed. Carol and I had just gone into the living room when we heard the car pull into the driveway. We went downstairs.

Dave turned the car around. Carol walked to him and said something as she opened the car door on his side of the car. Billy, Carol and Dave and I all walked over to the patio and sat down. Robert and Richard were playing and practicing their basketball shots in the back yard.

Dave said that they should be going before it got any later. The couple thanked us for the supper and buying the gas. They got into the car and started out of the driveway.

Billy and I started to sit outside for a while then I remembered that I hadn't cleaned up the dishes from supper. I said, "I'll go on upstairs and I'll be back in a few minutes."

Billy followed me inside and said, "I'll help you."

We saw the baby as we passed the bedroom door. At the same time, we breathlessly exclaimed, "The baby, they forgot their baby." There she was sound asleep.

Billy turned, ran down the stairs about three steps at a time, and ran out the front door whistling and shouting at the top of his voice, "You forgot your baby! Wait! Stop!"

Well, thank goodness, their old car was having trouble getting up the hill. By cutting across our front yard and the next door neighbor's front yard and the side yard of the house at the top of the hill Billy was able to catch them even though they tried to keep driving. I picked the baby up in a hurry and she was still sleeping. I was not able to run very fast with her in my arms but was following on behind Billy carrying "Punkin" and the bundle of towels.

Carol said, "We want you to have the baby. She is yours. We just can't take care of her. We won't ever give you any trouble over her or try to get her back. Just please keep her."

Robert and Richard heard Billy yelling. They came running around the house to see what all the commotion was about. They were standing in the middle of the street with us by the old car which was making a terrible racket. I was trying to give her the baby.

Billy said, "We cannot take her. If you have any relatives perhaps they will help you with her. She is precious. Let me call an agency and help you work out something."

The cars in the road were waiting to get by. Their old beat-up car was still making an awful loud noise; our neighbors were outside looking at us. They surely heard Billy whistling and shouting and now could hear all of us standing in the middle of the street appealing to this couple. What a sight we must have been!

Finally Billy took the baby from me and handed her to Carol. I laid the bundle of towels on the floor of the front seat. Billy kept saying, "Let me help you with this." But they evidently had made up their minds before they got here that they would not do that. They would not even listen.

The car was barely moving up the hill. The motor sounded like it was going to stop running any minute. We were almost to the top of the hill. Billy, Richard, Robert and I were standing in the middle of the street just looking at each other. We realized the cars had to go around us. As we walked slowly back down the street and into our driveway we asked each other questions about what had happened, knowing all the time we would never have the answers. The boys ran ahead of us to the front porch.

When we reached them Billy said, "That baby was the size of Larry, when God took him to heaven." I think for the first time they could feel the dreadful sting of death and became aware of the empty hollow void that it had left when it invaded our home. They stood quietly without moving before saying anything.

Then Robert asked, "Did Larry look like that? Were his eyes blue? Was he that little?" The longing for Larry made my heart hurt.

Billy said, "Larry's eyes were light brown and would have probably turned dark brown like yours and Richard's. He was that tiny but his hair was red."

In unison, they questionably said, "Red"? With that statement we all smiled and relaxed a bit.

Richard asked, "Why don't you have a picture of Larry?"

Billy explained that hospitals did not take pictures of babies at that time and we didn't know he would get pneumonia and be gone so quickly.

Billy said, "Let's go into the kitchen and I'll draw you a diagram of what the doctor said happened to Larry's lungs.

Since Larry was an eight months old baby instead of nine, his lungs were not developed. The hospital placed him in an incubator for seven days. Then twins were born prematurely also. The small nursery in Kingsport only had two incubators.

Thinking Larry was strong enough the doctor said we could take him home.

Hospitals keep babies now when they are born prematurely. When this does happen, the baby is placed in an incubator and kept there until the lungs are fully developed. Sometimes several weeks and even months."

We gave the boys a goodnight hug and turned in for the night. In our bedroom Billy and I reflected on the happenings of the evening; finally drifting off to sleep with our minds full of unanswered questions.

A few days later while reading the paper we were filled with sorrow. There was a small notice that a baby girl had been abandoned in a hotel lobby in Jackson, Tennessee. (About 140 miles west of Nashville) She had been found soon enough that after being checked by a doctor he said she was in fine physical condition. An agency was placing her in a home.

Could this be the little stranger that was in our home and slept on Robert's bed for a few hours? Should we have tried to keep her? Or did God have her 'special' for another family who needed her love and she was just for them?

What mixed emotions we experienced, such a longing for our little son who was taken. We wanted him so badly. Now here this baby and many other children were just left with us. "Oh, God, I don't understand it at all."

Many times through the years when situations would arise that I didn't understand, my dad would say, "Leta, you must have faith in God and realize that He knows what He is doing. There are some things you will never understand. God doesn't have to give you a reason for what He does. You probably wouldn't understand even if He tried to."

Then he would always remind me of the scripture, from which I have heard him preach many sermons, "For my thoughts are not your thoughts, neither are your ways my ways, sayeth the Lord. For as the heavens are higher than the earth, so are my ways higher than your ways, and my thoughts than your thoughts." (Isaiah 55:8-9)

"Your business is to trust Him and His Word. You must always remember, no matter what, God is faithful." Often he would pull me to him and smile saying in a teasing yet firm manner, "Leta, You are going to have to accept the fact, God knows more than you do about a few things!"

There is no substitute for the power and authority in the scriptures in helping us cope with the complexities of life. We still feel the sorrow in our hearts when we think of Larry, but we sorrow not as those who have no hope. (1 Thessalonians 4:13) This brings healing and gives us great assurance.

Gods' restoring power turned the hurt through the death of Larry into one of the greatest opportunities of our ministry; that of sharing our home, our lives and our love with many lonely, unhappy, frightened children. Watching them settle down, start smiling, and enjoy playing again was most rewarding and for a while they became a part of our family.

CHAPTER SIX

HOLY TERROR

At last, there would be time for Billy and me alone. Robert was 26 years old. He had already graduated from Middle Tennessee State University in Murfreesboro and was attending the Nashville School of Law at night. He had a good job as Business Administrator for Metro Public Libraries. He was married and buying his own home on Carter Avenue just four blocks from us. His wife, Wynnelle, was a hairdresser and worked at Hair Fashions. So, they were doing fine.

Richard was 22 years old. He had also graduated from Middle Tennessee State University and was elected as Associate Student Body President his senior year at MTSU. He was in his second year as Assistant Manager of Commerce Union Bank on Gallatin Road not far from home. He was doing fine there.

It had been a couple of years now that no one else had been in our home and I did feel relieved of the responsibility which we seemed to have inherited.

I was just beginning to realize how good it felt to be free from someone else being in the house. And there even was a little extra money to spend on things I wanted and had been unable to do so before because there just wasn't any left after the necessities were purchased. I could breathe easy. It felt good.

It was the first day of our Vacation Bible School and there was no need for me to go until later in the day since everything seemed to be going so smoothly. This 1977 VBS was just going to be perfect. Every worker had been on time this morning. We were pleased with the attendance. The classes were keeping to the schedule, with a certain amount of time allotted to each lesson and activity.

All the children (and even some of the teachers) were looking forward to the snack time that was coming later. I had gone by the craft shop to pick up some extra supplies needed for the younger craft class.

With everything being taken care of there was time to run by the house for a few minutes. The phone was ringing when I got there. The director of the Vacation Bible School was on the line. She had a loud yet unsteady voice. She was pleading for help!

She said, "We need the pastor immediately. We have a problem that we can't handle." Billy was not at home but by God's favor, he called shortly afterward. I gave him the message. "You are needed at the church immediately. A little boy is causing problems."

Billy went directly to the church. The perfection of the early morning had given way to chaos when a 10 year old boy named Bobby arrived on the scene. He had thrown a large rock and dented the front door of the sanctuary. He had eaten the refreshments and was fighting with all the children. Bobby was ready to defy anyone and anything for any reason.

To show distinction between our son Bob and this Bobby we referred to him as "Little Bobby." He proudly took on this name and he goes by it until this day. Billy put his hand around Little Bobby's shoulder. "Why don't you step into the church office with me where we can be alone? That way no one will interrupt us."

At this, Little Bobby straightened up trying to stand tall. He looked around at the other children to see if they noticed what a great honor had been bestowed upon him. Billy told me, "He raised his eye brows, tilted his little head back and walked right into my office." Billy followed closely behind. "Sit down here on the couch with me, "Little Bobby."

Before Billy could say another word, "Little Bobby" said, "Everybody always picks on me. They always start trouble with me."

It took an hour and a half in the Pastor's Study but Billy and Little Bobby finally had an understanding. Billy told Little Bobby that he would try to get everyone to leave him alone and not bother him.

Little Bobby, in turn, was not to disrupt the Vacation Bible School again. By this time VBS was over for the day and everyone was gone. Billy spent the rest of the day of what turned out to be the first of many, many days with Little Bobby.

Billy found that Little Bobby lived just across the street from the church in an apartment with his mother and older brother. Often, because the door was locked, he could not get in. Little Bobby was the little boy that we had often seen playing on the curb across from the church and in our parking lot but would never talk to us. He said the VBS had taken his place to play. "This is my turf." He wanted them to leave and not ever come back. Billy explained to him that the children were there to play with him and they would not take his place. Little Bobby said that would be okay, as long as it was just for that week.

Little Bobby attended VBS every day the rest of the week and there were no problems, even though he would keep his sparkling blue eyes on the kids with a sort of frown on his face. He didn't have any more fights.

We later learned that Little Bobby was not allowed to ride the school bus to and from school because he fought with the children on the bus. We also learned that the school let him out 15 minutes earlier than the other children and that he had to report to school later in the morning, again because he was in so many fights. He fought with the children going to school and coming home from school.

One day he hit a teacher. In his music class he took viola lessons, using the school instrument. The viola was too small for him, he said, and it caused him to miss notes. One day when this happened, the teacher told him to stop hitting the wrong notes and he said, "The teacher yelled at me, and I became so angry I swung my arms smashing the viola into a chair and then I hit the teacher." He had to pay, literally, for that act of temper which was to our dismay one among many. We were to find out how many.

When the summer was over he began dropping by the church office every day, usually in the afternoons. I worked in the church office and Billy was usually back from his calls by the time Little Bobby got there. We often ate out at a little restaurant across from Vanderbilt University called Mack's. We would take him with us.

Little Bobby said, "If you don't see me outside when you go to eat just call for me and I will hear you because I am always somewhere around close." Many times he was out after dark playing on the curb. When we asked him why he wasn't in his house, he would always say, "My mom has to keep the doors locked." But I asked him, "Is your mother at home?" He usually answered, "I don't know." I quit asking about her after the first few times.

Billy started taking him with him when he had errands to do. He would even plan his day so that he could include Little Bobby, if at all possible. Little Bobby would bring his report card for us to see it and asked us to sign it. We told him his mother must do that. If he got hurt at school they would call us. We took him to the doctor many times. He fell in the alley behind the church one afternoon while playing "King of the Mountain" in a wooded area. A knife was in the ground and he fell on it, cutting a deep gash in his leg. He came into the church with the blood running down his leg and his hands dripping with blood. He had taken his shirt and tried to tie it around the cut. That had not stopped the bleeding.

Billy was there, thank God, and took him to the emergency room at General Hospital. His leg needed eight stitches. We would change the bandages and clean his leg every day until it healed.

Before too long, we started bringing him home with us for the weekends. He would come on Friday afternoon and stay until after church on Sunday night. He brought his dirty clothes and I washed them on Saturday. We bought him what we could and gave him lunch money and work books that he needed in school.

Billy talked to him on his first visit about taking a bath regularly and washing his hair. Little Bobby answered, "I can't take a bath at home." Billy asked, "Why?" "Dirty clothes are always in the bathtub." Billy would ask him to take a shower as soon as he got to our house. Then on Saturday and Sunday we asked him to shower again. He would argue and complain, "All you want me to do is take showers."

When he came, he usually brought modeling clay that we had bought him. He had and has now a marvelous gift of creating perfectly beautiful models of animals with minute details. It was unbelievable how real he could make them look. He could mold other things for us as well. We encouraged him to develop this wonderful skill by reading books or taking a class, in which he would have done well. However he didn't want to and didn't want us to talk about it.

He would make his models and put them in the refrigerator to harden. He did not want them moved from where he placed them so if you did move them you had to be very careful to place them back exactly as he had them or there was trouble.

One afternoon, just as I was getting into my car, I looked up and here came Little Bobby dragging a big cardboard box. He was running so fast he was out of breath. The store where he had been given the box was two blocks away from the church. Since he knew was it time for us to leave, he wanted to get there before we left.

I could hear him yelling, "Mrs. Langford, Mrs. Langford." I could hear him before I could see him and I thought something had happened. He ran up to the car, saying, "My mom said that you all could have me. It won't take five minutes to get my stuff in this box." Then he added, "If you want me." His blond hair was all messed up; sticking to his sweaty forehead like it had been glued. His deep purple-blue eyes were literally dancing with excitement. His dirty face, with freckles across his nose had a big grin from ear to ear. He was looking straight into my eyes waiting for an answer.

I said, 'Oh, Little Bobby, I don't know." He quickly added, "I won't eat much and I'll get up by myself to go to school and I won't fight and a big box of cereal will last a long time."

With a deep sigh that I tried to hide, I said, "Let's go talk to Rev. Langford about this first. Okay?" I felt as if I were smothering. I can't believe this. I silently prayed, "Dear Lord, what can we do? I don't want another heavy responsibility of a child. Please, God, No."

I told Little Bobby to get in the car and we would wait for Billy. "Just leave the box right there." He was dragging it with him. Finally Billy drove up with a big smile on his face and said, "Bobby, you ready to go eat?" Without waiting for the car to stop, Little Bobby ran over to Billy dragging the box behind him. I watched him telling him his exciting news to Billy. He was standing on one foot, swinging the other one back and forth.

From the very first day of his meeting Billy, he has always called him Reverend Langford. The expression on Billy's face let me know that he was having trouble finding the words to say. He pushed Bobby's hair back off of his forehead and patted him on the head. I thought, "How in the world is Billy going to handle this?"

Billy by this time had stopped the car and they were both walking over to the car where I was sitting. I wanted to get out but I could not move. With Billy's hand on Bobby's shoulder, Billy said, "I told Little Bobby that we would have to wait on this for a while. That you and I needed time to talk about it and try to work something out."

Little Bobby didn't seem too disappointed. He said, "I can get another box anyway if my mom won't let me keep this one." For several months everything went about as usual as far as Little Bobby was concerned. He was getting better grades in school and he would tell people that we would introduce him to, "I don't fight much anymore."

The next spring on a beautiful cool crisp morning, Little Bobby came into the church office. He said, "I need to talk to Reverend Langford." He sat down in the chair across the room from my desk. I told him there were magazines he could look at and handed him some paper and a pen. He said, "No, I don't want 'em." Billy was counseling someone. When he came out of the office, he said, "Hi, Little Bobby, are you ready to go?"

Little Bobby said, "I need to tell you something before we go. I have some good news and I have some bad news. I'll tell you the bad news first. My mom is moving to another state. The good news is...you can have me. You will have to take me now."

Little Bobby had already caused some problems at our house. He would not do what we asked him to unless he wanted to do it. Now to take the full responsibility of a renegade 11 year old boy already known to our congregation as "A Holy Terror," what are we getting ourselves into?

We have taken so many into our home that we made our garage into two bedrooms and for many months out of each year they had been occupied. Billy rationalized, "Honey, if we give Bobby one of the rooms we will still have an extra bedroom if an emergency should arise and we need another one."

I am here to tell you that many emergencies did arise, not just for another room, but with Little Bobby. If we had anyone as guests in our home, he would be rude to them, no matter how much we talked with him. I shall never forget the Friday afternoon he came to stay. I was standing in the kitchen at the dishwasher, taking out the clean dishes, when I heard the familiar sound of the car driving into our driveway into our back turn-around and stopping near the patio next to the den door. I then heard the car door shut.

You cannot see the driveway or back patio from our upstairs kitchen window but I had learned the sound of our car and knew Billy was home. I stopped stood quietly and listened for the car door to shut, hoping I would not hear a second one. But there it was. Billy had brought Little Bobby home this Friday, not for just the weekend but for who knows how long.

I thought Billy had understood that we had decided we would help Little Bobby as much as possible but we would not bring him into our home permanently. I felt weak in the pit of my stomach.

By the time they had reached the top of the stairs, I was composed enough to say, "Hi Bobby," with a forced smile.

Bobby said, "I left my dirty clothes down stairs by the washer. Rev. Langford said I should take a bath before supper." By the time he had finished talking he was back down to the bottom of the stairs.

Walking back into the kitchen Billy walked over to me and put his arm around my waist. Before he could say anything I said, "Billy, I don't want this responsibility." He squeezed me and said, "Honey, just pretend that he is here for the weekend."

I knew this would be the longest weekend in history. It proved to be just that. "I know Bobby is a real problem and it is irritating the way he does things, but it will get better." Billy assured me.

We were always running out of milk because Bobby would drink all of the milk and put the empty carton back in the refrigerator. Cereal was the same. He would put the empty box in the cabinet and I would think there was plenty. These were just two of the things we had to work through. Sometimes I would get so upset I would just get in the car and drive. I didn't go anyplace special, I just had to go.

When we ate breakfast, lunch or supper, Bobby made everything into a sandwich. Fried chicken with mashed potatoes or any vegetable, it went onto a piece of bread and became a sandwich. If we had rolls on the table he would say, "I need two pieces of bread."

We could not keep potato chips, cookies, or any kind of snacks where he could find them, even pickles and olives. He would eat the entire package or jar so I soon learned to put out what we could eat, then hide the other in my closet or under one of the beds so that we would have some to eat at the next meal. I usually bought half a gallon of ice cream at a time. I would go to serve it and there would be the empty carton, all that I bought. When I bought more than one carton, the extras would also be empty.

I remember the time Billy and I went to a Minister's Retreat in Gatlinburg. We left Bobby at home with a sitter. When we returned, as we started into the den, you could see books all over the floor. He had taken all the books out of the book case (which covers one entire wall).

"Bobby, what in the world is this? Why did you do it?"

He said, "Well, I thought there might be something hidden in the books. So I thought I would find out. And besides I was bored." Billy and I had worked months to get the books arranged according to sermons, study sources, auto-biographies, concordances and prophecy.

Bobby said, "1 can put them all back."

I asked him, "Where are the radio reel-to-reel tapes that were on the top shelves?" Our radio program, The Belmont Hour on each Saturday morning had been on for five years. We had kept them and they were arranged according to dates.

He said, "I played some of them and the others are under the couch and on the piano bench."

He continued, "What's the big deal?"

Even now, 15 years later, we still do not have them arranged in the proper order as they were before Bobby "struck," and I seriously doubt that they ever will be.

My prayer or question to God was "Why did you deliberately send Bobby into our home? Why can't we get through to him? It is hopeless."

With the stress that Bobby was causing in the home I was becoming as much of a problem as Bobby was. I was becoming resentful of him.

Then one day as I was running downstairs exhausted in complete frustration, to awaken him (for the fifth time) when the Lord spoke to my heart, and said, "You are investing in lives." When I reached the bottom of the stairs I stopped, stood there for a minute then wrapped my arms around myself, took a big deep breath and said, "Thank you Lord." My struggle with me was bearable. I could handle the frustration better. God restored my joy.

Even when Bobby ignored us when we spoke to him, even when he deliberately did things that Billy had told him not to do. Even when he broke the windshield out of our Assistant Pastor's car because he didn't want him to be at our house, [he left his car and rode with us to a funeral], when he broke the lock on our self-cleaning oven door, to show how strong he was, these are to mention only a few things, we continued to love him.

The years that Little Bobby lived with us brought about a lot of adjustment in our home. Everyday something unexpected happened. I don't know if I ever really got to him. His lifestyle and early upbringing created a problem. It was so totally different from the rearing of Bob and Richard.

However Little Bobby did graduate from Stratford High School (thanks to Billy and our son Bob). They had a "never tiring courage and patience." When Little Bobby would get into trouble at school he would say, "I'll call my brother the attorney, and he will represent me."

Little Bobby needed an extra credit to graduate. He wanted to take Home Economics. They worked his schedule around so that he was able to do it. He made an absolutely perfect and beautiful needle point design of a double barreled shot gun. He was so talented and gifted in this area.

Richard was away at college and worked during the summer while Bobby was in high school. When Richard was home he would always include Bobby in his activities. He also had a lot of patience with him. The boys and Billy deserve all the credit.

Little Bobby is now 5 feet 11 inches tall. He says he weighs 235 pounds. We are all sure that he weighs much more. But if you ask him about it he says, "It's all muscle," as he holds his arms up to show you.

Bobby has had several good jobs. He was in the Army for a while. He moved to an apartment and lived with Wayne, a friend who also grew up in our church. Later he went to Indiana when Bob went there to open a business. He was going with a girl who lived in Texas and may be moving there.

Bobby comes by occasionally and visits. Sometimes he will stay just a few minutes and at other times he will stay all day. When he was over the other day I asked him if he had time to read over "Castaways." He said, "Sure, I've got all day." His comment as he finished reading was, "Boy, I was a holy terror, wasn't I? I'm sorry, mom Langford, I really am."

Then he continued, "You didn't tell 'em about the keys."

I didn't remember the keys. "What keys?"

He said, "You know. How when we would go anywhere, I would always ask you and Reverend Langford for your keys. And after I was here for a while, I told you why."

He continued before I could answer. "It was because of that time in El Paso, when we lived in Texas. When one day I went with some people and we drove out in the desert and they left me. Don't you remember? I told you how I had to walk for hours and hours to get to a house to get somebody to take me back to town. It was so hot. I got blisters all over my feet, the top and the bottom from the hot sand."

He turned his head toward me and looked straight into my eyes . . . and I was remembering . . . that it was such a regular thing for him to ask for the keys that Billy or I would automatically hand Bobby our keys when we went somewhere, always adding, "don't lose them." He assured us that he wouldn't, however I had an extra set made and kept them in my billfold, just in case.

I remembered the day that I started to hand him the keys and I was so surprised when he said, "Nope. Now you can keep the keys. I know you or Reverend Langford are not going to take me off somewhere and leave me."

Bobby still had the look of that little 11 year old boy. Bright shining deep-blue eyes and the big grin from ear to ear that I remembered seeing in the church parking lot. He slowly closed the notebook, paused a few moments and said softly, "I'm glad I'm a part of your book." He got up out of the chair, came over to me, bent down and kissed me on top of my head.

He asked, "Why didn't you write about the three boys that we didn't know their last name? Or Leslie, the little 6 year old girl you took from Tennessee Preparatory School? Or the Judge's daughter, or the girl that came from Kansas, or the one that took your High School Class ring?" He added, "You should write about all of them."

He blinked his clear bright purple blue eyes and added, "And especially about the time we spent most of our Christmas money that we got from the church for some kids that were here, for clothes and stuff."

Still holding my notebook, he turned his head, looked out the window and sighed deeply. While still looking away, he said, "You know what? I loved living here and I loved it when you told me those stories. I think about 'em sometimes. They are so neat."

August 26,1994 -

It had been three years since hearing from Little Bobby. I answered the phone at 9:45 Friday morning. The voice on the phone said, ""Hey Moma Langford. Do you know who this is?" "I don't believe I do. Keep talking and I'm sure I'll recognize your voice." My mind was racing with questions. He continued, "What do you mean, keep talking?" When he said this, I recognized that it was Little Bobby. He said, "I sure have missed you all." He is living in Texas now.

He and Karen, his girlfriend attended a birthday party that we were having at our house that night for Ashleigh, Richard's little girl. Bobby looked great. After the party as he was leaving we were standing on the patio. He reached out with his big muscular arms and hugged Billy with one arm and me with the other. He pulled us to him and said, "I sure love you guys."

We watched Little Bobby help his girlfriend Karen into the truck, walk around the truck, get in and drive out the driveway with a big wave and a thumbs up signal. Billy put his arms around me and squeezed me real tight.

Standing there under the clear sky filled with twinkling stars I started thinking about the difficult years we had shared. It was hard to believe or even imagine what a storm that he brought into our home and that he could have been such a "Holy Terror."

All the while that we had Bobby as well as the many other people in our home, Billy and I tried to maintain as normal a relationship as possible, considering all the responsibilities of the church, and wanted it to be harmonious and good. It was most difficult at times.

Our home life and our plans were interrupted many times. The principles of daily living that we learned were simple and practical, not at all complicated. We prayed daily and leaned hard on the Word of God for guidance. Our marriage not only survived but was strengthened. God gave us hope to see beyond the present circumstances.

We had to guard the home that was being used to help others so that it did not collapse and had to realize that our marriage was just as important as the church, the house guests, and any other problems that presented themselves.

In the ministry and his secular position with a shoe company, Billy had such a demanding schedule; the rearing of the children and keeping the house was mainly my responsibility. It was very lonely at times. Billy was home too little and I would become frustrated and overwhelmed.

One of the worst feelings was to be surrounded by people, involved in activities, and yet to be experiencing hidden deep feelings of loneliness and frustration because there was never enough time. Something unexpected was always coming up and I could feel the stress taking its toll on me

Our back yard swing has been a place of retreat many times. If I was unable to get away from the house I would go to the back yard to the swing which was in the very back of the yard. I would sit on the swing and quote Psalm 121, my favorite. While looking over the valley and across the river up to the hills that surround Nashville, my feelings of depression and anxiety would be replaced with confidence and contentment.

"I will lift up mine eyes unto the hills, which cometh my help.

My help cometh from the Lord which made heaven and earth.

He will not suffer thy foot to be moved; he that keepeth thee will not slumber.

Behold, he that keepeth Israel shall neither slumber nor sleep.

The Lord is thy keeper; the Lord is thy shade upon thy right hand. The sun shall not smite thee by day nor the moon by night.

The Lord shall preserve thee from all evil; he shall preserve thy soul.

Thy Lord shall preserve thy going out and thy coming
in from this time forth, even for evermore."

September 1992

Little Bobby's first marriage didn't work out. Robert our older
son asked him to help him in opening a new Shoney's Restaurant in
Lafayette, Indiana and also one in Kokomo, Indiana. He was delighted
to go and to be working with him. He has always idolized him.

Little Bobby was a wonderful set-up person and a great kitchen
manager except when his temper would get out of control. He lived
with Robert during this time.

December 1995

Later he moved back to Nashville and back with us and back
into his old bedroom downstairs. In 1996 he started working with
the Metro Sheriff's Department as a guard. Billy's health started
deteriorating following a heat stroke while we were building our new
church. He had a heart attack and a triple by-pass surgery in October
10, 1990. This was just ten days before we were planning to have our
Retirement Service at church.

Later a permanent IV Stint was placed on the inside of his wrist
in the vein that went directly to his heart. The medication had to
be mixed and administered daily. The home nurse from Vanderbilt
instructed Little Bobby how to mix and administer the medicine from
the little vile that was kept in the refrigerator. She came three days a
week to irrigate the IV tube and Bobby would explain any problems
to her. He stepped in and took complete medical care of Billy. He did
this every morning before going to work. During the day he would call
and check with me to see if everything was going okay.

He never complained or acted as if he resented taking care of him.
He did this until Billy went to sleep on Saturday night and went to be
with the Lord early on Sunday morning, February 23,1997.

September 1,1999

While working at the Sheriff's Department he met a wonderful girl Dana who was from Jackson, Tennessee. They were married on September 1, 1999. They live in Heron, Tennessee about ten miles from Jackson. Her parents live close enough to take care of the children while they work. Lyndsey, their little girl is nine years old and their little boy, Brayden is three. Bobby works in the warehouse and shipping department at the Pringle's Plant and Dana works with ABRIA Health Care.

June 11, 2009

Little Bobby just called to see how we are doing. He said, "Mom, be sure to write about our new house. It has four bedrooms, two baths, two decks and it has an above ground storm shelter. It is on 1.3 acres. I'm getting ready to paint the decks today."

What a sigh of relief as I write this and to think what a terror he was but quickly my mind raced to the thoughts of how gentle he was and to his never-ending tender loving care for Billy. Then with a bigger sigh I felt my thankfulness for him.

March 5, 1999

Since Billy's death I have worked as receptionist/secretary at the Tennessee District Council of the Assemblies of God. The phone rang in my office and to my surprise the excited voice on the other end was so very familiar. "Hi mom, it's Little Bobby. I got married."

Before I could say anything, he continued, "And mom, she's about your size. She is a little ball of energy. "

I said, "Bobby, what is her name and how old is she and where did you meet her? How long have you known her?"

The questions kept coming to my mind but I finally said, "Little Bobby, bring her over to the house. I will look forward to meeting her."

He said, "Don't worry mom, you'll love her. Her name is Dana Williams"

She said her father knew Dad Langford." They had ministered together at the Mission, down town. His family had attended Belmont Assembly when Dana was about three years old (Little Bobby has just started calling Billy, Dad Langford since Billy died). Oak Hill still actively participates in this `outreach program.'While still in shock, I managed to ask, "When did you get married?"

He replied with unmistakable excitement in his voice, "Yesterday."

"I have known her for about two years and we just decided to get married. She is twenty-seven years old and she is really pretty but best of all she has a wonderful personality. I know you are going to like her."

Then I asked, "Little Bobby, Who married you'?"

"Would you believe our good friend, Bill Covington? (Metro Court Clerk) I called him and asked him if he would and he said, just come on over. So we went over to his office and he married us right there. He kept on talking about Dad Langford and said he remembered so many things that they had talked about. One time during the ceremony he had to stop and he had tears in his eyes. He said to be sure to tell you that he loves you and if you need anything to be sure to call him."

Last night he brought Dana by the house so Richard and I could meet her. She walked into our den in front of Little Bobby. He had his hands on her shoulders. To my surprise she was much prettier than I had expected. She was wearing blue jeans and a red and white blouse and her blue eyes were sparkling. Her short hair was curled. She sort of pulled it back as she gave a timid beautiful smile which showed her perfect white teeth.

Little Bobby still had his uniform on. He is a Deputy Sheriff and a correctional officer for Metro which includes Nashville and all of Davidson County.

Little Bobby said, "Dana, tell mom, go ahead and tell her,"

Dana squinted her eyes and said, "Tell her what'?"

"You know." Little Bobby cut his eyes to me then over to Richard, "Tell them, you asked me to marry you."

My mind flashed back to the many times that Little Bobby had heard Billy say to me, "Honey, you know you asked me to many you,, followed by his unique jolly laugh. I smiled back at him. I thought, maybe we have had more of an influence on Little Bobby than we realized. Oh, I hope so.

May 26, 1999

Little Bobby and Dana came by the house. Little Bobby said, "Well, we got some good news today. We are going to have a baby. I must not have responded as quickly as I should have. Because he continued, "What's the matter ? Mom, aren't you glad?"

Dana didn't take her eyes off of me while Little Bobby was telling me the good news.

CHAPTER SEVEN

STORM CLOUDS OVER MUSIC CITY

There's rain behind those clouds. A storm watch is in effect. A severe thunderstorm with a fast moving front is approaching. Nashville lies under a heavy veil of gray clouds. In the dark clouds hovering over Music City are violent devastating winds, dangerous lightening and heavy rain.

Raging storms land severe blows leaving many lives, homes and families in ruin. Homes are ripped apart and left in shambles, without love, and helpless. Conflicts of life become a grim reality.

Disappointment fills the air with a silence almost deafening, except for the roll of heavy distant thunder. A tornado is forming right before our eyes. Disaster can strike anytime, any home, and in any city.

Disappointments and anxiety brings division in families and leads to great stress. Loneliness and depression becomes the companion when great expectations turn into shattered dreams.

Hope vanishes right before their eyes. Heart searching questions, doubts and uncertainties flood their minds. Violence can then follow. Daniel Webster puts it: a storm is an atmospheric disturbance characterized by a strong wind, thunder, lightning, and heavy rain also a strong emotional outburst, to rage, to rant as in anger, agitation, turmoil and violence.

In spite of precautions, jealousy and bitterness can destroy everything in its path. The hopeful entertainers are often emotionally unprepared for the failures, insults, rejections and insecurities that are a part of the country music industry. In our earlier ministry we dealt with those having a problem with alcohol; now in later years drugs have become an even more serious and dangerous habit which causes a lot of destruction and a lot of pain.

We have witnessed the emotional pressures and problems and have become personally involved in very tense and uneasy situations sharing their grief, disappointment and frustration. Through the ministry of the Word we have brought hope to shattered lives.

Through the years we have seen many who have come to Nashville and attended our church who were trying to climb their way to stardom in the music field. They were sure their song, whether country or religious, was just what the publishers were wanting.

They also felt they would be discovered as a great artist, either singing or playing, telling us of their plans with great excitement in their voice. Offering to play or sing their song anywhere to anyone who would listen. There were so many who came to church and wanted to sing in the church services that Billy made a rule that only one visitor could sing their new song during each service.

We have listened to many in the church parking lot, restaurants, and our back yard. They usually carry their guitar with them everywhere they go. Sometimes it is another instrument but most often it is a guitar, maybe an old one with a battered, beat-up, case or a brand new one just purchased for their trip to Nashville.

One day while driving down music row we noticed a crowd of people standing on the street corner across from the Hall of Fame Museum. We slowed down to see what the commotion was about. There was a tall slender young man who looked to be in his early twenties, dressed in a plaid shirt, jeans, boots and cowboy hat.

He was holding a broom as you would hold a guitar while playing it and singing at the top of his voice. He would give a big beautiful smile and wave at the people passing by in their cars and then continue to play on the broom.

Days would become months, and months would become years. In the humid heat of the summer sun and the dreadful freezing cold of the winter, they would be walking up and down the street in front of the church holding onto their song. By this time many had spent all their money and had pawned their instrument. We know of those who pawned everything they owned, even their car. Eventually their clothes became worn. They are bone tired. The expression on their faces show they are weary. They have nothing.

First they rent an apartment, then go to one room, then try to rent with someone and eventually use their car for their home. For some it took longer than it did for others, depending upon how many were in the family and how much money they brought. We have seen families do this.

They come to Music City, USA by the hundreds from farms, small towns and large cities. High on hopes, having dreams of making it as stars on the Grand Ole Opry, singing their songs on the radio and being on TV. Those wanting to break into the music field often think that when they get to Nashville they will automatically have it made in the music industry. The competition is unbelievable. There is no way to tell them. We found from experience early in our ministry there is really no use to try.

Some would leave and we wouldn't see them for months or even years and then one day they would return again with a familiar note book or satchel under their arm. With renewed hope in their heart and excitement in their eyes; forgetting the hardships earlier endured.

A couple days a week Billy would go door to door in the neighborhood inviting people to church. Mrs. Smith lived in an apartment directly behind the church. She said that she had never been invited to attend church since she moved to Nashville until Billy invited her. She attended the very next Sunday. She became a faithful member and attended every church service, unless she was ill, until she died, almost twenty years later.

One afternoon Billy was visiting on Seventeenth Avenue close to Division Street. Sitting on the porch swing was a nice looking well-dressed middle aged man and a little blond headed girl, about five years old. Sitting on the top steps were two little boys. One was six and the older one twelve years old.

Billy walked up to them and introduced himself. They talked a few minutes then Mr. Lowe said that his wife had gone to the little grocery store on the corner of Division and Seventeenth Avenue, two nights before and had not returned. Supper was cooking on the stove and they needed a loaf of bread. She told Mr. Lowe to watch the food.

She would be right back. She said that she could get back quicker than the boys or he could.

He said, "We kept waiting for her to return. Finally, I walked to the store to see what was taking her so long. I looked all through the store and when I didn't see her, I asked the clerk if she had been there. The clerk knows us and said that she had purchased a loaf of bread and had been gone about thirty or forty-five minutes."

They started attending the church and became very close to us. The younger boy, Joey, stayed with us a lot through the years. He started calling me 'Mom' from the very first. The older boy, John, was always with his dad. The little girl, Lynne, stayed with an aunt during the week. They attended church regularly. They were a very close family.

Mr. Lowe always seemed preoccupied with his thoughts. His wife has never been heard from and the detectives never found a clue as to what happened to her. Even though he spent nearly all he had trying to find her. Several years later he did marry a wonderful lady. Billy officiated at the wedding ceremony in his home. The children participated in the ceremony.

Mr. Lowe has one of the gentlest spirits of anyone that we have ever met. Both of the boys resemble him in looks and attitude.

One evening after John had already gone to bed a couple of boys came by his house. They said they were going driving. He got dressed and went with them. He didn't return and Mr. Lowe became worried about him.

He called us early the next morning and said, "John didn't come home last night. I'm afraid something bad has happened to him."

After lunch we went over to their house and in the early afternoon word came, "John has been in a wreck and was killed instantly." The other two boys were also killed when their car ran off of the highway and flipped over. They were just inside the Florida state line.

Not often but every once in a while Mr. Lowe talks about the disappearance of his wife and then the death of John. He always concludes with, "I'm so glad and I'll be ever grateful for that afternoon when Brother Langford came by our house and walked up to us when we were sitting on the porch. His understanding and love and wonderful outlook on life has made all the difference for us."

It was another ordinary Tuesday morning and time to type the Sunday school and church attendance record from the previous Sunday. It was 9:15 and time for my second cup of coffee. I was getting up from my desk to get the coffee when someone was running up the front steps and fell hard against the door. I looked through the glass out of the top part of the door. There was a blond headed girl, wearing a crisp white blouse and blue jeans clutching something tightly to her chest. It looked like a white package or a large white book.

She was leaning so hard against the door that she would have fallen if I had opened it. Coaxing her to stand, finally she held herself up until at least the door could be cracked open enough that I could talk to her. Easing her in a little at a time and resting in between I was finally able to open the door wide enough for her to come in.

She was unable to hold her head up. Her long blond hair was covering her face and so I had not been able to see who it was. As the door pushed open, she fell into my arms and I looked into her face and recognized her. "Oh, no " It was Jan. I felt my strength drain and felt sick at my stomach.

She almost knocked me down and we both fell against a chair sitting by the door. She dropped the book that she was carrying and became limp in my arms. On the front of the cover was a beautiful wedding picture of her in her wedding gown, and under the picture was the words "My Wedding Album". Also a beautifully framed 8 by 10 picture of her and her husband fell, breaking the glass.

Slowly we straightened up and we made the few steps over to the couch. She was saying over and over, "Please help me. Oh, please help me. Please pray for God to help me."

She then passed out on the couch for a few minutes. As she would awaken she would start again, saying "Please help me. You gotta help me."

I said, "Jan, please tell me what is the matter with you. How did you get here?"

She said, "1 drove our car." Speaking clearly but slowly she added, "I just kept telling myself. I had to get here and you would help me." Then she drifted off again.

"Jan, have you taken any medication? Any pills?"

"Yes, I took a whole prescription of Valium and I drank a lot. She was out of it again.

I shook her and when she finally roused up again. I asked her, "What did you drink?" By this time I was shouting and shaking her really hard. "Tell me what did you drink?"

"Some whiskey."

With one hand I reached the phone on the desk and still shaking her with the other. I called Vanderbilt Hospital which is only four blocks away. Then called David, her husband at work and told him to come quickly. David said, "When I left for work this morning she seemed fine."

When I explained to her that she needed to go to the hospital, she started screaming, "No, no, no. I won't go to the hospital. I came here. I thought you would help me." She kept trying to sit up but she kept falling back.

"Sister Langford, it's my marriage. I've broken my marriage vow. I was at a motel last night when I decided I would commit suicide. On the way home I stopped by the liquor store and bought a bottle. You know, I have never drunk in my life. I decided after David left for work this morning and the kids had left for school, I would end it all. My life is so messed up. There is no way. I don't want to live, but, I'm not prepared to die without Jesus. I brought my wedding album and picture for you to pray over."

She started crying and sobbing and trying to hold her head up but passed out again.

David came in while she was still passed out. He looked over at the wedding album lying on the floor and then looked at me and said, "What's that doing here?"

Jan roused up at that time and I didn't have to answer him. She said, "David, please don't take me to the hospital." She said, "I don't want to go to Vanderbilt Hospital. Don't take me to Vanderbilt Hospital."

We had to get her to a hospital and do it quickly. I suggested several other hospitals. For some reason when I mentioned Donelson Hospital she perked up and said, "I'll go there and then added, "Only if I can ride with you, and David goes in his car."

David picked her up and carried her to my car. I was so afraid that we might not make it to Donelson Hospital which was several miles away and through traffic. Her speech was really becoming slurred and she was almost completely unconscious.

She sat up enough to barely see out the side car window as we were pulling out of the church parking lot. She drawled out "Sing Amazing Grace for me." Her words were running together. I started singing the first verse of Amazing Grace. After the first line she interrupted me. "Don't tell David." I promised her I wouldn't.

I didn't start singing again. We just drove a few miles then she said, "Sing louder, so I can hear you." I started the first verse again. I was just finishing the last verse as we pulled into the emergency entrance. David arrived before we did and told them we were coming. They were waiting for us to help get her out of the car.

Jan wouldn't get out of the car until I did. David came around and parked my car. The nurses got Jan into a wheel chair. She held on to my arm so tightly. She said, "Stay close to me. Please don't leave me."

The Doctor was very understanding and permitted me to stay with her. If I moved just a little she would say, "Don't go." When she opened her eyes they seemed glued to mine.

David called Billy and explained to him where I was and the reason for leaving the church office without leaving a note as to where I had gone, which I always do.

It was late in the evening and getting dark. Her hospital room was above the parking lot. Cars were pulling into the lot with their lights on. I stood looking out the window almost all afternoon.

Jan was resting. The doctor said Jan had passed the crisis and would be alright in a day or two. David and I went down to the cafeteria to get something to eat. We had not even thought about eating all day or even drinking anything.

When we returned to her room she lay motionless. I walked over to the bed and leaned over to see if she was breathing. She roused up and raising the hand with the IV in it, reached for my hand and said, it's getting dark isn't it?" Trying to look out the window she continued, "You better get home before it gets any later. You can leave if you come back if I need you."

I went to the nurses' station and asked a nurse to come to her room. When the nurse came in I said, "I'm going to go home now.

Will you call me if Jan asks you to?" She said she would be glad to. I gave her my phone number and spoke loud enough for Jan to hear.

Then Jan said, "You promise to come back tomorrow?"

I promised her I would. I held her hand and said a short prayer and she had fallen asleep.

Many hours were spent at Donelson Hospital over the next few days. The doctor whom I had met the day as we entered her into the hospital called me concerning her. She would not talk to him but said she would talk with him in my presence.

There is not a more frustrating feeling that we experience in our life than that of loneliness. Loneliness produces fear and fear can destroy us. Because of a terrible experience that I had with fear early in our ministry; I felt the gripping pain, and understood her confusion and feeling 'out of control.'

During that experience my only hope and strength came from relying totally on the scripture, "For God hath not given us the spirit of fear; but of power, and of love, and of a sound mind." 2 Timothy 1:7 I showed her how it was marked in my testament and related to her how God gave me victory and He would do the same for her. I explained to her that when my mind won't stop thinking that I place the testament under my pillow at night. Her pretty purple blue eyes were staring into mine.

She said, "Would you let me put it under my pillow?" I told her I would gladly do it because I knew what peace it brings when you do.

I also told her that when she got home to open her Bible to that scripture and leave it open. Until this very day when God gives me a scripture needed for guidance, I keep it open as a reminder of God's faithfulness. If there is a problem or an unusually hard situation, you will find an open Bible in every room in the house. Billy could always tell when I was praying about something special. There is always one open in the kitchen and on the foyer table as well as my bedroom. I inform those who ask about them, "I'm not doing this to impress anyone. I do this for my peace of mind out of necessity."

Before being released and leaving the hospital, she and David worked through their problem. She related to him everything that had happened and that she was trying to escape the unhappiness and fear that comes from pressures and uncertainties of many things. He was very understanding. They have a wonderful relationship today and have shared many years of happiness.

With the help of the Lord and the guidance of the Holy Spirit I was able to reach her and give her the assistance she needed until she developed a trust in the doctors who treated her over several months. She re-established her identity with herself, her family and God.

Twenty-one years later: This past Friday Billy, Robert and I saw David and Jan. They were just beaming as they came into the office. David said, "I'm so glad to see you guys. Jan and I are so excited. We are going to be grandparents in two weeks. Brother Langford, remember when you dedicated our baby?"

Billy said, "I sure do. It doesn't seem possible that she could be old enough to be married and having a baby."

Jan said, "We are doing fine, just getting older fast. God has been so good to us." She smiled her big pretty smile and continued, "We are members of Two Rivers Baptist Church and we attend the services regularly. But you all will always be our pastor." She hugged me and whispered, "Thanks for saving my life."

The rush hour traffic seemed unusually slow this afternoon. The Shelby Street Bridge had a lane closed which didn't help. Supper was going to be late. We didn't have to be anywhere for an appointment. So I just settled back in the seat, put the car in neutral and decided to enjoy listening to the radio.

The only thing that bothered me was the two couples that were staying at our house during the Quartet Convention. They had sung for us at church Sunday a week ago. The next Monday they called and said that they had been unable to get a hotel room as everything was filled. They asked if they could possibly stay with us. The convention had been over two weeks. They were making no signs of leaving. They had not helped with the groceries, and four more to cook for was really making it difficult. We kept thinking, "They will leave in the next day or two."

The announcer on the radio said he had a singing group from Texas, called Beaumonts that he was going to interview. What really got my attention was his next statement, "they are making their home in Nashville and you can contact them by writing them at their new address, 107 Tiffany Drive."

I sat straight up and said to myself, "Surely I didn't hear what I thought I heard." It seemed as though that song would never end. Finally the announcer said, "Welcome to our show and to Nashville."

As he introduced each of them, the familiar sound of their voices were loud and clear. They were our house guests. I put my head down on the steering wheel and thought, "I'm not believing this. I need to tell Billy about this."

The traffic was beginning to move and I felt nervous inside. But I needed to get a couple more things for supper and the drug store was next door to the grocery store so I decided to pick up my prescription that the doctor had called in. I was hurrying home to get home before our guests. I wanted to tell Billy what I had heard on the radio before they got here. Billy had not gotten home yet. Finishing up supper, everything was ready except the tea. I sweetened the gallon of tea with sugar and saccharin tablets.

Everyone arrived home and we were eating supper and they kept asking for sugar to sweeten their tea. I informed them that I had already sweetened it.

Cleaning up the dishes from supper I decided to check the saccharin bottle to see the strength of the tablets. To my dismay when I had gotten home from the grocery store I had put my prescription bottle in the cabinet next to the saccharin. In my hurry to prepare supper I had sweetened the tea with my hormone pills. That night everyone eating with us received a hormone treatment!

The next day a box of records arrived with their picture and our address on the front of the album cover. That night Billy suggested rather strongly that they should make other arrangements for their lodging. They left at the end of the week. Oh yes, they also had an eleven month old baby that they would leave here during the day. It took a few days for our house to finally settle down again. How sweet it is for everything to be in place around here!

Billy was leaving to go to the church office and as he was turning the car around he started honking the horn. I thought he had forgotten something. I ran out to the car.

He said, "Honey, why don't you get things together around here and I'll be back around ten o'clock and pick you up. You can make my hospital visits with me today. It's too nice for you to stay inside all day;

and this is your favorite time of the year. The orange and red leaves on the trees are absolutely magnificent. They will start falling before long."

Without much coaxing I agreed with him and told him, "I will be ready when you get back." I was really looking forward to being with him all day as well as enjoying seeing and drinking in all the beauty of the trees.

The hospitals are located in different areas over town so we would be seeing all the various sections and neighborhoods of Nashville. It would pretty well take the entire day. This is the reason that I did not go very often with Billy to make hospital calls.

It was six-thirty in the evening when we drove into the parking lot at Memorial Hospital. We made this our last visit since our house is located on this side of town not very far from the hospital. We decided to eat supper at a restaurant following our last visit. It was on Gallatin Road just up from the hospital. We could get home early that night and relax. There were no services scheduled, so tonight was free, which was unusual.

The elevator came to a stop on the first floor and we were waiting for the door to open. Billy squeezed my hand and said, "Thanks for making my calls with me today." I replied, "The pleasure was mine."

As we stepped out of the elevator a nurse grabbed Billy by the arm and started practically pulling him down the hall. Almost shouting, she exclaimed, "You are a minister, aren't you?"

Billy said, "Yes, I am. Could I be of help to someone?" By this time we were practically running down the hospital corridor toward the emergency room. Billy and the nurse were a few steps ahead of me. The nurse was short of breath as she was talking to Billy.

"There is a baby that has just been brought in and we need you." The nurse and Billy disappeared behind the beige curtain in an examining room.

A young man wearing jeans and a pullover knit shirt was pacing back and forth. He and I were the only people in the emergency waiting room. Questions were flying through my mind. "What could have happened to the baby and how had he gotten hurt?" I thought, "If this young man will look my direction I will ask him about it." He avoided looking anywhere except the floor. He was staring at the floor.

Ten or fifteen minutes later the doctor came out, the nurse came out then Billy came out from behind the curtain. Billy walked over to me and said, "Honey, they are transferring the little boy to Vanderbilt and the doctor has asked if I could meet the rest of the family there?"

On our way out of the hospital, we went by the snack bar where there were cold drinks and knickknacks to eat. We each got a coke and a package of snacks to eat as we drove back across town. We did not experience all this anxiety when we visited Vanderbilt earlier in the day. Two police cars were parked out front and several policemen were in the emergency room. Billy told me what the doctor had suspected. However they were not sure of the details. The baby boy was 14 months old.

The young man that was in the waiting room at Memorial was already there. He was pacing back and forth just like before. The young man was a former boyfriend of the infant's mother. The baby had bruises about the head and shoulders where he apparently was beaten. There were also five or six pin punctures in his testicles. The mother had taken the child to him to be taken care of while she and her husband were at work. The little boy lived only a few hours after being transferred to Vanderbilt.

The young man was arrested at two thirty in the morning following the death of the little boy. Billy held the funeral service which was scheduled for the next day in the Forest Lawn Memorial Gardens on Dickerson Road. The grave was located near the road.

Just at the close of the service the mother started running toward the busy four lane highway screaming at the top of her voice, "Oh God" over and over. The funeral director and her husband started running after her but didn't catch her until she was in the middle lane. She turned and started running toward Nashville facing the traffic. The other funeral director had stopped the traffic in all the lanes. They finally caught her and managed to get her over to the side of the road.

Billy visited her several times following the funeral. On one of his visits she told him that she had remarried. When Billy saw him, he recognized him. It was the young man that had been walking back and forth in the emergency room and brought the baby to the hospital.

Billy went to visit them. He checked with the neighbors but no one seemed to know where they had moved. Billy wrote a note on the back of his card which he usually does, telling them to call if they need him. He put it in the mailbox. They have not called.

The sleet and snow was falling on a freezing cold Sunday morning in December. Following the morning worship service we had all (20 in attendance) gathered around a big pot belly stove to keep warm. This little old lady came over to me and asked, "Would you come to my house for dinner?" Mrs. Mayes, Jackie, her son and Dora, her daughter had walked five blocks to church.

They had just recently moved to Nashville and had attended church for the past three or four weeks. Robert and Richard wanted to walk back with them. Billy and I waited for the others to leave then we turned off the lights, checked on the stove, locked the doors and drove on down.

There was black smoke coming from the chimney of their apartment. We hurried from the car to get into the warm house.

They were expecting us and threw open the door as soon as we reached the porch. There was a strange, strong, almost overcoming smell within the house. I gave an inquisitive look at Billy. He whispered, "That is tires, rubber tires burning in a fireplace. I thought, "Rubber Tires?" Then I questioned "Why?"

"They are using them for heat."

In the living room was a fire place filled with black smoldering pieces of burning tires. Setting next to the fireplace was a twelve by twenty four cardboard box piled to the top with pieces of rubber tires. On the other side of the fireplace was another box filled with rubber tire pieces.

The furniture in the apartment was so very simple and the surroundings so humble but the warmth of their love made up for the lack of furnishings. So we were not as aware of the bad strong heavy smell of rubber burning.

Dinner consisted of fried chicken, watered gravy, and biscuits. It was delicious. Everything was so clean. The tablecloth and napkins were starched and ironed with painstaking care. She had gone to a lot of trouble and taken time to prepare for us. We shall never forget her kindness to us. She had a gift for each of us, handkerchiefs for Billy and me and little cardboard toys that they had made for Robert and Richard.

Dora and Jackie had entered into the activities during the day. They were unusually well mannered. To this day Robert says Jackie made a great and indelible influence on him by the attitude he displayed.

They attended church regularly. The first of April Jackie and Dora came to church one morning without their mother. After church Jackie asked if Billy could go by and have prayer with her. He said, "She is awfully sick."

Billy went by on Sunday afternoon and had prayer with her. When he got home he said "I think she has pneumonia. She needs medical attention. She said her older children will be in this week and she will go to the doctor then." On Wednesday night we thought they were coming to attend Bible Study but they had come to tell us Mrs. Mayes had passed away.

Billy conducted the funeral. Her older daughter accepted the Lord at the cemetery, following the service. Jackie and Dora went to live with her out of state.

Several years later we got a phone call from Jackie. He wanted Billy to marry Dora. Dora and Jim, her fiancée came by the church. He was nice looking and doing well financially. Plans were made for the wedding and the date was set.

Jackie had done well financially also. He had graduatedfrom high school and had a good job. He was tall, well built and handsome. Still having one of the most beautiful smiles Dora graduated two years after Jackie. She was a beautiful girl. She was as radiant as ever and so excited about the wedding. The rehearsal was scheduled for Thursday night and the wedding Friday night.

The church was decorated with flowers and candles galore. It was one of the most lovely and magnificent weddings that we have had. Dora's wedding dress was gorgeous with the long flowing train. The reception was held in the fellowship hall and it was beautiful also.

The following Thursday we got a phone call from Jim, he was crying so hard we could hardly understand him. He said, "Please come to the hospital. There has been a terrible accident." We rushed to the hospital emergency room. Standing by the door was Dora and Jim. They ran over to the car. Dora almost fell into my arms and Jim put his arms around Billy's neck and said, "He's dead! Jackie is dead!"

Billy asked them if they wanted to talk to us in the car or go inside. They said, "Let us talk here." Jim began his tragic story, "This morning Jackie and Dora were arguing about something. I heard them downstairs. They were so loud they woke me up. I dressed and got my gun and started down the stairs to see what the commotion was all about.

Dora started running up the stairs and Jackie started to follow her. Jackie grabbed her hair and she pulled away. I told Jackie not to follow her upstairs that I would shoot him, if he did. He kept coming up the stairs after Dora and I shot him. I didn't mean to kill him. It all happened so fast! I can't believe what has happened. Brother Langford, I didn't mean to kill him. Please believe me. I didn't mean to kill Jackie."

Dora and Jackie had always argued and even wrestled with each other when they were fighting. Jim was not aware of their 'brother and sister' fights; which they had done since childhood. They didn't seriously hurt each other, just scuffled around.

Dora was staring out the windshield into space. I don't know if she even heard what Jim was saying. She sat motionless. Not moving the least bit. She had stopped crying. Every once in a while she would take a big deep breath. Plans were being made for the funeral the next day.

She finally spoke very softly. "Here is what I think Jackie would want."

Speaking each word distinctly she outlined the entire service. She scheduled it late in the day so those coming from out of town could attend.

A week has passed since the accident. It is hard to even imagine, one week ago today Jackie was the best man in his sister's wedding. Today Billy is preaching his funeral.

That was one of the hardest and most difficult funerals that we ever conducted. The sorrow that is felt by the loss of a family member makes every funeral sad. But we thank the Lord for the promise, in I Thessalonians 4:13-14: "We sorrow not, even as others which have no hope. For if we believe that Jesus died and rose again, even so them also which sleep in Jesus will God bring with him."

One Saturday night about ten thirty as I was preparing my Sunday school lesson someone knocked on our den door. I wondered who that could be this time of the night. I pulled back the curtain, opened the door and there stood Ron. He was a disc jockey and had come directly from the radio station.

"My wife and I had a terrible argument before I went to work. I packed everything I own in the car. 1 told her I wouldn't be back. We argue all the time. I cannot continue to live like this. I am going back to Kansas City. I just wanted you to pray with me before I left town. I'm sorry to disturb you so late."

When I could finally get a word in I said, "Let's sit down on the couch and talk a few minutes before we pray. By the way, can I get you something to eat or drink?"

He said, "I would like a cup of coffee if you don't mind. I haven't taken time to eat all day."

I suggested, "Let's go upstairs and we can talk while the coffee is being made." He followed me upstairs without saying anything.

By the time the coffee was ready, I had made him a sandwich. He hesitated at first when I handed it to him but he ate it like he was really hungry. Billy was reading in the bedroom. He joined us in the kitchen when he smelled the wonderful aroma of hot coffee brewing. We drank coffee and ate cookies and listened to Ron pour his heart out.

Two hours later we were still sitting around the kitchen table. Ron was the only one still drinking coffee. Billy asked Ron to spend the night with us. At first he declined but then he said, "I really would like to spend the night here." Billy asked him not to make a hasty decision while he was upset. Ron decided to go to church with us and maybe talk to Judy tomorrow afternoon before leaving town.

While Ron and Billy were talking I went downstairs and put the pillow, sheet and blanket on the couch. The big gold couch in the den has been a bed many times for a lot of people. It always looks so comfortable and inviting. Often when I was making it up for a bed, Robert or Richard would say, "Mom, I want to sleep on the gold couch sometime." It is so soft you just sink down into it. We don't dare even think about getting rid of it and getting a new and better one. However we have been thinking about putting it in Billy's office and gradually getting used to it being gone. It truly feels like part of the family.

Ron and Billy came downstairs. We called it a night. Billy and I slowly climbed the stairs. We were exhausted and fell into bed, expecting the regular hectic pace of a busy Sunday to greet us in the morning.

Ron and Judy met after church and reached an agreement. Things worked out for them and they are still together!

There is that girl again! Every time we drive up for church she is here. I was getting so put out with her. She always stands on the sidewalk next to the church door. Billy always gives her money, every time she asked for it. She never had time to talk or have a conversation with Billy. She would ask for money and when he gave it to her she would hurry back across the alley to her apartment.

The first few times I didn't mind and it didn't bother me, then when it became every week, I began having problems with it.

The money Billy gave her was for Robert and Richard to buy their school lunches. When we didn't have money for lunch meat they would have to take mayonnaise sandwiches. Sometimes he would give all the money that we had for groceries that week. We would have to do with what we had. The church was small and we didn't have money for things that we needed

much less give her nearly all that we did have. I wondered, "Who does she think she is to think we have to support her? Where is her husband? What is she doing in Nashville? Why does she come here every week?"

Then I'd answer at least one of the questions, "She knows Billy will give her money."

It became a routine. When we left church I would ask Billy, "How much money did you give her this time?"

He would respond with, "Oh, just a little."

Then I would follow with the next question, "How much do you have left?"

He usually said, "Well Honey, I only had fifteen dollars so I gave her all but five."

"You know we need it for groceries and what will Robert and Richard do for their lunch money?"

His answer was always the same. "I don't know why but I really feel like I should give her the money."

I questioned farther, "Every time"?

Billy added, "Well maybe she can get things worked out right away." I knew there was no need to say anything else.He was going to keep giving her money.

I would speak to her as I went in the church but wanted to avoid her. This feeling of resentment would swell up inside me. I dreaded going to church because I knew that she would be there then Billy and I would argue. I tried not to have these feelings and think I had them under control then I would see her and the anger would start again. My attitude concerning other things began to get detrimental. I would start an argument with Billy over absolutely nothing.

The girl had never done anything out of the way. She was always modestly dressed, not forward at all. In fact she appeared to be shy and as I think back and see her so vividly in my memory I would say she was timid and lonely and desperate. I can still see her. She stood about five feet four inches tall. Standing right next to her was my resentment, tenseness and anger.

One Wednesday night she wasn't standing out front. I thought, "Well, finally." But during choir practice I looked up from the piano and I saw her come in the front door and go to Billy's office. In a few minutes Billy and one of the board members were talking. They followed her out the front door.

Before we finished choir practice Billy and Harry came through the door each carrying a large box. They left and returned shortly with two more large boxes. They were carrying them as if they were really heavy. Billy motioned for me to come to the back. The boxes were on Billy's desk. Billy was standing by his desk with his hand on one of the boxes.

Billy said, "Honey, that girl gave us these. She said they had been given to her. She had hoped to use them in the ministry someday. She had wanted to marry a minister and entertain people." She said, "You can use them and they will be in the ministry. I want to give them to you for buying milk for my baby, baby food and diapers."

Being in the ministry had not worked out for them. Her husband decided to try the music field. So they moved to Nashville. That too had seemingly failed. He is going to stay here and continue 'pitching ' his songs.

Billy said, "The money I gave her tonight is going to buy her and her baby a ticket back home to Indiana. She said she just couldn't stay here any longer. She is packing up the few things she has and is leaving."

Billy was opening the boxes as he was talking. He pulled out a plate and unwrapped the tissue paper that was around it. He held it up. It was beautiful. Those four boxes were filled with beautiful china. In the ARITA pattern Number 928, Dukagawa. Small silver and gold wheat pattern in the center and edged in silver. It was a ten piece place setting, which included water glasses, ash trays, coasters, two candle holders, two salt and pepper sets, sugar and creamer, three platters, three oblong and three round vegetable bowls, napkin holders, gravy boat and stand and six extra cups. There are one hundred and forty four beautiful pieces of fine china.

I was in shock. I was ashamed I was humiliated.

Billy said, "She also sent you this tablecloth. Her grandmother crocheted it for her to use when she used her china." He opened up this large absolutely gorgeous white crotchet table cloth.

This cut my heart deeper. Such remorse I have never felt. I was so sorry for my selfish attitude toward her and all the harsh words I had spoken to Billy. I was so wrong.

I prayed for forgiveness from God and I will forever be begging for forgiveness from Billy.

Now the questions about her are, "Why didn't I reach out to her? Why couldn't I see her hurt and pain? What was her name? What was her baby's name? Was it a boy or a girl?"

I never once went to see her. I never took the time to talk to her much less show her understanding and love.

I was going to church to win people to Christ and yet I left someone hungry, hurting, and lonely standing at the church door; reaching for help, grasping for love and understanding when all of her hopes were dashed away.

That was the greatest and hardest lesson I ever learned.

Today we have a beautiful dining room suite and in our China Cabinet in the dining room stands a memento filled with beautiful china. Many times I pause to think of the girl for which it stands, hoping that someone will show her kindness and give her love and understanding.

And I wonder if somehow in her heart she could forgive me. If I should meet her on the street I would not recognize her yet she taught me the greatest lesson in my life. She taught me the importance of praying the prayer in Psalm fifty two and verse ten: "Create in me a clean heart, 0 God; and renew a right spirit within me."

As I write this my eyes are filled with tears and my heart is beating faster. I am filled with such remorse. If she should ever read this book, this is to her. "I ask you, will you please forgive me. I failed you miserably and I'm so sorry."

The first of June a call had come to the church office asking us to schedule a wedding to be held in the sanctuary for January fourteenth at six o'clock.

The cold piercing wind was blowing and icy patches were still on the streets. Snow was falling ever so lightly. The bride was dressed in her wedding gown. She was carrying her veil and train over her arm and the groom was dressed in his tuxedo came dashing through the church doors.

Earlier in the day the couple had come down and decorated the sanctuary and the adjoining fellowship hall. The chairs were lined up against the wall. The long table was set up and in the center was a beautiful crystal candelabrum with red and white candles. They had left room in the center of it for the wedding cake and the plates on one end and the punch bowl and cups on the other. The personalized napkins were lined up in the center next to the candelabrum. The red and white ribbons, flowers and candles were gorgeous.

Billy was not performing the ceremony. The couple had looked at many other churches but had decided to use ours. They invited Billy and me along with our two associate pastors to attend the wedding. We all stayed over from work to attend. The organist and the soloist arrived. It was snowing a lot harder now. The snow really blew inside as they ran in. The minister and his wife and the bride's family arrived at the same time. They had driven up from Birmingham, Alabama.

The wedding party assembled down at the altar and talked quietly a few minutes then they all sat down on the front pew. The organist began playing the soft and sweet wedding songs. Through the windows you could see the light shining from the street lights and reflecting off of the snowflakes. It was toasty and warm inside. We have never had a more beautiful setting for a winter wedding. It was absolutely perfect.

The minister's wife, the five family members and the wedding party were seated on the first two pews by the altar. They would turn around occasionally to see who had come in.

The bride looked absolutely radiant. Her long white flowing dress with sequins in contrast to her dark shoulder length hair was gorgeous. The maid of honor wore an exquisite long red dress with red sequins. The dresses sparkled in the candle light. Only the overhead dome light over the altar was on.

The groom was very tall and stately in his black tuxedo and red cummerbund and red tie. The best man also wore a black tuxedo with red cummerbund and red tie. The minister wore a black robe with a white stole. The wedding party consisted of the bride, the groom, the maid of honor, the best man, and the minister. The soloist and organist also wore dark suits and a red tie. They were on the platform.

6:15: Billy, our two associates and I pulled our chairs close to the door and waited in the fellowship hall for other guests to arrive.

6:30: We all check our watches and look at each other and listen to the beautiful organ music. The candles grow brighter as it gets darker outside. The cold from the outside seems to be drifting inside.

6:45: The puzzled look on our faces reflected the questions in our mind; could the invitations have gotten lost? or perhaps a misprint? maybe the invitations read 7 o'clock instead of 6 o'clock.

What in the world could have happened?

No one is here!

7:00: The organ music becomes softer and the soloist began to sing. He had a beautiful clear soprano voice. He sang two songs. The wedding party then stood and slowly walked to the altar.

7:15: Following the ceremony they proceeded down the aisle and went into the fellowship hall. Richard, our son and associate, cut and served the wedding cake. Jim, our other associate made and served the punch. 7:30: Candles are blown out, punch is poured, the cake is put back into the box and the decorations are put back into bags. The wedding party, the minister and his wife, and the family are gone.

The church is empty, dark and filled with disappointment. We feel a deep ache in our hearts. We join hands and pray a special prayer for them as they start their life together already experiencing a great disappointment. We see the couple occasionally when we are eating out or at social functions. They are doing well in their business. We never question or even mention to them anything about their wedding day.

Questions fill our mind and we can't help but wonder, what in the world could have happened that cold January day?

Billy promised Charlie that we would go with him and his wife Joan to see his recording studio after the Wednesday night prayer meeting. He bought a big two story house and turned part of the first floor into a huge recording studio. They lived in the apartment upstairs. He had done most of the work on the building and remodeling himself.

When church was over and everyone had gone Billy turned off the lights, locked the doors and we were on our way to see one of the first recording studios on Music Row.

Charlie showed us all the neat equipment and how it was controlled by this huge complicated board. Microphones were all over the place. The walls and the ceiling were carpeted just like the floor. He said this made the sound much better.

Joan was expecting in the next few months. She was busy taking care of the other two small children and she was letting Charlie do most of the talking and explaining about the studio equipment. She took her boys and our boys upstairs for a snack. They were not too interested in our conversation.

The day came for Joan to deliver her baby. Charlie called and asked me to go to the hospital with them. He offered to come by and pick me up on the way to the hospital but I insisted that I drive my car. He asked me if I could come immediately. It was in the late afternoon and Billy was home so he would be able to watch Robert and Richard.

I arrived at the hospital just a few minutes after they did. She was ready for delivery and they took her immediately into the delivery room. Charlie did not want to go in with her. He said that he would stay in the waiting room with me. In just a couple of hours a beautiful little girl was born. The nurse said that Joan would be in her room shortly.

Charlie said, "As soon as Joan is in her room and she sees you, you can leave. I wanted you to stay here to prove that I stayed here while she was in the delivery room."

This was the first indication of trouble.

Soon more warning signs arose. One day he called Billy and said that he had to talk to him. Billy was the manager of Family Booterie Shoe Store in Green Hills, but he said he could get away for a little while. Charlie said that he would pick him up and they could talk in the car.

Charlie, Joan and the baby drove up a few minutes later in their Cadillac. Billy got into the back seat. They drove into a service station and Charlie stopped the car. He handed

Billy some change and asked him to get them a cold drink out of the machine on the outside of the station. He was getting the drinks when Joan came over to him and said that Charlie

had changed his mind and wanted to get coffee. While Joan was still talking to Billy, Charlie drove off with the baby leaving Billy and Joan stranded at the service station.

Not being aware of this incident it seemed nothing out of the ordinary for Charlie's car to drive up in our driveway. I ran down the stairs to the den door just as Charlie was getting out of the car with the baby.

He said, "I would like to leave the baby here for a while. I'll be back shortly. Don't let anybody have this baby." That did seem strange for him to say that.

He was driving out of the driveway when the phone rang. It was Billy. He told me what had happened and said, "Honey, can you come get us? Charlie left Joan and me at the service station in Green Hills. We thought he would come back for us, evidently he isn't going to do so."

I told him about Charlie bringing me the baby. Tell Joan not to worry, the baby is fine. I'll bring her with me.

The baby and I drove across town and thank goodness, she fell asleep as soon as we started driving. The traffic was heavy and it took us forty five minutes to get there.

Billy went back to the shoe store to check up on things. Joan came home with me. We were finishing supper when we heard a car drive up. Charlie had returned for the baby. We invited him to eat supper. He did eat and we sat around the table talking for a while. Then he said that he was taking the baby with him and that Joan could stay with us.

Joan was holding the baby and Charlie tried to take her away from her. They were standing in the middle of our living room pulling on the baby and she was crying. Billy stepped over and got between them. My heart was really beating fast. They were arguing so loudly and were saying such mean things to each other.

Joan said that she would not let him take the baby. He said that he wouldn't leave without her. Billy asked them to hand me the baby and for both to sit down on the couch for just a few minutes. I took the baby downstairs to the den.

He began talking to them about their differences. He pointed out that the baby was being used to cover up the real problem. They should accept the responsibility of realizing and accepting the fact of their differences. Marriage is seventy-five percent not fifty percent giving. Each person has to be willing to go that extra twenty-five percent. Billy always says, "If each person gives seventy five percent the marriage will be one hundred percent better." That is the secret of making a marriage work.

About midnight they had aired most if not all of their problems. Billy knelt down beside them and prayed with them. They hugged and became civil to each other. They walked down the stairs side by side. They picked up the baby and left with the baby sound asleep. She was never aware of the fury of the strong winds of turmoil that had just passed so close to her.

Billy received a call in the middle of the night from Glenn, a Methodist minister. He asked him if he would go with him to make a call to a house where someone had been killed. Billy said he would be ready and meet him at the church.

Glenn told Billy that someone called from the house and asked him to come. Because of the situation he wanted another minister to be with him. He said that he was not acquainted with the people and didn't know who the man was that called him.

Billy and Glenn arrived at the house before the police. Billy said there a man was lying against the rail on the back porch. He was covered with blood. They went to the front door to go in. Blood was in every room of the house. The lady of the house was very calm. She spoke to them and said that she was glad that they came. She told them to look around and they would see what happened. There was no one else there and she said that no one else had been there. While they were talking to her the police arrived.

She told the special investigator that her husband had been viciously attacked ten days ago by her German shepherd dog. They said the victim had lacerations on his scalp and face, scratches on his shoulder, bruises on his chest and the only bite mark was on his side. She also stated the husband had been attacked previously several months ago.

She said, "Somebody said I shouldn't keep the dog in the house, but it's spilled milk now and there is nothing I can do about it."

The animal was described by her veterinarian as the "largest of the breed he had ever seen."

The lady stated that the dog had never bitten anyone else and especially liked to play with children. She said her husband suffered from hardening of the arteries and she believed

that had caused his death and not the dog bites. "I'll have the dog put to sleep, but it's too late now."

While Billy was at her house she asked him to conduct her husband's funeral. Following the funeral she asked us to come by her house for a little while. She served us coffee and cake. We were surprised when we found that no one else was invited.

Several months later she called the church during service. Billy could not leave the platform. Robert heard the phone ring so he took the call. A lady said, "I need help now. Someone is trying to kill me. Please come as soon as you can."

Without our being aware of it, Robert, our son who was seventeen and Brother Hooper, one of the board members took off to her house. When they arrived there a man was holding

a gun to the lady's head.

It was the lady whose husband had been killed by that big dog just a few weeks earlier.

When no one came to the door, he and the board member opened it and went in. Robert said, "I did what I thought Dad would do. I walked over to the man and said, "Give me the gun.

You don't want to do this."

He said, the man handed the gun over to him. They talked to him a few minutes and came back to church. We had not dismissed yet. After church he came over to me and said, "Mom, get dad. I want you and dad to come into the office."

The board member and Robert were waiting for us when we walked into the office. We could not imagine what could have happened. Robert told us about the call and about them going out to the house. Then he pulled out this loaded German Luger pistol. Robert said when the man handed it to him he said, "I'll give this gun to my dad to keep for you."

We did keep the gun for several years. One day the lady called and said, "Do you have my German Luger pistol?"

Billy said, "I don't know. Who is this?"

She told him who she was and about the Sunday morning incident. She said "I'd like to pick it up today."

In about an hour she drove up to the house and picked it up. She said that she couldn't stay and visit because she was in a hurry but would get back with us soon. That was thirty-one years ago. As yet we have not seen nor heard from her.

We had finished eating supper. The boys had gone to their rooms to get their homework. Billy and I were lingering at the table talking. It felt good to just sit and talk awhile. But the conversation was interrupted with the phone ringing.

It was Tina. She had been calling nearly every other night for several weeks. At least tonight it was at a reasonable hour. The calls have been from one o'clock to three o'clock in the morning. She asked Billy to meet her at the church in an hour.

He kissed me bye. As he was going down the stairs he said, "I'm taking Little Bobby with me." I told him that I would have the kitchen cleaned up by the time he returned.

Suddenly, I felt a compulsion, "Go with them." I ran down the stairs and caught them as they were pulling out of the driveway. "Honey, I'm going with you."

Billy thought something was wrong so put on the brakes. I started to climb into the back seat but Little Bobby insisted I ride up front. He got out and got into the back. Going down the stairs I had yelled and told Robert and Richard that I was going with Billy and Little Bobby to church for a little while.

On the way to the church I told Billy that I didn't know why I felt so strongly that I should come along. He said, "You are always welcome to come along with me." I am aware of that but I don't usually go.

The anxious feeling bothered me. I began to pray silently as we drove and was not entering into the conversation with Billy and Little Bobby. I hadn't taken time to get ready.

Billy said, "Honey, what is the matter?"

I replied that I had no idea why the sudden turmoil inside. He said, "Well, I'm glad you came. We might need you to pray while I counsel her."

Tina was already there when we arrived. Her car was parked right next to the church door. We greeted her and walked into the church together. I went to my office, Tina and Billy went into his office, Little Bobby pulled a chair close to Billy's office door. Little Bobby always felt as if he was our protection. He especially watched out for Billy.

I motioned for him to come to my office and told him there was really no need for him to be that close to Billy's office. I was sure everything would be alright. He questioned me about my uneasy feeling the feeling I could not explain.

About an hour had passed when Tina and Billy came out of the office. Billy motioned for me to come with them as he walked by my office. Little Bobby had fallen asleep in his chair. I followed them into the sanctuary. When we were half way down the aisle, Tina turned and just stared at me without saying a word and then turned back around and walked to the front of the church. They stopped at the altar.

Billy said, "Tina wants to kneel at the altar and pray. Will you pray with us?"

They knelt on the right side of the altar and I knelt across the aisle on the left side. Billy asked Tina to repeat after him the 'sinner's prayer'. Both of their voices were clear then her voice became gruff, mean and loud. I looked across the aisle just in time to see Tina jump up and reach for Billy's neck. She was almost in a standing position leaning over Billy with both of her hands stretched trying to choke him. He could not get up without grabbing and pushing her back.

In a loud gruff whisper she said, "I'll kill you. I'll kill you. I hate everything you stand for and I hate you."

I jumped up from the altar and started toward Tina.

Her eyes had a glassy stare. I shouted at the top of my voice, "Oh God protect us. I plead the blood of Jesus over us."

She stood up straight and looked even taller than her five foot ten height. She turned and started over toward me. My five foot one inch seemed shorter than it ever had. Her mouth was snarled as she was saying, "You have ruined everything. You! Why did you have to come? Now I'll have to kill both of you."

I did not move or step back. She stood right over me staring down into my face. I stood, bending over backward and thankful for God's power over demons. (Mark 1:8) "God stop her on the authority of your Word, In Jesus' Name, stop her."

She took a step to the side and then to the other side and then went to the front seat and fell into it. When Tina came over to me Billy was able to get up. She had a terrible look of disgust in her expression. We didn't know what she was going to do next. We were standing looking at her as she was all slumped over in the seat, gritting her teeth.

"Why aren't you afraid of me? You know I have a knife in my hand and I have every intention of using it."

She slowly raised herself and got up off the pew. She very slowly went up the aisle toward the door. Billy and I were walking slowly behind her. Tina turned around as she was going out the door and said, "I won't be calling you anymore."

Fellow ministers and friends have asked us, "Have you ever heard of a very tall, slender, pretty girl who calls ministers and asks them to meet her at their church and pray with her? Then she tries to kill them? Did you know that some have had to be taken to the hospital? Things like that happen only in books, confined between the covers, don't they?"

Billy and I glance at each other, we took a deep breath, nodded our heads and replied, "Oh yes, we have heard of her"!

CHAPTER EIGHT

PREACHER'S KID

PLEASE NOTE: LARRY (IN MY CHAPTER/GOD DOES ALL THINGS WELL)

He was born prematurely at eight months and lived only ten days.

ROBERT

◇◇◇◇◇◇

When you say, "my dad's a 'preacher' it is usually acknowledged with a surprised look and the reply, "oh, really?" You are never really sure if that is a compliment or an inquisitive response. You learn to accept it as a compliment, however it was intended. So you answer with a smile in the affirmative. "Yeah."

Growing up in a preacher's home brings problems and rewards. Have you ever wondered what it is like being raised in a preacher's home? One of the rewards is being exposed to an intimate relationship with the Lord by our example.

We moved into the heart of Music City and before we knew it Music City had moved into our hearts. We lived in the back of the church located on the back of the property at 914 Eighteenth Avenue South for five years then we moved into our house on Sentinel Drive where we lived five years. We moved from there into our house on Tiffany Drive on September 16, 1961 on Robert's tenth birthday.

I am still living here and enjoying every minute. Billy and I took the boys through the house and told them "whoever has the larger bedroom will have to give up their room when we have guests. When visitors are passing through town or those holding services at the church your bedroom will become the guest bedroom."

Robert quickly spoke for the smaller bedroom. Richard has shared his bedroom many times since then. Our home has been open to many students from the different colleges. They have made our home their home through the years. This also has enriched our lives. The privilege of sharing our home has been our joy.

Even though we live in a proverbial "fish bowl" The boys know there is a prayer covering every situation. It is impossible to live up to everyone else's expectations, so don't even try. God is the one who directs our lives.

Billy worked at Family Booterie Shoe Store six days and two nights a week to not only provide for our family but also help with the church payments. That is why the boys and I would go with him as often as possible so we could be together.

Driving down West End Avenue on our way to church one morning when Robert was six years old, he stood up in the floor of the back of the car with his hand over the front seat and said, "Momma, why don't we get another daddy? One to stay home with us and the other daddy could work?"

Billy took one hand off the steering wheel and placed his other hand on Robert's head and said, "Hey, if we get another daddy, he is the one that is going to work and I'm the one staying home with you guys". Robert straightening his beautiful red hair said, "Daddy, you messed up my hair".

From the time he was born when we have been eating out, we have had people come to our table and ask, "Is this your little boy?" Then they would look straight at me and then at Billy and I would tell them," On my dad's side of the family everyone had red hair."

Children feel very early on our vibrations concerning church, worship, and our prayer life. If we love it, they will. If we resent it, they will. If we gossip, they will. Children are great imitators. They had to miss their favorite TV programs, they had to sit and listen for hours when we were invited to dinner at someone's home. They live by are judged and condemned by an unwritten set of rules.

Many times because of engagements, counseling or emergencies, Billy was unable to attend school activities, sports events and has missed celebrating our birthdays and other special occasions.

Explaining that "Daddy had rather be here with us and he will be here just as soon as he can because you are very important to him" wasn't always easy.

As they were growing up they never left the house before I had prayer with them. Until this day they will call and ask for prayer for direction from God in their lives.

Robert, Richard and I have spent many hours waiting for Billy while he was making hospital calls. We would ride with him to be with him. He was with us very little because the church was small and he went to work at Family Booterie Shoe store. While sitting and waiting we played every guessing game imaginable. We would not turn on the radio. This became a special time to talk without disturbances and interruptions. This gave us quality time together. If they became tired one of them would eventually fall asleep. I consider those special times as a very precious gift. I hope Robert and Richard remember them always.

As they became older we would take them into the hospital waiting room of Vanderbilt, Baptist or Saint Thomas. To keep them occupied, so that I could make the visit with Billy, he told them they could check the phone and drink machines for change. When we returned they were always excited to show us how much money they had found from the machines and explained to us where they had been. Later it became a contest between the boys and I guess it still is!

They always looked forward to making the hospital visits with us. When Richard was tall enough to reach the phone, he would take one floor and Robert would take the other. The hospitals were much smaller then. Now when we are together and pass drink machines, one of them will invariably reach down and check for change and then look at us and smile. A warm feeling fills our heart as we think back remembering all those visits. We smile, wink and keep walking.

Early in our ministry Billy and I both learned one of life's most rewarding truths for happiness is learning to laugh. It made all the difference in our home and marriage to realize the fact that it will be okay. Tomorrow will bring hope and God will still be there.

My special time with the boy was every night after the busy day with their activities and their home-work finished and they were in bed, I would go into their bedroom, sit on the edge of their bed and there we would talk, sometime late into the night. I learned a valuable lesson in their very young years, that was the time they talked and I listened.

What a wonderful opportunity we have as a mother to build a relationship with our small children that will direct them all through their life. This is definitely, "a time to love."

"ROBERT" BECOMES "BOB"

◇◇◇◇◇◇

The Fall Semester had just begun. Robert was so excited to be in the sixth grade and was explaining to us about the school class room and his teacher Miss Jackson. Then he said, "You might have to start calling me Bob or Bobby from now on." We asked, "Why, do you want to change your name?" He said, "We were getting mixed up all day".

Miss Jackson said, "Since there are three Roberts in the class, she is going to write Robert, Bobby, and Bob on three pieces of paper. You will draw out a piece of paper and whatever name is written on it that will be what she will call that person. Each one of you will draw a name out of the box."

He said, "It really doesn't matter with me. I hope it's okay with you if I get Bob or Bobby." We anxiously waited for him to get home from school. When he got home without saying anything he handed me the folded slip of paper and on it was written "Bobby." In school from that day he was known as Bobby.

However, the transition was not so easily accomplished. When he took a part-time job he was called Bob. Until now, I still call him Robert as often as I call him Bob. When he answers his phone he instantly knows who is calling: Robert-the church, Bobby-the school, or Bob-the attorney and business.

He was baptized and started making hospital visits with Billy when he was six years old. Often he would be asked by the patients whom they were visiting to lead the prayer.

When Bob was eight years old we were getting ready to leave after the church Wednesday Night Prayer Meeting. My arms were loaded down with books and my purse hanging on my shoulder when Bob pulled on my arm and said "Mom will you go back down to the altar with me? I feel like we should pray." I told Billy to get Richard and go ahead and get into the car Bob and I would be there in just a few minutes.

While walking down the aisle Bob said, "I don't think we should go home before praying". We knelt at the altar and I asked him, "What do you want to pray about?" With a half frown with his eyebrows raised, he finally said, "There's just something not right."

So we began to pray this prayer, "Lord, whatever the situation is, wherever it is and whoever it pertains to; we ask your intervention and protection. We thank you for answering this prayer and commit to you. Amen." This was the beginning of many prayers that we have prayed together over the years even until today.

We went home and went to bed as usual but I was awakened at 3:15 in the morning feeling the same feeling that Bob felt at church. I prayed until daylight and could not go back to sleep. Everything seemed normal. At breakfast, Bob was off to school, Billy left for church, Richard had been taken care of and I was cleaning the house. I was still aware of the feeling that both Bob and I had earlier and was wondering what we would hear today.

In the afternoon at 3:15 the earth shook, screams followed and bolts and pieces of steel and steel bolts were flying around our house. Sirens began to blast. There were fire trucks, ambulances, police cars coming from all directions and people running through our yard screaming, "Are you alright? Is everybody okay?" The new tall WSM Tower was being erected and was just about completed. We would watch them working on it and could hear them talking to each other during the day. It was located two blocks behind our house. It had fallen with four workers on it.

The news reporters said "How it crumbled and fell, looking like a huge pile of spaghetti was absolutely a miracle." My heart started beating faster and in the midst of all the excitement, I knew for sure that it was a miracle. Our prayers had been answered. Every time the incident was reported on every station they mentioned that it had to be a miracle. Bob said, "Mom, aren't you glad we went back inside and went down to the altar and prayed?" I pulled him up close to me and gave him a big hug and said. "Thank you, thank you, thank you."

There are four huge steel bolts in a box under the couch down in the den that will always be a reminder when our faith needs reaffirming.

Little League Baseball became part of our busy schedule. Bob played first base and Richard was the bat boy. When Bob was twelve years old during one of his medical exams, which he had to have every year, a tumor was found in his upper chest area. The doctor scheduled the surgery at Baptist Hospital for the next Monday. We prayed for Bob to be healed at church on Sunday morning during our worship service.

On Monday morning we arrived at the hospital and on the desk just inside the glass window we could see the orders. Bob's name and the time of surgery were on top of the stack of papers and we could see it clearly. The doctor came up to us as we were sitting there and said, "I would like to examine Bob one more time to see exactly where the tumor is and check the size of it again. Then we will proceed with the surgery."

In about ten minutes the doctor returned and said, "Bob is getting dressed. He will be right out. We could find no sign of the tumor when I examined him. Surgery is cancelled the tumor is gone. This is a good way to start the day." Before Bob got all the way out of the door that opens into the waiting room he shouted, "Now I can to go to ball practice today. I put my glove in the car."

His team made Tennessee State Champions and they went to Winston-Salem, North Carolina. They played and lost to Florida on August14th, 1964.

Babe Ruth came next and he got to play first base with Mike Gooch and Wayne Garland as the pitchers. They had a wonderful connection all through Little League and into Babe Ruth. They knew each other's play perfectly. Wayne Garland went on to play with the Baltimore Orioles. His record of 20-7 was the best winning percentage of any pitcher in baseball at the time. Coach Schmittou approached them about going pro and they were considering it. Bob had planned to but was injured in a riot by Fisk University.

"Curfew"

We had a youth social at our house and he and a friend were taking some kids home. They lived across town and instead of going around the town they decided to come back through town which led them directly in the path of the riot. He was injured by a jagged stone that was three inches by nine inches. It was thrown from the wall around Fisk University. It was on April 8, 1967 on a Saturday night, thus the "Curfew" was enforced. I wrote this story concerning curfew which was published in "The Pentecostal Evangel" August 18, 1968. Reprinted by permission, copyright 1068 by the General Council of the Assemblies of God."

Seven o'clock CURFEW tonight! Could you believe it? We were under a curfew! The rioting had been all night Friday and all day Saturday. In an effort to control the situation this beautiful city was under a 7 o'clock curfew.

What about meeting the teenagers at church? At 6:30 we were scheduled to give out tracts, inviting people to attend our special youth service that was coming up, downtown on Broadway, and go from door to door around the church area. We already had the tracts. We had stamped them. We had planned where each group would go.

Suddenly, all activities stopped. Not a thing could be done. There would be no opportunity for this evangelistic outreach tonight. We were under a curfew.

A few minutes before 7, I was hurrying home from the grocery store. The lights in the business area started going off. The service station, the drugstore, and the open-air market were all dark. Almost all cars were off the streets.

My heart was pounding with such an anxious feeling and at the same time it was breaking as I thought of the words of Jesus. "The night cometh, when no man can work" (John 9:4).

Oh, no! Surely this wasn't happening on this Saturday night! It didn't make any difference how badly we wanted to meet and give our tracts, we couldn't. The curfew applied to everyone. The night was coming and we couldn't work for the Lord that night!

What about tomorrow and tomorrow night? We take for granted that Sunday means church, but not this Sunday. We would be told in the morning over the radio whether we could have service.

When we awoke on Sunday, it was quite different around our house. Everyone was up early awaiting the announcement concerning church.

It came, "Churches will be permitted to have services this morning, but the curfew is still on. Curfew begins at 7 o'clock tonight; and no one is excluded." "The night cometh..."

The rebellion we are experiencing is not only among college and other young people; there is something underneath, an inner disturbance.

We may be forced to close our church doors unless we Christian parents get a new touch of fire in our souls that will spread to the youth of our country. They want something worth fighting for and our attitudes toward God and His Kingdom are reflected in their lives.

Rebellion can come to Christian homes. When we see it, we should pray very hard and not let it go unnoticed; for what we have in our homes is reflected in our society.

Be genuine in your beliefs, and the young people will see that you are alive. They want something alive, a reason to live. Jesus gives us life and life more abundantly.

My mind went back to Saturday night, April 8th last year. Some young people had come to our house for the evening. Our son Bob and a friend Ronnie, were taking home some of the kids who lived across town. Bob said, "We'll be home by 11."

We walked up the stairs and turned on the TV to get the news and there was a bulletin! A riot had broken out in the section of town the young people would have to go through. There was no way to get in touch with them, and we knew they had no idea of what they were running into. We earnestly prayed for their protection and committed them to the Lord.

Eleven o'clock came and no word; 11:30: still no word. At 12:05 the phone rang. Bob said, "Mother, there is a riot. I've been hit with a big rock, but I'm okay." Rocks had been thrown through the car. The car was all dented in. The windows were broken, except the windshield. One of these rocks hit Bob in his shoulder. Ronnie was driving and hadn't been hit but was terrified. The police were unable to check for us.

As soon as they got home we took them to the hospital. The doctor said, "If the rock had hit Bob any higher it could have paralyzed him or killed him instantly. It was a miracle he had not been permanently injured".

Dr. O.G. Nelson, Surgery Physician, sent Middle Tennessee this notice to the ROTC Instructor: This will verify the Vocation Rehabilitation status of Robert Myers Langford. He has been given a scholarship on account of an injury to his spine which creates general weakness on exertion. I have recommended light work in his case. Sincerely, 0. G. Nelson, MD' September 10, 1970.

In an instant we had become part of a terrible riot with no warning whatsoever.

I kept thinking about these incidents of violence, rebellion, rioting and crime so near us now. I was unable to sleep and had prayed until early morning. Then the Lord Jesus spoke so clearly to my heart: "As the clouds precede the storm, as the thunder precedes the rain, so this turmoil and violence precedes My coming. I am nearer than you think."

Then I saw a long, beautiful linen tablecloth, with crystal, fully set. Of all the banquets I have attended never have I seen one so elaborate and beautiful. The Lord was walking behind each chair. He was looking at each place setting and making the final check. He was almost at the end of the long, long table

It was the marriage supper of the Lamb. Oh, my heart is no longer heavy when I hear the announcement of violence or rioting, because I am looking just a few steps beyond this turmoil and rebellion. Just as quickly as the rain drops begin to fall after the thunder rolls, just that quickly our Savior is coming. "As the lightning cometh out of the east, and shineth even unto the west; so shall also the coming if the Son man be......So likewise ye, when ye shall see all these things, know that it is near, even at the doors"(Matthew 24;27,33).

The group "Up With People Rhythm of the World" was giving auditions at a hotel down town. Bob played the trumpet and was first trumpet in the Stratford School Band all thru High School. He auditioned and was accepted.

They traveled in many countries and he would miss school for practices and productions. We told him to make the decision and we would respect his desire. He went to a couple of practices and then one morning he came in to breakfast and said, "I told the director of the group that I wouldn't be back but expressed to him how much I appreciated their accepting me. He said he understood how I felt about missing my credits and school projects. I told him about the Babe Ruth Tournament coming up that I would miss and I was really looking forward to playing in it. I have played first base since Little League." His Little League Team won Tennessee State Champions. They had played in Winston-Salem, North Carolina on August 13th and 14th. They were beaten by Florida by one of the guys trying to steal second base.

While attending Middle Tennessee State University his third summer there, he had been selected to represent the school. He and those going to high schools to talk about the features of attending MTSU had an Associated Student Body Planning Retreat for 1972 at Camp Holy Lake Resort.

Bob was the head of the Student Ambassadors. Before the meeting there was time to take the canoe across the lake and back. Bob hesitated to get in and told them, "Hey guys, I can't swim and I'm afraid to go across because this lake is so deep." They insisted and promised him that they would be very careful and not do anything to cause the boat to turn over. He reluctantly stepped into the unsteady canoe.

It was a beautiful late summer afternoon in September. The red and orange leaves had begun falling. The cool air was fresh and crisp. The workshop would begin at six p.m. Everything was already setup so this left a couple of hours to relax and enjoy the beautiful mountains surrounding the lake. The lake is located sixty miles east of Nashville just out of a little town called McMinnville.

Bob had looked forward to this workshop all summer. Teachers and Student Council officers meet and make plans for the coming college year. He attended last year and loved every minute of it.

He reminded the guys again, "I can't swim. I'll just stay here and enjoy this beautiful and peaceful place. I won't mind. Go on guys." He started to step out of the canoe. They insisted they would be cautious and "you sit in the middle of the boat. We will sit at opposite ends and paddle. We will go to the center of the lake and come right back."

Bob had taken swimming lessons at the YMCA. We had Richard taking lessons in the same class. This was a mistake. Often if brothers or sisters are in the same class the older will watch after the younger and will not learn to swim. That is exactly what happened. Peter and Dwight assured Bob that they would be careful. Sure enough Bob had gotten over his nervousness and he was glad that he had decided to come along. The forty foot deep lake was calm and looked like a gigantic mirror with the blue sky's reflection. The canoe was not moving. It was really neat.

Suddenly from nowhere, a canoe was rushing up behind them with a couple of guys goofing around. Peter shouted, "Watch out. Bob can't swim," But they were already too close. Their canoe struck Bob's canoe with such an impact that both canoes went out of control and hurled all the boys into the center of the deepest part of the lake.

Bob fell sideways and tried desperately to catch hold of the rim of the canoe as it was turning over. As the water was closing over his head he was holding his breath and trying to keep from swallowing any water.

He began to sink to the bottom of the lake remembering some of the swimming lessons he managed to come to the surface only to discover he was under the overturned canoe. After struggling trying to grasp something he started sinking again. He said, "So this is how it is to drown." In exhaustion he quit struggling and felt himself sinking farther and farther down.

He said that pictures flashed thru his mind. Like watching a screen and thought, I've read about things like this before. He and Wynnelle had been married just six weeks and he said, "I saw Wynnelle standing in the door of our house on Carter Avenue."

One of the canoes had been turned upright and the water emptied. The boys were frantically looking for Bob but were swimming past him without finding him. Dwight said, "We have to keep going down, deeper and deeper. Let's go to the bottom." Peter said that he felt something suddenly pass his hand and he grabbed it. It was Bob's hair.

He began pulling up his limp body with one hand while pulling up to the surface with the other. Finally he surfaced with Bob's reddish brown hair clutched in his hand. All four boys took hold of him. They pushed and shoved him finally getting him into the canoe while Peter was getting his strength back still trying to help.

They were hitting him in the back and finally he began spitting and coughing up water. His breathing was very shallow and uneven. He was still limp but was looking around and gradually able to sit up. He looked across the lake. They had reached the shore. This was on the opposite side of the lake.

They had to go back across the lake which had seized and taken possession of Bob and brought him face to face with death. The guys after diving into the 40 foot deep lake regained their composure talked awhile and rested on the grass. After a prayer they thanked God for helping them and asked for safety back across the lake.

The boys climbed back into the canoes and headed back to the lodge. They seemed surprisingly calm as they entered the conference room and explained to the stunned group what had just happened. Everyone understood their being late and joined in a big applause with whistles and gasps. The workshop was a success and one that was never to be forgotten.

Robert and Richard have always been very active in politics. They each ran for President of their classes all through their school years. When Robert was in his second year of college, and Richard was running for Vice President in his junior year of high school, Robert wrote this letter to him:

"Richard: I know that the next couple of days will be very trying for you as well as everyone associated with you and involved in your campaign.

There are lots of things to be learned during a campaign for a school office. As you know I had a couple of campaigns to go that myself. Luckily I was able to come out ahead on the first time around but I wasn't so fortunate the second time. I do feel however that the experiences I had, warranted my effort in running both times.

Remember one thing Richard, you don't have to win an election in order to have a successful campaign. The election is just one aspect of the entire ordeal. Try if you can to put everything into your campaign without worrying about defeat. Be nice to everyone, and especially to your opponents. Do not however, be superficial because people somehow can see through a 'glass smile'.

Another thing to consider is you and your opponents may have the same friends. After all, the position of boys' vice president is slightly more than a title while friendship is a purpose for everything and if defeat should come there is a definite reason for it. You know there's a lot of truth in the saying anybody can win but it takes a big man to lose. When I lost in running for President I was somewhat disappointed yet I feel as though I gained a valuable experience in accepting defeat and learning to face reality in the best way.

Of course there is the possibility of victory. If you win you should also take it in a nature of humility. As you yourself said, it is the people putting you there and you are their representative. You should at all times be responsive to their desires and tolerant of the faculty's supremacy.

This is by no means a written lecture but rather a simple guideline to go by. I wish you all the luck in the world. Work hard, keep a good image and most of all keep a good Christian attitude regardless how the election turns out. Remember, "The Lord will perfect that which is his own," as "all things work together for good to them that serve the Lord." Your friend as well as brother, Robert." P.S.: Someday people will pay to have a copy of one of my handwritten letters. See ya'.

Richard did not win that year but his senior year he ran for Student Body President of Stratford and won.

We could not believe what we saw in our front yard as we were returning from a hospital visit. Bill and I drove in front of our house getting ready to pull into our driveway and there were two brightly colored signs. One red and yellow sign was on the right side of the yard that read, E. Marvin Fleming for Representative and a bright blue and white sign on the left side the same size sign that read, Bill Boner for Representative. The only house on the street with two signs in the front yard.

Bob was Campaign Manager for Bill Boner who was running for Representative in the 52nd Legislative District for the House of Representatives in the state of Tennessee. The only problem, Richard was also Campaign Manager for Representative in the 52nd Legislation District the incumbent E. Marvin Fleming.

Bob and Richard have always been close and very supportive of each other in what ever project in which they were involved. .They both loved being active in politics

An iron-clad rule was invoked at our house concerning mealtime: no discussing politics during any meal. Absolutely none.

By the way, that rule still exists.

Bill Boner won by a slim margin. Bob called Richard who was sittin' in his car in front of his campaign headquarters where everyone had already left and said, "Richard, I feel sad and can't enjoy our winning because I know you put forth so much effort to win. I do appreciate you and how hard you worked and I love you." Bob went to Washington with Bill for several years. Bill later became Mayor of Nashville 1987 — 1991.

Bob attended the YMCA law school here in Nashville at night. He always included his Bible when he carried his books to college and law school. During that time on his off nights he taught at Trevecca Nazerine College and also taught two classes at night at the facility located in Only, Tennessee which is about fifty miles west of Nashville. During the day he worked at the Downtown Library as the assistant manager. In just a few months the manager, due to illness had to retire and Bob was appointed as manager. He was the youngest person that had ever held this position.

The Constitutional Convention was being held and Bob was encouraged to run. This Convention would change the laws written for the State of Tennessee and he was the youngest delegate to ever run for this position. I'm reminded of time that he ran for Delegate in the General Election.

As the rain was hitting me in the face, I asked myself the question," Why will we sit here in a down pouring cold rain with freezing wind blowing our umbrella inside-out to watch a MTSU Homecoming football game on a busy Saturday afternoon?" The reason: love - clear and simple.

My son Richard was President of the Student Body at Middle Tennessee State University and he was to participate in the halftime activities. Here we sat drenched and not complaining at all.

A few days later the alarm went off at 5:00 a.m. It's November 2, 1976 and the great day of the General Election for Davidson County, Tennessee. We are up, dressed and ready for the busy day ahead. Here I stood in the freezing cold 29 degree weather, in the dark watching for the sun to come up at the Dalewood School Precinct waiting for the voters to arrive. Billy was at another Precinct. Richard and his friends from his SAE fraternity were going from different locations to check if any of the workers needed water or anything to eat.

Bob was running for the Delegate to the Constitution Convention. The first time in over 100 years the Constitution of Tennessee was being revised and rewritten. I wanted Bob to win so here I was at a voting precinct before dawn.

Bob had already asked me, "Mom, can we have the victory party at our house?" Of course the answer was, "Sure, no problem, that'll be fine." With Bob winning the election he will help determine the writing of the new laws and review the other laws. We did have the victory party at our house. Bob made the statement to his dad and everyone present, "Dad, I'm going to be a man of my own ideals and standards. I may be one of the youngest Delegates but I'm going to stand firm for the principles that I know are right."

A letter I sent to Bob:

Remember Bob, when I sat up in bed in the middle of the night saying, "God bless Bob's ministry." You were living in Lafayette, trying to decide about Macon. The words came forceful. "The direction for Bob to take is the opportunity to use the ministry and gift that was given him. There will be opportunities opened up in ways by me for this gift to be manifested. He will not have to push. The door will open and opportunities will be presented."

You have proven yourself in integrity and have proven your ability in business. Waiting for direction is the hardest of all and this period of time was very necessary for your gifts to be operating in your life. The place for you to be is the place thru which the opening of the power, in the operation of faith and healing. Keep this channel open. The direction will be clear to you without a doubt. God has placed you where you are and your influence is phenomenal.

God will confirm this in and by His own way. I am reminded of the prayer for your dad in the Sunday school room, when the doctor said he had a mass in the back of his head and would require surgery. You and Richard prayed for him. When he went back to the doctor the next day, there was no sign of it on the x-ray. You prayed for me while I was playing the piano and the temperature that I had for weeks left. These are just two examples. You were a junior in high school.

You are just exactly where God wants you and doing exactly what He wants you to do. You may decide another direction whatever it is, Macon, Nashville, whatever, let the deciding point be, "God, it's where you will use the ministry you have given me." Don't hassle with it. Just rest in His leading and have the peace that is beyond our understanding. God's gifts are freely given.

Bob, you have great faith and that gift of faith is touching many lives that would not be reached by so called 'religion' but by your testimony, your confidence and unwavering faith. God is using you in a wonderful ministry. You are investing in lives. The bottom line is, and will always remain; God is your motivation for living.

Love you, Mom.

February 1994 this article was published by the Hendersonville Area Chamber of Commerce.

Robert Langford tells why he loves Hendersonville.

As CEO and President of Restaurant Management Services, a Macon, Georgia based chain of 125 restaurants with sales in excess of $100 million and a franchisee of Shoney's Inc. since 1985, Robert M. Langford could live just about anywhere he chooses. He and his wife Wynnelle have chosen to make Hendersonville their home since 1992 and he will speak to those attending the February Chamber luncheon about why.

Mr. Langford was a senior partner with the Nashville law firm of Bone, Langford and Armistead, P.C. As counsel for government affairs for Shoney's Inc. Mr. Langford developed an active and successful Political Action Committee.

He is very active in his community having served as a church board member and in the past has been on boards of organizations like Tennessee State University and Teen Challenge of Nashville. He also served six years on the board of trustees of Central Bible College, Springfield, Missouri and has been active in the Rotary.

As a Shoney's franchisee, Mr. Langford has consistently been one of the top performers. The sales average of his units have been among the highest each year since 1986 and his company, Langford Enterprises, Inc. has been recognized in virtually every category since his first unit opened.

Many business opportunities have come his way through the years and with those opportunities there have many opportunities for him to be a living testimony for the Lord. He has always had great faith. He fasts often and spends time in prayer.

In January 2012, this article appeared, Denny's recognizes Langford for leadership role. He received the inaugural "President's Guiding Principle Award" from Denny's President and CEO. He was recognized for his leadership with the more than 1,600-unit Denny's system.

Presently, he and his partner are the principals of Dynamic Management and own and manage 60 restaurants including 23 Denny's in Florida and 31 Black-eyed Peas in Texas. Kori owns the Black-eyed Pea in Hendersonville.

A letter to Bob on his 47th birthday.

"My dearest Bob, on a beautiful fall September morning forty seven years ago God sent a most blessed and precious gift to our house and we named him Robert Myers.

I felt that I could never love you more than at the moment the nurse placed you in my arms but through the years that love has grown. We have shared much joy and laughter, tears and sorrow, and today I love you more and words cannot express how truly thankful I am for the joy and the love you have brought to our home and my life.

Bob, I want you to know what I was thinking about today as I was having my daily prayer time.

We often feel that we have a handle on life. But, life is a funny thing. Unless it has as its center "Christ" there is no handle. Christ is the handle that turns the key to success or failure.

We often get so busy in 'living' that we forget the giver of life, who in turn gives us joy and peace and rest. I know that you are constantly giving of yourself which you have always done but you must make yourself available to the Holy Spirit to be renewed daily and let him direct your steps.

You have made me so very proud of you in every way. I am so glad you are my son. I have drawn from you strength and many times through the years you have been my only confidant.

I want the very best that life has to offer for you with happiness and contentment always.

You are so very dear to me and have always brought that something 'special' to me.

Jesus is coming so soon. We can see the predictions happening about wickedness in high places and sex running rampant in our Nation. This world with its filth, turmoil and disrespect for God and everything sacred is quickly coming to an end.

We will soon be with daddy. Remember, he said, "Look for him around the throne of God that he would be watching for us." That day is fast approaching when we can spend eternity together.

May God keep you in His care and shield you from every hurt and anything that would ever harm you!

Following the events of the day we make our usual bedtime call. I am unable to talk to him now in his bedroom. He has moved on with his life and now has a beautiful wife, Wynnelle. They have a precious and beautiful daughter, Kori. She graduated from Vanderbilt and is involved in the family business. They live in a lovely home on Old Hickory Lake just across from Taylor Swift.

Upon finishing his law degree he was appointed as Legal Counsel for Metro with his office in the Courthouse. While representing Metro he was contacted by Mr. Ray Danner, the owner of Shoney's and Captain D's and he asked him to join his company. Bob was a Shoney's Restaurant franchisee in 1986. He joined Shoney's Inc. company in 1995. He also served as CEO of Restaurant Management Services in Macon, Georgia, a franchise operator of 120 restaurants. He has kept his Law Degree current and still practices law.

At this present time he is President of Dynamic Company.

During this past winter when the flu viruses were so bad, he had been flying a lot and was trying to get over the effects that last forever. He kept going, trying to get his strength back and it would not let up. About the time he thought he was over the symptoms would return and he could hardly breathe. He could not get relief.

We had been praying for his healing. He did not want to expose me to the flu so I had not been near him for over a month. After weeks and weeks, one Saturday night, the Lord spoke to my heart and said, "Call Bob and pray for him over the phone to be healed." I felt it so strongly I did not hesitate. When I called him, he said "Mom, I just can't get my strength back." I said, "Bob, I have never done this before.

CHAPTER NINE

RICHARD

How excited Billy and I were. We were going to have another baby! We were on our way to see Doctor Cayce, whose office was downtown on Church Street, in Nashville. The street was bustling with business. The office building was located next to Castner Knott's Department Store. We could see the sign from the parking lot, which was located behind the store and we then knew where to go. We had no trouble finding the doctor's office. Parking downtown was a problem even then, in 1954, and so much more so now.

As we got off the elevator on the third floor, the doctor's office was facing the door. My heart began to beat faster and my thoughts, suddenly turned to fear. I felt weak in my stomach. I stopped in my tracks, remembering and feeling the hurt deep in my heart of losing Larry only six years earlier. Billy said, "What's wrong, honey, do you feel sick? Why are you holding your stomach?" Taking a few deep breaths and not wanting him to know what I was thinking, or to be alarmed, I squeezed his arm tighter and said, "No, I'm fine."

The nurse was standing by the reception desk at the doctor's office. She smiled and asked, "Are you Mrs. Langford?" With a deep sigh and trying my best to smile, I answered in a weak voice, "Yes, ma'am." She put her hand on my shoulder, and said, "Come on in. We're ready for you." After the examination, as the doctor was leaving the room, he said, "You can get dressed."

In a few minutes, the door opened. Doctor Cayce, his nurse, and Billy were coming into my room. I knew something was wrong. The nurse closed the door. The doctor looked at Billy, and said, "Sir, your wife is three months pregnant; however, her womb is turned upside down and I don't think she will be able to carry this baby. She could lose the baby at any time."

Billy reached down and held me tenderly in his arms. After what seemed like an eternity, Billy calmly replied, "Doctor Cayce, we will pray and believe that God will help her carry our baby full term." Doctor Cayce put one of his hands on my shoulder and his other hand on Billy's shoulder and said, "I'll join my prayer with yours!" He then continued and said, quite clinically, "I've already sent your name with the information to Baptist Hospital. They have reserved a room for you. In case you start to bleed, you will not have to call them. Go immediately to the second-floor nurse's station. They will take care of you and they will call me." I know he followed the medical protocol, and felt very concerned for me, but Billy and our faith in God had to be revealed, for our baby to be born.

From the time that we knew that we might lose our baby, until our baby was born, I had to be extremely careful of what I was able to do. The activities that I loved so deeply were curtailed at the church, yet our prayers continued, and our faith got stronger. Since I was unable to play the piano at the church, former Supreme Court Justice Charles Galbreath's wife, Joyce, stepped in and filled that void. The last two months of pregnancy were spent in bed most of the time.

My mom and dad had retired from the Ministry and were living in East Nashville on Burris Avenue, in the Inglewood area. That was the place of refuge that Billy, Robert, and I were able to retreat. Thanks to God's provision, they took care of me and Robert who was four years old at the time. Billy would come each night for supper and spend the night and be with us. Even though he was busy during the day, as the pastor of Belmont Assembly of God, he felt the need to provide for our struggling family and was also the manager of Family Booterie Shoe Store on Union Street, which he worked, two nights a week.

Having to stay off my feet and in bed, made it feel like time stood still, but with God's grace and His strength, we were doing our part of what the doctor said we must do to have a healthy baby. To help pass time I counted every flower on the wallpaper and sang every song I knew and tried to read books. It would have helped if we could have had a television, which had not yet made its grand appearance. I was glad that I had a radio in my room and I listened to WENO, which was known as the country music station. It was the only station that just played Country Music at that time. The other stations had mostly talk shows and news. WSM was the largest station and known as the clear channel and played popular country music, talk and news.

The thoughts of Larry were always in the back of my mind and also the fear that I might not make it to the hospital in time for the delivery. My prayer everyday was, "Lord, please let me know when it is time."

Finally on Thursday night at 11:30 on May 5, 1955, my water broke. We made it to Baptist Hospital and Richard's arrival was at 12:15 on May 6th. Doctor Cayce laid Richard in my arms and said, "Here is your six and one-half pound miracle baby and you carried him the full-term!" With a big smile and nodding his head affirmatively, he looked across the room at Billy and said, "We know why, don't we?"

Six weeks later, I could not wait to get to my scheduled routine check-up! Richard had gained weight and was doing fine. What a relief, for me, Billy, my family, everyone who prayed, and even the doctor's office. When we took Richard back for his scheduled visit, we signed in at the desk and the nurse stepped through the door. She took Richard in her arms and told the other patients that were waiting in the office, what a miracle had happened with me carrying Richard full term.

Following the examination, Dr. Cayce asked the nurse to get Billy. I said, "Oh no, now what?" Then the doctor reminded me saying, "Following the birth of your baby you will still need surgery. We will have to correct the position of your womb." In the excitement of having a healthy baby, I had forgotten about the conversation that potential surgery was going to be needed. He looked away and then looked at me and was squinting his eyes with a surprised and pleasant look of amazement. He then asked me, if he could examine me again. My heart was pounding. "What is happening?" I thought. Billy and the nurse came in. The doctor and the nurse were looking at my record folder. Then they both nodded their heads as if to say, "yes" as they compared notes.

The doctor raised his voice, cleared his throat and with a puzzled yet enthusiastic look exclaimed, "Your wife's female organs are perfect. This is truly a miracle." Then he continued, "If I didn't know that you were the same person, I would never believe you are the person that I examined before you had your baby. Your female organs are perfect, as if you had never had a baby, absolutely perfect." He leaned down and gave me a big hug. He shook Billy's hand and said, "I'm now convinced that prayer definitely works." He looked back at me and said "I was expecting to do surgery on you." He added, "Someone else, higher than me, performed surgery." Doctor Cayce, his nurse, Billy and I gave thanks with grateful hearts. This wasn't a long prayer, but more of a great sigh of relief, that God stepped in and had already corrected the problem without surgery! This was the beginning of many miracles that we were going to see and experience during our ministry in Nashville, Tennessee.

Richard was a robust child and was growing up normally. However, at the age of four he was scheduled for a tonsillectomy at Baptist Hospital. This was a routine procedure for children, at that age, at this time of our culture's normal procedures. After entering the operating room he suddenly began running a high fever. Dr. Vaughn, his pediatrician, came back downstairs to our waiting room and said, "I don't understand what happened, please take him home and check his temperature every hour and call me back with each reading." As usual, we did what the doctor said.

On arriving home as we entered the house the phone was ringing. We didn't answer right away because we were taking Richard's temperature as soon as we could. It showed perfect, no temp at all. The phone was ringing again. It was the dietitian from Baptist Hospital. She worked at the hospital and was a member of our congregation. With excitement in her voice she said, "I'm so glad you answered. I thought this was the day for Richard's tonsillectomy. Something happened in the operating room and the medication given for clotting of the blood caused several children to hemorrhage and they are in serious condition." Billy explained to her our activities of the day. How thankful for the promise of God in Psalms 121: verse 4, "He that keepeth thee will not slumber nor sleep." We checked every hour and his temperature remained normal the rest of the day.

Several years later when he was ten years old, he would wake up in the middle of the night terrified, shaking and shouting, "Help me. Momma, help me. Please help me." This started happening every night. I realized we needed an intervention to keep his mind clear from being tormented. So, each night as I prayed his goodnight prayer with him, I began to add, "God keep Richard's mind clear and do not let him have a bad dream tonight." Once again, claiming a promise this time in Psalms 127 verse 2. "He giveth his beloved sleep" and II Timothy chapter one verse 7;"For God hath not given us the spirit of fear; but of power, and of love, and of a sound mind."

One night, after several weeks of prayer right in the middle of my prayer he said, "Momma, my bad dreams are taken care of but just keep on praying just in case." I still add that to my prayer for both of my boys every night. He began waking up in the mornings singing a song either in English or another language and he still does.

We had a Missionary staying in our home and while we were eating breakfast, he heard Richard singing. He asked him to come into the kitchen. He asked him to sing the song again and said, "You are singing the native language of the area where I am serving. You even have the exact, distinct dialect of my area of that part of Africa."

Because of the agreement when we first moved into our house on Tiffany, Richard had the larger bedroom, so he had to give it up, and sleep on the couch in the living room when we had guest speakers at the church, which was very often. Robert took the smaller bedroom so he wouldn't have to give up his bedroom. However, even though he chose the smaller bedroom he still had to give his up too. That is the reason we added two bedrooms and a half bath downstairs where the garage had been.

In November 1973, the day before Thanksgiving, we entered Baptist Hospital because Richard was losing weight so fast. His body had become just skin and bones. After the tests, it was diagnosed as Leukemia and he needed immediate treatment.

Another doctor was called in and he also agreed with the findings. We asked if they would postpone treatment until the next Monday and they asked, "Why do you want to wait? This is profoundly serious and needs to be addressed now."

We told them there is a Youth Convention being held downtown in Hume Fogg Auditorium of four to five hundred young people from different churches across the state and there would be prayer there. We will call those in charge of the services to please place Richard on their prayer list at each service. I was scheduled to play the piano for the opening of each service. I would go and leave as soon as I could. When I got back to the hospital Billy and Robert would go. They attended with the group from our church.

Before the scheduled treatment began on Monday morning, Billy asked the specialist to take another test if possible. He agreed that it would not be a problem. While in the waiting room we saw our family doctor talking to the specialist. They both came into the room. The specialist said, "I don't understand this, not at all. Everything is fine. We can't find a trace of Leukemia and his blood count is up to normal. It's just a miracle!"

Here we are in the same hospital where I was handed my miracle baby seventeen years ago. Seeing with my eyes and feeling the wonderful love of a healing Jesus in my heart another miracle had been performed. This miracle was given to Richard, my seventeen-year-old son.

He finished his term as class president of Stratford High School in 1973. He entered Middle Tennessee State University the next fall. In his senior year at MTSU he was elected as president of the student body. He received his first degree from Middle Tennessee State University. After graduation, he pursued a career in banking and received his BA in Banking from the University of Tennessee. After a couple of years of finance, he decided he wanted to be in a field where he could help people and give of himself, so he enrolled in the Central Bible College in Springfield, Missouri and followed his calling into the ministry.

He holds three BA degrees, two Masters Degrees, (MA and MTS). He received his MA in Biblical Studies from the Assemblies of God Theological Seminary and a Master of Theological Studies from the Vanderbilt Divinity School. Richard finalized his theological training with a Doctor of Ministry from AGTS with an emphasis in Organizational Leadership. He married. Billy performed the ceremony and Church located on Gallatin Road. Richard had already been appointed as the Business Administrator at Calvary Temple Church in Naperville, Illinois under the senior pastor Robert Schmidgall. Following the honeymoon, they went directly to Naperville to start their ministry. They ministered there about four years.

We at Belmont Assembly needed an Associate Pastor and Music Director and we asked if they would consider coming here and working with Billy and our church on Music Row.

They decided they would do that hoping it would strengthen their marriage. They have two beautiful daughters, Jennifer Jane, who was born, January 8, 1982 and Ashleigh Elizabeth who was born August 28, 1987.

The word "Divorce" never sounds good! It seems that it always has far reaching consequences. There was separation from his girls. This also included our whole family. They were not permitted to be a part of our ministry, our home or our activities. Billy especially missed being with them. Thankfully, now they are a part of his life and ours. Richard enjoys being with his grandchildren. Jennifer has two boys, Carson Luke and Cameron Langford. Ashleigh has a little girl, Audrie Elizabeth.

The Ministry of Missions has been on Richard's heart for as long as I can remember. This dream came true on Wednesday, December 6, 1989. He was carrying Christmas gifts and medicine to churches in Nicaragua. At the Miami International Airport the people working there said the packages could not leave. While Richard was talking to the clerk at the window she said, "Excuse me, I have a call." Then turned back to Richard and said, "The gentleman on the phone said, you have permission to take the packages with you when you board this plane." She stamped his tickets. While waiting on the runway before taking off Richard called the airport back to thank the gentleman for granting permission for the packages to be taken. When he asked to speak to the gentleman by name, the reply was "Sir, there is no one that works here by that name!"

While pastoring at Oak Hill Assembly, we were privileged to send as much as $50,000 annually to a Central American country, usually at Christmas. For several years Richard would recruit and accompany a team of doctors, dentists and nurses for a volunteer short term stint in Colombia. On one of these trips he and a companion missionary were rescued from rebels who had put them in jail in El Salvador.

He was also privileged to take a group from our church and build a church in Asunción, Paraguay. He spent two years in French Harbour, Roatan, Honduras. In 1999 he was approved and appointed by the

Assemblies of God Missions Department. He was a pioneer in this field as he became the first Missionary Associate to be appointed with his circumstances.

On one trip, he sent us a message that he was on his way to Nairobi. He would only teach two classes until he had some time to get adjusted and to find how things are done at "EAST" (East Africa School of Theology). He would also be working with the "Kenya Kids, street children orphaned and living with AIDS, and he would be teaching the Maasai, in southwest Kenya. His budget was raised through friends and the Assemblies of God churches in Tennessee.

As he was preparing for a subsequent mission trip, he, and we, received a big disappointment! The day before his departure from Nashville he received an e-mail from Kenya. The staff was awaiting his arrival. However, at the board meeting of the Kenya Assembly of God, on the day before his arrival, someone mentioned Richard was joining the staff and the classes he would be teaching. It was noted that Richard was divorced. The KAG has a rule that they will not allow someone to teach who has been divorced.

The American Missionaries, who had worked there for twenty years tried to explain that Richard was credentialed and approved by the Tennessee District and the General Council and had made a commitment to remain single. It was to no avail. They asked him, "Please convey their apologies to your mother and your family for any hurt or disappointment that may have been caused."

The missionary continued, "There are other places in Africa where the policy is not so rigid. I will certainly recommend you and he then mentioned Ethiopia. We know God's ways are higher than our ways. If the Lord of the harvest wants you to serve as a missionary in another country, then so be it. Maybe the Lord is leading you on such a journey as Apostle Paul's journey to Rome via prison in Palestine, which will ultimately bring greater glory to Him as you find out where you will be."

Richard's reply, "I appreciate all your prayers, thoughts, energy, and support. I will wait for your direction. If you remember, one of the first things that you told me is the need for someone to be flexible. What a prophet!"

He immediately received an e-mail from the director of Ethiopia stating they had been praying for someone to be contacted to come to Ethiopia to teach at Addis Ababa College. They stated that almost every school needs teachers and he was sure there would be a position in another advanced bible school.

Richard was accepted at ABC, "Addis Bible College" in Addis Ababa, Ethiopia and enjoyed every day there. He learned to write and speak the Amharic language. The missionaries there accepted him into their families. He still corresponds with them.

He had been home spending a few days with us. On his third flight returning to Addis Ababa, he had a heart attack on the airplane and was taken to the hospital in Amsterdam. We had to make a quick decision; come home or continue on to Ethiopia. The missionary in charge called me and said, "if it is at all possible for Richard to continue his trip, we sure do need him here. When he arrives we will check with the hospital here to make sure he is okay. We will take good care of him."

At that moment I did not realize that the hospitals in Africa are no comparison to the hospitals in America. At least not the hospital he was going to. With this made clear, I agreed for him to continue on to his destination. He had some extremely hard days but by his being there the government let the missionaries stay. There is a law strictly enforced that someone either with a Doctorate Degree or working on a Doctorate must be on the missionary team. With lots of prayer and a great determination Richard was able to serve four years. The college is now fully staffed and operated with Ethiopians.

The adjustment of leaving Africa and coming back home into the American culture was incredibly stressful. Also, the divorce was taking its toll on him. Upon his arrival back home a high school friend began spending a lot of time here at the house. I was glad that he had someone to be with him downstairs. They would watch TV and talk. They spent a lot of time upstairs with us also.

Before Richard started his mission tour, he had his colon removed because it was abscessed. The doctors were treating him for nervous stomach. The colonoscopy did not show the hidden abscess and it spread into his entire colon. Thankfully, they were able to attach his stomach to his small intestine which causes him to have frequent bowel movements. Fortunately, they didn't have to attach a bag to his stomach. Since that surgery, he has had stomach problems and he has to be very careful as to what and when he eats.

I needed to be out of town. I felt comfortable leaving and asked his friend if he could be here and check with Richard and let me know how he was doing thru this adjustment. He said "I'll be glad to do that. After work, I will run by and I'll let you know." However, that was bad news because the friend brought something to help Richard relax and get some much-needed sleep. It for sure did that.

On my returning home, we began making our visits to the Hospital Rehab Centers. First we went to VITA (Vanderbilt Institute for Treatment for Addiction), then on to Burns, Tennessee, and, next, to a hospital in Fort Lauderdale, Florida. Finally, it seemed as though Richard had gotten his medicines worked out and we were so relieved. He has a wonderful Doctor at Vanderbilt Hospital.

Richard has always enjoyed holidays. He starts playing and singing Christmas songs before Thanksgiving. It was Christmas Eve. Everyone had come to our house for our traditional dinner and opening of presents. The youngest one present always reads the Christmas Story (sometimes with a little or maybe a lot of help), and then we let them distribute the gifts from under the Christmas tree. The gifts had been given out and were stacked by each of our chairs.

In the middle of our opening our presents, a loud knock came on our den door. You could see thru the door. There were two nice looking guys standing there. They could see what we were doing. Bob answered the door and asked them, "What do you want?" They said, "We know this is Christmas Eve and we don't want to intrude on your family but we just wanted to talk to Richard a minute. We just need to tell Richard something." Richard went outside for just a minute. When he came back in he said, "I've gotta go with these guys. I'll be back in just a few minutes. Don't wait on me to open presents; I'll be back as soon as I can. I'll open mine when I get back." We could not believe what had just happened. I ran to the door. Bob reached out and hugged me and as he was holding me he said, "Let's say a prayer for his protection. Something is not right." The whole family who was here for our Christmas Eve celebration joined hands as we cried and prayed together. Satan had attacked our family again. He was certainly working overtime to destroy Richard and his ministry.

The dark cloud again invaded the privacy of our home. The beautiful Christmas tree, the colorful decorations, the lovely presents and the joy of Christmas faded into disappointment, heartache and wonder. We asked each other, "Did they make Richard go with them? What in the world did they say to make Richard leave? Where did they go?" I knew that he didn't have his medication with him. We waited, and we waited, and still no word. Everyone left not having much to say as they were leaving and taking their Christmas presents. There seemed to be just "nothing to say," that kind of feeling.

Bob said, "We will stay with you and dad tonight." But we knew Wynnelle and Kori had cooked and planned for everyone to come to their house for Christmas Dinner at 1 O'clock tomorrow. I felt sure we would hear from Richard soon or he would be home.

We waited all night, yet we did not hear from Richard. The next morning still no word, all day, no word into the next days. There was still no word after four days. We were calling everywhere we could think of at the time. Bob found a wonderful couple who attended his church with the Ministry of Intervention.

Finally, we setup an Intervention with a couple who has experience with drug abuse. They called and said, "We have found him." They told us step by step what to do. Billy, Bob and I hurried to meet the couple. We talked just a few minutes in the lobby where they asked us to meet them before they went upstairs to do the intervention. "When we get to him, have someone ready to drive the car. You wait in the lobby."

"When you see him come out of the elevator you go stand by the car. We will walk out with him to the car. Don't say anything. Give him a hug. Then Bob you get in the car while he is with your mom and dad. They are expecting him in rehab in Pikeville, Tennessee, just out of Crossville. There should be no problem." How grateful and thankful we are to them for their dedication to God for their special ministry. They found him and the other two guys on the sixth floor at the Lowe's Hotel located across the street from Vanderbilt University; the University from which he had earlier received his Master's Theological Studies Degree. He was unable to call, but after a few days, we received a letter. He said, "Mom, I am so sorry. I have made such a mess of things. I was really trying to die. I am so ashamed and I am so sorry. Please forgive me for messing up Christmas and for not calling you. I am so sorry. I love you, dad and the family so very much."

Later we received another letter, then another and another. He said, "Please come see me and will you bring my dog Sam?" When we returned home, he did not accept the many phone calls from the past 'friends.' He met a great sponsor that went to meetings with him every day.

Our hearts were broken. But the good news is, broken hearts can be mended and healed with God's love and believing God's Word. There is hope in distress. The Lord spoke to me during this time and gave me the same promise that he gave David, when he wrote, Psalms 91: verse 14-16 "I have heard your cry and I have seen your tears. My revelation will be made known to him. He will be a golden vessel through which the Living Water shall flow. He shall bind up the broken hearted and bring hope to the dying. Salvation shall be within thy household. I will find up all the broken fragments of his life and put them together and there will be joy and contentment."

The Lord is our healing Jesus and has so beautifully restored, refreshed and definately renewed Richard, his life, and his ministry. We accept what is recorded in Malachi, Chapter 4, and Verse 2, "Unto you that fear my name shall the Sun of righteousness arise with healing in his wings."

On Palm Sunday, Richard and I met Bob, Wynnelle and Kori at the Community Church in Hendersonville. We were going to have lunch together following the morning worship service. During the congregational singing Richard turned to me and said, "Why did you put your hand on my shoulder?" I said, "I didn't." When we stood up to sing another hymn, he turned to me and asked me again with a puzzled look on his face, "What?" I shrugged my shoulders smiled and said, "I didn't touch you." The third time when he felt the hand on his shoulder, he also heard a noticeably clear voice say; "This is where I want you." He put his hand on my arm and then patted my shoulder. He had a big grin on his face and we continued listening to the singing. It was not until we were eating lunch that he told us what had happened during the service. He said, "There is no doubt about where I'll be attending church."

On a beautiful October Monday in 2009 Richard entered the hospital. He needed a knee replacement but took the journey of a lifetime. He had a (NDE) Near Death Experience. The surgery went successfully, and he was back in his room and are supper. One of the shepherds from the church was staying with him. We came on home before it was dark.

The next morning the phone rang at 5:30. It was Bob, who lives in Hendersonville. He said, "Mom, we need to get to Vanderbilt as soon as we can. The hospital just called, and Richard has ARDS (Acute Respiratory Distress Syndrome) and he is in Surgical Critical Care. He has a lot of meters surrounding his bed. He is in a coma. I will come by and pick you up. How soon can you be ready?" I said, "I'll be ready as soon as you get here." He said, "See you in about ten minutes."

We could not go in when we arrived because the doctors were working with him. There is a very small room just outside the Critical Care rooms that has four chairs in it. They told us to wait in there until the doctor came to talk to us. The nurse said that it could be a while. My heart was racing, and Bob was holding my hands in his. Hearing every sound and watching every movement around the door we anxiously waited to see if it opened. But it didn't. Finally, Bob said, "We need to hear something from somebody. I'm going in those doors. I will be right back. You stay here in case I miss the doctor."

As he was turning to leave, the doctor knocked on the door then opened it He explained what had happened. Because of acid reflux, he had aspirated and his lungs were damaged. He has a large pic-line in his throat and other IVs in his arms and legs. There are 12-meter boxes and there was a pump on his feet is to release the pressure every few seconds. The breathing tube is giving his lungs oxygen. He has 16 IVs going into his body.

The nurse in charge thought he was asleep from the anesthesia. The Shepherd staying with Richard called her attention to him. Then they called other help to assist them. When he didn't respond they immediately transported him to the Surgical Critical Care. He did not respond in the Unit. Only the whites in his eyes could be seen. They said he may have had an incident and they were concerned about his heart and his kidneys.

They began kidney treatment. They performed the 'brachial wash test' to get him off the high level of oxygen. He did not respond for several days. On the 17th the x-rays showed that he had bilateral pneumonia and had gotten worse. Saturday the doctor said, "If he doesn't respond and if his oxygen does not improve, we will have no other choice but to remove the tube. His lungs are not working. He is on 100% oxygen. The doctor told Bob, "Your brother is the sickest patient in SCCU and he is the sickest patient in Vanderbilt."

Bob arrived every morning by 7 a.m. to make the rounds with the doctors in the SCCU. Even the bed that is filled with water and moves constantly did nothing for him. He was moved to another room still in SCCU.

Community Church, Hendersonville, TN asked their congregation to pray at 2:00 p.m. for Richard and those that could, come to the hospital. They asked the Vanderbilt Administrator for permission to have a service in their chapel on Sunday afternoon to pray for Richard to be healed. The chapel was filled with people standing all around the walls. Bob led the service. We sang choruses and each one there said a prayer. The nurse opened the door so that everyone in the lobby could hear the singing. The chapel is located just to the right in the back of the main Vanderbilt Admission Office. This is also the main area for the family waiting room. We waited many hours and long days in the balcony over-looking the waiting room. We could only go in two at a time. Then we could not stay longer than a few minutes. The visiting hours were from 10:00 a.m. to 8:00 p.m.

On that Sunday night after prayer in the chapel, his oxygen began to come up. The doctor said, "I am amazed. This never happens like this. His oxygen began to gradually increase as if it were coming from an oxygen tank."

While we were praying here Richard took the journey of a lifetime. While he was lying in a coma in Vanderbilt Hospital, Richard was on a journey beyond this world.

He explained to us, there were two elements. First there was murky icy cold water in a huge lake, and it was black and you could feel the darkness. Evil was so strong, and fear surrounded me. There was a long line of people waiting to be baptized in it. The people being baptized never came up. I was terrified. I was tied in a chair and could not get out to help them. Then the second element suddenly appeared. I stood up and began walking out of the darkness toward a bright light shining just beyond where I was standing. The blackness began to fade until it was gone. The farther I walked the brighter the light became.

He encountered the majestic view. He saw and recognized someone in the Heavenly realm. He said he was standing by a beautiful, transcendent, iridescent crystal-clear river gently flowing past him. He saw and recognized Elijah, standing on the other side of the river. His arms were at his side. Elijah saw me and I could feel his piercing eyes, and he was looking at me. His gray robe was touching the ground. The brown shawl around his shoulders had a hood. It covered his hair. Everything was clear. The grass and the trees were dark green. The clear blue sky was filled with God's presence. I was not an individual anymore. I became a part of all the beautiful surroundings. It was the most beautiful and serene place far beyond any description. You could see miles and miles. There was joy and peace at the same time. There was a freshness coming from the sparkling crystal-clear water as it was flowing past me. (Revelation, chapter 22, and verse 1.) Describes what John said, "And he showed me a pure river of water of life, clear as crystal proceeding out of the throne of the Lord and of the Lamb." David also says this in Psalms 46:4, "There is a river, the streams whereof shall make glad the city of God, the holy place of the tabernacles of the Most High."

Richard said, "The first thing I remember when I could hear was, Robert saying, "Breathe, Richard." "Breathe." "Breathe." He was holding his hands over his mouth and breathing and blowing into them. I could feel someone holding my hand and I was hoping it was Jennifer. I had taught her sign language when she was in kindergarten. I signed into her hand. ICE. When Jennifer told the doctor that was in charge of watching Richard, what he had done, he said, "Where did that come from?"

Richard could barely whisper and he was asking the doctors and nurse to sing. He could hear people coming down the hall and he would call as loud as he could, "Can you sing? I want to sing and I want you to sing with me." Every time we went into his room he would say, "Let's sing. Sing with me."

He was transferred to the 7th floor after several days. A tornado warning was sounded over the loud speaker system. All the patients were hurriedly taken into the hall. The doctors and nurses shoved their computers in a little room adjoining the nurses' station. Richard had the whole floor including the nurses and the doctors, singing. They began to request certain songs to sing. When the warning was lifted everyone just stayed in the hall singing. Finally the head nurse said, "It is time to go back in your room but you can keep singing."

Just a few weeks ago at their Wednesday night supper before choir and prayer meeting, a nurse from Vanderbilt Hospital said, "Did they call your name Richard?" He said, "Yes, I'm Richard Langford." The nurse replied, "I was your nurse on duty that Saturday night. The charge nurse goes over the daily report with the nurse coming in and she told me not to worry about the patient in bed #3. He is going to die - he won't be here in the morning." "You can't be. I was working in SCCU and they said not to bother with you, that you wouldn't be here by morning. You were already 'clinically' dead'." He reached across the table to shake Richard's hand and said, "Wow, I'm glad to meet you! Wow, I am glad to meet you."

Richard is ministering at Community Church in Hendersonville in the Celebrate Recover Ministry. He sings in the church choir and also the Nashville Choir. "Sing praises unto God, sing praises: sing praises unto our King, sing praises." He certainly is doing what David recommends in Psalms 47:6 As I am writing; he is talking on the phone giving someone directions to the church for their meeting tonight. He is also a chaplain for the Hendersonville Police Department.

We now reminisce about his students and the settings in Honduras and especially his classes in Ethiopia which ranged from teaching computers, Theology and Greek. His love and compassion which is very evident. His heart is still at each location he has ministered. He has always loved to worship and to this day still feels his giftedness is in the area of music, teaching, and sharing his love of Jesus.

His birthday is May 6th. I asked him, "What do you want for your birthday?" He said, "Let's just have some friends over and have a "sing-along." So, this Saturday afternoon, May 10th, at 5:00 o'clock we are having a 'sing-along' in our backyard. Everyone is invited! From his near-death experience until now, Richard has not stopped and is still singing the wonderful old and new songs of the church.

Preacher's kids are ordinary, yet unique as they try to adapt to a very different, busy, ever changing schedule. However, it is also an extremely rewarding lifestyle. Perhaps, this saying by the famous poet and philosopher Henry David Thoreau could often be said of them, "If a man does not keep pace with his companions, perhaps it is because he hears a different drummer. Let him step to the music which he hears, however measured or far away."

A joy thrills my heart each time they give me a big hug and say, "I love you."

CHAPTER TEN

THE GLITTER OF AUTUMN

This beautiful spring day, I am reminded of another beautiful afternoon in late autumn 63 years ago, when Billy and I were sitting on our patio. With his beautiful blue eyes sparkling and his big broad smile said, with such a certainty in his voice, "You are going to love livin' in Nashville."

I can look out my kitchen window and see the beautiful blue sky, with a few white clouds passing by and every few minutes a large or small airplane coming and going from the Nashville International Airport. The trees line the Cumberland River. You can often hear the whistle from the Steamboat, General Jackson. It goes from Opryland Hotel to Riverfront Park on First Street downtown Nashville, across from L.P. Field.

Just above the trees, and across the river is Briley Parkway and at night the stream of lights shine brightly. The lights from Opryland Hotel shine a bit brighter. Often, deer from Shelby Bottoms come into our yard, as if they, too, sense God's presence and their open invitation to graze. It is not unusual to see wildlife in our yard. There have been as many as three to seven deer. Occasionally a wild turkey will wander into the back yard to visit the birds and the squirrels. The wooded greenway behind our house joins Shelby Park. Shelby Bottoms has bicycle routes leading from all areas of town.

From our living room, the loud booms can be heard when they have the beautiful fireworks display for the many activities at L.P. Field. When you look out that window you can see the smoke coming from the huge fireworks.

We have had many, many guests over the years. The comment most often heard is "Your house feels so comfortable." There is a motto that has always hung over our dining room table, "Christ is the Head of this house, the Unseen Guest at every meal, the Silent Listener to every conversation." On the bottom of the plaque it reads in small letters, "For to me to live is Christ"

Oak Hill Assembly has built a beautiful Family Life Center with a full-size gym and kitchen facilities. It was dedicated in January 2003 as "The W. C. Langford Family Life Center." We are truly honored and humbled by this tribute.

While Semi-retired we also had the privilege to serve a wonderful congregation in Eagleville, Tennessee located about forty miles from Nashville near Henry Horton State Park and just a short drive from Murfreesboro. We loved the opportunity to be with them.

There was a beautiful picture perfect, small white, well maintained Cumberland Presbyterian church surrounded by beautiful homes and farmlands. Across the road from the church was a large pasture with cows grazing just along the fence line bordering the road. What a peaceful scene we were greeted with every Sunday morning. The little white house behind the church is also maintained and has only been kept as a reminder of days gone by.

The church is located on Mount Vernon Road about five miles from the little town of Eagleville, Tennessee. It is not far from the community of Rockvale. Billy received approval from the Cumberland Presbyterian Board in Murfreesboro, Tennessee to serve as the pastor of Mount Vernon. The membership is around 100 and average attendance 50 to 75.

It was a joy and delight as we looked forward to the beautiful drive each Sunday morning. From our driveway to Mt. Vernon church takes exactly one hour. Judy Sides was the soloist. Her husband Greg played the piano. She also was a High School teacher.

Billy talked with her and encouraged her to pursue her calling for the Ministry. She is now the Pastor of Mt. Vernon. Each Sunday morning she wears her father-in-law's pulpit robe. He was also in the ministry before he went to his eternal home.

The Rockvale Community always has a combined Thanksgiving Service with all the area churches participating. I had the privilege to play for these services. Billy ministered at Mount Vernon four years. He was honored to have preached his final sermon there on a beautiful fall Sunday, October 1996.

I talked to Judy's dad, Buddy Taylor, just today and he said, "Judy is now the Assistant Principal of Riverdale High School in Murfreesboro." Judy and Greg met while touring with John Connelly.

As I reflect upon our incredible and rewarding journey, sometimes situations made life seem impossible and difficult. We always relied on the strength of the promise God gave to Zachariah, chapter 4 verse 6: "It is not by might, nor by power, but by my Spirit, says the Lord of Hosts." It is inscribed on a wooden plaque over the kitchen sink and sits on the window sill. The letters have turned yellow with age. We read it every day!

The memories we shared, brought us many tears and heartaches, but no comparison to the peace, joy and genuine happiness beyond words. We were so privileged to be a part of the lives that crossed our paths while living and ministering in this beautiful little city which has become Music City.

Billy has lived in his eternal home since February 23, 1997. He went to sleep here on Saturday night at our home and arrived in heaven early Sunday morning. Earlier on Saturday evening he put on his suit, coat and tie. He went downstairs and asked Richard to drive him to Centennial Hospital to make a hospital visit and to pray for someone. He said, "Your mom doesn't think I should go. But I am fine." I said, "If you are going, I'm going with you."

Richard drove us back by The Centennial Mall. The lights shining and glowing in the background from the Tennessee Capitol is absolutely gorgeous. Billy and I had never seen it at night. Billy said, "Richard, can you stop and give us time to gaze on that magnificent setting a few minutes. It is hard to realize how really beautiful it is."

Richard said, "I'll pull over into the parking area and we can stay as long as you want."

We stayed there and talked about twenty minutes. Billy said, "How about stopping by Captain D's and ordering our food to go?" It was about eleven o'clock when we got home. We ate, then Billy went into the bedroom and I put away the left-over food. When I went into the bedroom he rose up in the bed and said "What time is it?" I said, "It is 12:45" He squinted his pretty bright blue eyes, then he gave me his beautiful smile and asked, "What are you doing up so late?" I replied, "You kept me out all night." I finished rolling my hair and went over to kiss him good-night but he had already fallen asleep. I didn't want to disturb him so I very carefully and quietly crawled into my side of the bed.

Around 5 o'clock in the morning I thought I heard him say something. I jumped out of bed and went to his side of the bed. When I placed my hand on his forehead he was already cold. I knew he had made his heavenly journey and that he was in his eternal home on this Sunday morning. The coroner was called. He said, "There was no struggle. I can tell by the position of his body. He just went to sleep."

The funeral home director came into the living room where we were waiting for them to take his body from the bedroom. He motioned for me. He asked, "Do you have the bed nailed down? The four of us cannot move the bed. We can't move it to get the gurney by the bed." I told him, "No." Then I asked him, "May I have a few minutes with him alone with my boys?" He responded, "Of course."

We went into the bedroom and I sat on the side of the bed next to him. I ran my hand through his beautiful silver curly hair and held his hand. I talked to him about the home he was going to and told him me and the boys will be there before too long. We talked between thirty and forty minutes. Robert, Richard and I went back into the living room. The funeral director went immediately into the bed room. He called out, "I moved the bed over. You can come in after Reverend Langford with the gurney."

My heart overflows with love and gratitude for the gift from God to let us be a part of Nashville as it has grown into Music City, USA. It has been an incredible and rewarding journey. God directed our journey and we were blessed to have been a part of it. The sound of music continues, the songs continue to be written and the quest of the dreams will be accomplished.

God's wonderful gift of music is experienced as the rhythm of life continues.

Billy was so right. I do love livin' in Nashville. I'm so glad we 'Moved to the Music!'

Apartment House when first Arriving to Nashville

Family living in the back end of the church

Little Bobby

CPSIA information can be obtained
at www.ICGtesting.com
Printed in the USA
LVHW011207120422
715979LV00002B/181